MW01034625

TURKESTAN SOLO

Born in 1903, Ella Maillart is a Swiss national and traveller *extraordinaire* who, when static, makes her home in Geneva. Her occupation is described in *Who's Who* as 'explorer', but she has also achieved success in the guise of a yachtswoman — who sailed for Switzerland in the Olympic Games of 1924 — and a skier.

This book is set in 1932. A time when by normal standards, to someone who was both a Westerner and a woman, extensive travel within central Asia could be only a mystical pipedream. Thus the journeyings Ella Maillart describes so vividly in *Turkestan Solo* are the product of a truly determined traveller's spirit. Like a latterday Marco Polo she spends six months travelling from Moscow through Russian Turkestan, encountering en route difficult terrain as well as the problems engendered by a general food shortage. Throughout she retains her conviction that the life of a nomad is the best life, and never regrets the European civilisation which she has left behind her.

For us, Ella Maillart's observations are full of a beauty that is rendered exotic by the inaccessibility of the far-off lands she travelled over fifty years ago. But *Turkestan Solo* is more than a traveller's tale: it is a record of social history that is still pertinent today about regions in the grip of historical chaos as three great powers — Russia, China and the British Empire — and their peoples struggle to live alongside each other.

This edition of *Turkestan Solo* is introduced by Julia Keay, who has travelled widely in the Indian sub-continent and the Himalayas. Educated in England, Switzerland and France, she has four children and has written a quantity of material for BBC Radio. She is currently researching a book on Mata Hari.

TURKESTAN SOLO

*One Woman's Expedition
from the Tien Shan to
the Kizil Kum*

ELLA MAILLART
Translated by John Rodker
Introduction by Julia Keay

CENTURY PUBLISHING
LONDON

LESTER & ORPEN DENNYS DENEAU
MARKETING SERVICES LTD
TORONTO

"Real strength, real courage, and the only genius in this huge ant-heap of ours, lies in going where one wishes, when one wishes, and as rapidly as one wishes."

GEORGES DUHAMEL

Introduction copyright © Julia Keay 1985

All rights reserved

First published in Great Britain in 1934
by G. P. Putnam's Sons

This edition published in 1985 by
Century Hutchinson Ltd
Portland House, 12-13 Greek Street,
London W1V 5LE

Published in Canada by
Lester & Orpen Dennys Deneau Marketing Services Ltd
78 Sullivan Street, Ontario, Canada

ISBN 0 7126 0439 1

The cover shows a detail of a Persian lacquer book cover

Reprinted in Great Britain by
Guernsey Press Co. Ltd, Guernsey, Channel Islands

INTRODUCTION

'TO PUSH THE nose of my sailing boat into every creek and to point my skis down every possible gully of the mountain.' Ella Maillart was born with adventure in her soul. Her conventional middle-class upbringing as the daughter of a Swiss businessman seems, at first glance, an unlikely start to a lifetime of travel and exploration. But she was born in 1903 and the full horror of 'man's inhumanity to man' was brought home to her by the First World War which, coinciding with her most impressionable years, filled her with a burning need to live every minute of her life to the full.

She missed her final school exams because she was too busy founding the first ladies' hockey club of Switzerland. She was a member of the Swiss Olympic Sailing Team at the age of twenty-one and a member of the Swiss National Ski Team from 1931-34. With three girlfriends she sailed the length of the Mediterranean, crossed the Bay of Biscay, and then, looking for the next challenge, thought 'Why stop here? Is not the very vastness of Tibet waiting to be conquered?'

The image conjured up by these details of her early life is of a hyperactive daredevil, plunging wildly into excitement in an attempt to escape from a reality she didn't wish to face. Doubtless there has been an element of escapism in her wandering life, but that, like the physical energy, was only part of it.

Her lifetime of travelling has brought her, in her eighties, to an enviably serene understanding of herself because the recurrent theme throughout her many journeys has been not escaping, but seeking. On her earlier travels, of which the subject of this book was one, her search was for the differences between the European culture of her sheltered Swiss childhood and that of the lands she visited. Maybe living among the primitive, nomadic peoples of some of the earth's remotest corners would show her where the West had gone so woefully wrong. Subsequent journeys, and the experiences of the earlier ones, taught her that the only valid and rewarding search was not for the *differences* but for the similarities between people of all races, religions and cultures. 'We must develop more interest and a greater understanding of the people we meet. Like us they are passengers on board that mysterious ship called "Life". The sooner we learn to be jointly responsible on that ship — instead of blaming the staff — the easier the sailing will be. Forgetting differences but emphasising traits common to each human being . . . we can find an inspired solution to the inner and outer chaos disintegrating us.'

Certainly if escape from chaos had been her motive for travelling to Turkestan in 1932 she would have been sadly disappointed. For sixty years, since Tsarist Russia's advance towards the Persian and Afghan frontiers had incorporated Central Asia into the Russian Empire, the assorted peoples of that remote region had been buffeted by conquest, revolution and civil war. For centuries before this expansion the Uzbeks and Tadzhiks, the Kazakhs and the Kirgiz, the Turkmens and the Karakalpaks had been in a more or less permanent state of war, not only with each other, but with neighbouring Persia, Afghanistan and China.

Their new status as part of the vast empire of the Tsars for the first time introduced a level of stability into the region by removing the threat of further invasions from outside. But gradually it became apparent that one burden of feudal exploitation had been replaced by another. Their ability to resist was severely limited by their lack of a common national identity or loyalty, but resentment grew into outrage, and in 1916 nomad and farmer, official and trader alike finally rallied under the one cause they did hold in common — Islam — to strike a blow for freedom and independence in the Great Revolt. Outbreaks of fighting throughout Turkestan resulted in large numbers of Russian settlers being killed and the inevitable reprisals were severe and bloody. The situation had barely been resolved when it was overtaken by the Bolshevik Revolution of 1917.

With their common adversary, the Tsarist Government, removed almost overnight, the rebels fell back into confusion. Internecine bickering dissolved any chance they might have had of avoiding the eventual Bolshevik takeover. But they could, and did, postpone it. For the next five years the rebels, or Basmatchi, waged bloody and savage war on the Red Army forces sent to subdue the region. Since the Bolshevik Revolution in the rest of Russia was making heavy demands on their manpower, Soviet forces in Turkestan were too thin on the ground to deal a swift death blow to the Basmatchi rebellion. The nature of the terrain, stretches of arid desert flanked by some of the highest mountains in the world, remote inaccessible valleys and barren and uninhabited plateaux, favoured the rebels — in fact the situation was an exact parallel of that in Afghanistan today, the Basmatchi being the equivalent of the modern Afghan Mujahedeen. But weight of numbers on the one side and lack of positive leadership on the other made the final outcome inevitable. Small groups of Basmatchi would roam the hills for some years to come, but no longer in sufficient quantities to pose a serious threat to Soviet authority.

By 1924 Khiva, Bokhara, Samarkand, Tashkent and Fergana had

been 'Sovietised', and amalgamated to form the Soviet Republic of Uzbekistan. Together with the neighbouring Soviet Republics of Kazakhstan, Kirgizia, Tadzhikistan and Turkmenistan, in other words the lands that under Tsarist rule had been known as Russian Turkestan, they formed what is now known as Soviet Central Asia.

The years of war and revolution had inevitably left the economy of the whole area in ruins. The first thing the Soviet government therefore had to do was restore it. But they were also determined to change its basis, to replace its previous near-self-sufficiency with an interdependence with the Soviet Republic as a whole. This process was still far from complete by the time Ella Maillart arrived and it made a fascinating and, with hindsight, horrifying backdrop to her journey. As she says, 'at every step the fourteenth century rises to face the twentieth'. Paradoxically the intensity of the social and economic upheavals involved in this reorganisation eased her path through regions that had seen few non-Russian European travellers for more than a decade. The authorities were too busy with the tasks in hand to pay much heed to a Swiss national who was unconnected with either the British or the Germans — two of the Great Powers regarded with paranoid suspicion by the Soviets. Characteristically Ella Maillart made the most of their preoccupation and, grasping every opportunity for progress with both hands and refusing to be daunted by the barriers she did meet, continued her search for a world where 'heat does not come in pipes, ice in boxes, sunshine in bulbs, music on black discs or images on a pale screen'.

One of the barriers that proved to be, for the moment, insuperable, was that across her intended route into Sinkiang, or Chinese Turkestan. But although bitterly disappointed at being unable to cross the Chinese border, she fully appreciated that another reason for the relative freedom in which she travelled through Russian Turkestan was that the eyes of the authorities were turned, in some apprehension, towards the dramas that were unfolding across that border.

For Sinkiang was in the grips of a civil war every bit as ferocious as the one that had recently devastated Russian Turkestan and in which the Russians themselves had a vested interest. They had no immediate wish to annex the province — their experiences of trying to achieve mastery over thousands of square miles of desert and mountains were all too fresh in their minds. But they were intent on maximising their influence over its corrupt government. The inaccessibility of the region meant that few people were aware of the real situation and it was in the interests of both the Governor of Sinkiang and the Russians to keep it that way. Two years later, in company with Peter Fleming, Ella Maillart would achieve her ambition of crossing Sinkiang on a marathon trek of 3,500 miles, the subject of her *Forbidden Journey*. But, for now, she had to turn away. With rather less fuss than the tourist might make on discovering, after a trip across town, that the Tower of London was closed for the day, she turned instead to the legendary cities of Tashkent, Samarkand and Bukhara.

Although package tours have now brought even Central Asia within the reach of Western visitors, few travellers either before or since Ella Maillart have had her freedom to explore it. A freedom not so much offered as won, by her dogged determination and insatiable appetite for the 'unknown destination'. It was Ella Maillart's good fortune that the timing of her journey enabled her to witness something of the metamorphosis of Soviet Central Asia from a scattering of disparate parts into a whole, like spread iron filings under the welder's torch. It is posterity's good fortune to have such a clear-eyed chronicler of an extraordinary era.

'To dawdle in my usual fashion, as if I had the whole of eternity before me'. Ella Maillart's description of her preferred rate of progress gives a misleading impression of little aimed for and little achieved. She was a passionate, hungry traveller, devouring every morsel of every experience. No crumb is wasted, no crust overlooked. And yet she had in such abundance the chameleon skill of the true traveller that the overall impression she gives us is one of quietness, of respect for, and total absorption in, the people and places she has chosen to experience.

Ella Maillart lives now in her native Switzerland, and she still travels, frequently and far. Never a year passes without a trip to some far corner of Indonesia, China, India or South East Asia. But if traces of her youthful hyperactivity still linger, she has long since replaced her early restlessness of spirit with a deep philosophical contentment. *Turkestan Solo* tells the story of a physical journey which was also one step in a personal journey to fulfilment.

Julia Keay
1985

CONTENTS

PART I — A VAGABOND ON THE WAY

PART II — A VAGABOND IN TURKESTAN

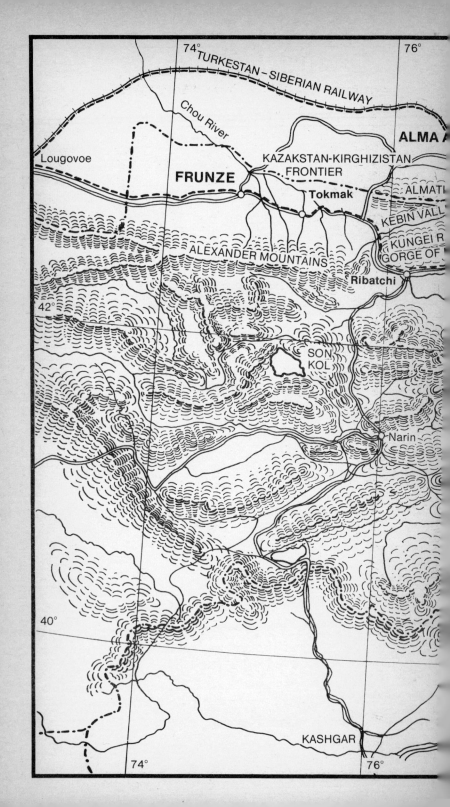

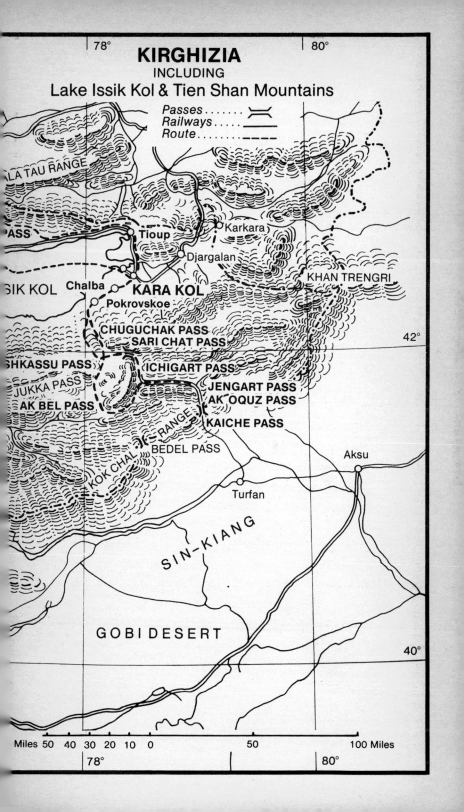

KIRGHIZIA
INCLUDING
Lake Issik Kol & Tien Shan Mountains

Passes . . . .
Railways . . . . .
Route . . . .

78°

80°

ALA TAU RANGE

PASS

Tioup

Karkara

Djargalan

KHAN TRENGRI

SIK KOL

Chalba

KARA KOL

Pokrovskoe

42°

CHUGUCHAK PASS
SARI CHAT PASS

SHKASSU PASS

ICHIGART PASS

JUKKA PASS

JENGART PASS

AK'OQUZ PASS

AK BEL PASS

KAICHE PASS

KOK CHAL RANGE

BEDEL PASS

Aksu

Turfan

SIN-KIANG

40°

GOBI DESERT

Miles 50 40 30 20 10 0   50   100 Miles

78°

80°

PART I

A VAGABOND ON THE WAY

CHAPTER I

LETS AND HINDRANCES

"No," ANSWERS COMRADE BLOCH, "no reply has come through yet from Kijev. Pograbetzki must have left on holiday."

The Ukraine Academy of Sciences is organizing an expedition which will spend the summer exploring Khan Tengri, a peak some twenty-three thousand feet above sea-level, in the Tien Shan mountains on the Chinese border.

"Do you think Pograbetzki will be passing through Moscow before he sets out? That would give me a chance of asking if he could take me with him."

"I don't know about that," is her answer. "Anyhow, now that all the details have been worked out, it's much too late for them to be able to take you."

"Then I shall have to give up my idea of seeing the mountains of Turkestan. . . . Very well then, I'll just go from town to town, wherever your organization has a ' base, and start with Tashkent."

I am in the central Moscow offices of the organization calling itself the Society of Proletarian Tourists, which has branches all over the Soviet Union. Thanks to that organization, two years previously I had been able to travel in the Caucasus and visit its mysterious valleys.

At that time the director's secretary, with whom I was talking, had been of the utmost service to me.

"All our ' bases ' in Central Asia are shut up this year," she adds, " they'd be no help to you for your rations. Why not go to Murmansk near the Arctic Circle, instead; we are beginning to work some worth-while mines up there. Or better, travel as correspondent with the *Malygin*, one of our ice-breakers, which for the first time in history is going to try to

13

make the passage from the Arctic Ocean to the North Pacific via the Behring Straits, in a single season. If it fails, you'll be forced to winter in the ice."

No. Cost what it may I am determined to go East.

The nomad's life enthralls me. Its restlessness pursues me: it is as much part of me as of the sailor. All ports and none are home to him, and all arrivings only a new setting forth.

And even as our remotest Asiatic ancestors, " that were in truth the race of iron of the ancient world, roamed the immensity of barren soil under implacable skies,"[1] so still the nomad journeys forth, accompanied by his flocks and tents of felt.

Besides, all I had been told by Commander Point, on his return from the Citroën expedition into Central Asia, amply confirmed everything I had imagined. " The Kirghiz are simple, hospitable, and above all free," was what he had said, and it was that quality which made its deepest appeal to me. Wherever I go, it is always the secret of such simple, straightforward races that I seek, peoples whom a fair sky is sufficient to content. Only by returning to their way of living, can we ever hope to find a way out of the bogs in which we vainly stumble.

There, on the western slopes of the lofty ranges, the Soviet regime, with extraordinary suddenness, has plunged the nomad straight into the twentieth century, collectivizing, socializing, sedentarizing him ; and bringing in its wake schools, hospitals, newspapers, wireless, tractors, and the cinema.

Yet, on the Chinese side of the very same ranges, the Mohammedans are rising in revolt, and the governor of Urumtchi goes in peril of his life. Tourists are treated as suspicious characters with imperialistic intentions. As for the Soviet Union, though feared, the country depends on it, since practically all commerce passes through its hands.

Was there a chance, I wondered, of my insignificant person, backed by its Swiss passport, being able to travel freely

[1] René Grousset, *Histoire d'Asie*.

through the land? Then I should know whether it was Britain or Russia, or Mussulman fanaticism, or possibly a nationalist awakening, whose object was to restore again the ancient Turki-Mongol unity, that was behind the revolts.

" Not all the barbarians fell beneath the Merovingian axes. Immense reserves exist in Asia still. The stories brought back by travellers describe the Mongolian steppes as now inhabited by peaceable, inoffensive peoples, now full armed, awaiting the call to rally of some chief. The descendants of Timur and of Jenghiz Khan are a source of much alarm to us, and keenly our eyes sweep the plains which they share with wolves." Thus wrote Père Huc, concerning them.

Is there indeed a yellow peril, latent though it be? And will a West, some day drained of its human reserves, begin to tremble before these hordes, which Japan seeks to influence ever more strongly?

" No," Krylenko said. " Impossible to add to the number of our party. Even as it is, we don't know where to get hold of six saddles and five horses."

Krylenko is People's Commissar for Justice. This is the man responsible for the signing of so many death-warrants, whose name is a word of terror to multitudes.

A powerful head, bald, stern featured, surmounts an undersized body on spiral legs squeezed into khaki puttees, that makes one think at moments of a caricature come to life. Clear and direct, though at times teasing, his glance darts forth like a spurt of metal from the blue transparent irises. An enthusiastic alpinist, year after year he organizes expeditions into the Pamirs or Alai Mountains.

" And look at what you have written here about the Caucasus. Just consider. How could you? ' The bases in Suanetia are clean though simple,' you say. But in my opinion they are simply filthy." And highly amused by my favourable opinion, he bursts out laughing. " Can you leave it with me? I should like to read it? " he adds, turning the leaves over.

" I'm so sorry, I need it. It is the only copy I have. But I am expecting some soon from Paris, and I'll send you one then."

" So you would have liked to come with me? And I don't frighten you? " It seems that Krylenko's reputation is rather that of a Don Juan. Gut before I can say anything, he breaks in :

" Yes, yes, I know, you're a born mountaineer, and as strong as a man. All the same I can't take you with me. No, it isn't your sex that's in the way; let me introduce you to Comrade Rosa who has been in my party three years running now, and I think I'm lucky to have her."

Rosa is a solid creature, with gaps in her teeth, checking over a list of stores.

Nothing remains but to take my leave. As I am opening the door, Krylenko calls after me :

" Go to the offices of the ' Tajik Group '; the man in charge is Gorbounov. He has gone off to study glacier formations. You won't need a horse for that, because there are motor-lorries which will take you into the Pamirs as far as Khorog."

Raging, I walk down Bogoyavlenski Street. Am I never to come face to face with the Kirghiz peoples? On this occasion, anxious not to waste the moments of a man as busy as Krylenko, I had taken an interpreter with me. The young Jewess with black plaits makes no attempt, however, to spare my feelings.

" You go about it the wrong way," she says. " You should have done as Madam Viollis did. No one could resist doing what she asked of them. To begin with, you should have presented Krylenko with a copy of your book, charmingly inscribed."

" Yes, I know. Good-bye. Many thanks for your help."

Everything I try fails: there's no doubt I must be lacking somewhere, or else I don't seem worth bothering about.

Nevertheless, I am determined that the few pennies I have earned by the sweat of my pen shall take me further than Moscow, with which I am thoroughly familiar by now.

There in the distance is Samarkand awaiting me. The fabled ruins of Tamerlane crumble day by day, and I must hasten. Like the pilgrims in *Hassan*, I go on my way murmuring to myself :

"We take the golden road to Samarkand."

Like them, my desire is to cross the desert to the slow gait of camels, and, in this age of aeroplanes, enter into the thoughts and feelings of the padding caravans.

Four days later, busy, intelligent Comrade Krausch telephones me on behalf of the Tajik Group.

"We've had no reply from Professor Gorbounov to the telegram we sent concerning you. He must have left his base therefore, and we can't now get at him. But anything else I can do, please count on me at any time."

My ill-luck continues, it seems.

This confirms what I have heard already, that foreigners, some possibly hostile, are considered undesirable in the frontier regions bordering on India and Afghanistan. The problems of victualling the population still offer grave difficulties, and there are always uprisings of the 'Bassmatchi' to be feared. These are adversaries of the Soviet regime, who, with or without the encouragement of foreign powers, are attempting to organize a Nationalist movement in those regions once called Eastern Bokhara.

Visits

Greatly discouraged, I decide to pay a couple of visits in order to distract my thoughts. Away back in Paris, my friend Vera, whose husband is an exile and taxi-driver, had entrusted me with a coat to take to her mother, and so I go to see her at the other end of Moscow where she has rented half a room. It gets more and more difficult for her to make a living, and the ninety roubles a month she earns at the office is two months overdue already.

She has shrunk almost to nothing, it seems to me, and has given up expecting anything from existence at all.

" I bartered my last silver spoons in the ' Torgsin '.[1] shop for soap and sugar, but how am I to manage next winter? "

I decide to go along and see what's happening to the young folk, my old comrades at sport . . . and find the Park of Culture and Rest[2] on the Moscow river as animated as ever. Fedya the instructor is there still. He is so astonished to see me that he stands transfixed, his jaw dropping, and looks so droll that I can't help laughing. Even so, I manage to take a snap of him. He is now in aviation, and our mutual friend Serge, he tells me, is in Leningrad doing his military service.

I go on questioning him.

" And are the Changui's still training here? "

" Oh, no! Quite a few are in Siberia taking the cure. They should be back soon though, in a year say."

That is as much as to say that they have been sent into exile.

" What have they done? "

" Who knows: maybe they let their tongues wag too much."

Along the boat-house wall I notice an enormous banner, bearing the words:

" Sportsmen! On to the conquest of the Five-Year Plan's most vital year."

" Maroussia is at the harvest front, one of a shock brigade," Fedya adds. " As for the others, I don't know what has happened to them."

---

[1] Shops which accept only foreign currencies in silver or gold, or valuables, for the commodities they sell.
[2] Cf. Ella Maillart, *Parmi la jeunesse Russe*.

LETS AND HINDRANCES

" Ella, we need someone to make up our eight. Come along, do! "

It is the Dramatic Artist's eight that thus calls to me. And, as in the past, I go with them, to swing up the long river to the measured beat of oars.

That evening I pay a visit to Pudovkin. Possibly he may be setting off for Mongolia, or he may be going to start on the sequel to his film *Storm over Asia*.

" What, you come from abroad and haven't even brought me some safety-razor blades? Or any of those new records of Mexican dances that I should so like to have? I hadn't the money to buy them myself when I was last in Berlin."

It was Pudovkin, worth his weight in gold in Hollywood, the producer of *Mother* and *The Last Days of St. Petersburg*, who was speaking thus. Nothing, however, would induce him to go and work at a distance from his comrades. He has even been accepted as a member of the Communist Party of late, and his time is no longer his own.

" Man is not adapted to develop in isolation; whenever he can do so, it is his duty to help those round him."

Yet does he himself, in the isolation of his creative ardour, feel the less alone? I dare not ask him, for the principal actor in his most recent film *Deserter*, happens to be present, accompanied by a woman of extraordinary pale beauty.

" No," he continues, " I shan't be leaving Moscow this summer; the cutting of *Deserter* is going to take up all the time I can give."

" Tell me," I ask, " what the critics said about the film *Life is Good* that you made a couple of years ago."

" Not released yet. The Censor isn't satisfied. It's had to be altered a good deal."

" What did you think of Dziga Vertof's sound film? "

" *The Donbas Symphony*? Most interesting, but too noisy for my liking. Chaplin says it's the first real sound film. On the other hand, the medical profession in the Ukraine got it suppressed as too trying to the audience's nerves."

" No, no," he says to me later. " I don't advise you to go
into China just now. There are brigands all over the place.
Southern Mongolia is still feudal, and the chiefs think they
are doing good business by selling their lands to the Chinese.
The natives are then turned off, and naturally have to become
thieves."

Pudovkin is pleased with his recent efforts. He knows at
last what he wants the sound film to do, and with that profound enthusiasm which is so peculiarly his own, he begins
to explain wherein the importance of counterpoint lies.

I find Boris Pilnyak in his little wooden villa, surrounded
by the most diversely cosmopolitan guests. Living in the
same house is an American couple, both on the staff of the
Moscow Daily News. That newspaper can certainly lay claim
to holding the record for the number of contributors on its
staff. I have never yet met an Englishman or American in
Moscow who did not to some extent, great or small, depend
on it.

There was also a Japanese musician preparing to give a
series of recitals, whom Pilnyak had brought back with him
from a recent voyage. She was living in one of the rooms,
and her lovely musical instruments lay strewn about the bare
boards.

Very humorously, Pilnyak began to relate how and why,
when he was in Hollywood, he had refused to pass the sup-
posedly Soviet scenarios submitted him.

He has also written a book about Tajikistan, and I was
anxious to get his advice about my own plans. We pecked
away at the red currants in his vegetable garden, and bent
our heads to search for the fruit from below, so that whenever I looked at him, there was his German-looking head,
with its shrewd eyes, looking at me upside down.

It was an opportunity well worth having, fruit being
exceptionally scarce, and apples costing a rouble or two each.
And there had been a leg of mutton at the meal which
seemed to me to have descended straight from heaven.

There have been great changes in the past two years, and on a moderate sum I am at a loss what to buy, or how to nourish myself. The cheap restaurants which used to satisfy me have become impossible now. In any case, you must take your own bread and sugar with you. But, leaving the cabbage aside, no epithet could qualify the rest of the food. Instinctively one senses it, and puts it aside untouched. The ' closed ' restaurants, reserved solely for workers in certain factories or organizations, are not much better either, and everyone makes an effort to eat at home, in spite of the perpetual difficulties which such a course entails.

Pilnyak has put his panama on, and is going to be useless as far as I am concerned. There seems no way of getting him to understand what I am after. Nothing will make him stop asking what day would suit me best to go walking with him in the woods.

All things considered, I decide to go to Tashkent, come what may, and even if I have to leave my bones there. But I need a special *visa*, and since my country has no consulate in Moscow I go along to the Commissariat for Foreign Affairs.

There I find Comrade Neymann, with his delicate distinguished features, his olive skin, and somewhat weary gestures. With the utmost amiability he tells me, " It is impossible for foreigners to visit Uzbekistan, except where specially invited. Two Englishwomen recently got off the train at Samarkand one morning, but were compelled to leave for Moscow the same night."

" But Vaillant-Couturier and Kisch went there all right less than a year ago."

" To begin with, they are Communists, and then they had applied for their *visas* long before. But there is nothing to prevent you going rather farther north, Kirghizstan say, which forms part of the R.S.F.S.R."

" Many thanks, but what I wanted to see were the Mohammedan women in their harems before they have all been liquidated. And to get some idea what the liberation they owe to the Soviet Government has meant to them."

Do what I may, it is impossible for me to get away in under ten days, that being the minimum period of delay necessary to obtain even the most trivial railway ticket.

The same evening, I pay a visit to that well-known journalist, Koltsov the ebullient, but only to find myself jeered at.

" What a long way you are going, and in pursuit of what? Adventure? Material for articles? Or in search of the picturesque or Shamanism perhaps? But we have real ' Shamans with bells on,' studying right here in the University of Moscow. Why spend six days in a train, when no farther than Astrakhan you can find a Buddhist monastery full of Kalmuks, who have spent the last twenty-five years poring over their studies?—and where, within a stone's throw, there are crowds of nomad tents . . . the man who kings it there is Litvinov the garage owner; he had the brilliant idea of supplying them with electricity to light their yurts."

Vast tables and innumerable books surround us, in the two spacious, sparsely furnished rooms, on the tenth or twelfth story of the immense modern block where live those who rule this land. Two thousand five hundred tenants are housed under the roof of the ' Dom Sovietov,' a building replete with every modern convenience invented by progress to facilitate existence, situated on an island of the Moscow river almost facing the Kremlin, as though strategically placed there.

Against a curtainless window, as though in a frame, appears suddenly the inspiring head of Schklovski the poet, and his frank, endearing eyes. Eisenstein, the great producer, seems sulky. The bumps on his forehead stand out prominently, and he is tightly buttoned up in a blue reefer suit. Alexandroff, his assistant, begins telling me about the unique films depicting native life they had recently been making in Mexico. They were unlucky enough, however, to have to return to

Russia in fulfilment of a contract. As a result, the film had perforce to be left behind, and now could not be prepared for exhibition, the Americans refusing to have it cut anywhere but on the spot.

Was I ever really going to set out for my unknown destination?

Greatly discouraged, I go to see a woman doctor I know, taking with me a portable Primus for mountain use, which she had asked me to buy for her in Berlin.

" Yes," she said, " I have to do photographic work at night, the two hundred and fifty roubles I earn a month not being enough to keep me and my child. The cost of living has gone up so much. And you? You don't look well. . . ."

" For the last three weeks I have been making every effort to get away to Central Asia, the Pamirs, or the Tien Shan, but with no success."

" The Tien Shan? But, I believe some friends of mine are leaving to-morrow for the High Plains of Kirghizstan."

My heart begins to beat. Perhaps this is my one chance, that has at all costs to be seized.

Follows a telephone conversation. . . .

" It's all arranged, is it? Listen, I've a first-class Alpine climber here . . . now, now, no protests . . . she's most anxious to join your party. . . . I'm sending her over. . . ."

CHAPTER II

A Last Throw

HASTILY I SWEEP up my handbag, as I say:
"Good-bye, dear! The heater? Ah, yes! Settle with me when I get back . . . if I do!"

My temples have begun to throb feverishly. The chance that has just offered itself must be turned into reality without a moment's delay.

At No. 36, Flat 112, in the street I have been given, I find the passage and rooms littered with packages, ice-axes, rucksacks. We become acquainted looking over some snapshots of the Caucasus, which we have all visited. Year after year, my new friends, availing themselves of the services of the Society of Proletarian Tourists, consecrate their two months' holiday, and their savings, to expeditions into the remotest mountains.

There are four in all. Auguste, who leads the expedition, has a round timid back, magnificent white teeth that gleam from under a clipped gingerish moustache, and the deep blue eyes of a child set in a clever rosy-complexioned face. He is a sort of Medical Officer of Health. His tiny wife, Capitolina, Capa for short, is as nervy as a kitten, impulsive, brusque, but with a sudden disarming smile. A graduate in physiology, her skilful needle is at this moment engaged in sewing up a bag of sugar, while she takes part in the conversation.

"Have you the necessary warm clothes, boots for mountaineering, stores for two months, and a Primus?"

"Why, certainly! And a Leica too, and English maps of the district."

"And have you your railway ticket for to-morrow night, your rope, ice-axe, and crampons?"

"Yes!" I reply, without a moment's hesitation, untrue though it is. "But I haven't a fur lining to my sleeping-bag like you."

Volodya is packing a medicine box. Tall and exceedingly thin, his head seems tiny by comparison. His calm and smiling expression denotes intelligence to an unusual degree, while his full, firm lower lip reveals great kindliness. Eminent both as a biologist and professor, he asks:

" Can you ride, and can you stick in the saddle twelve hours on end? "

" Yes . . . if I really know I have to."

More bluff. Thirty minutes is about all the riding I have ever done, and that was on a mare under the olive groves of Messara in Crete.

Volodya's wife Milissa, Mila, with her precise and calculated movements, gives an impression of succeeding in anything she undertakes. Her features are regular, and her pale eyes glow with generous light. The somewhat receding chin makes her eye-teeth stand out prominently. No doubt it is in her nature to ask the most important question of all.

" Can you put a good face on it, even at the last gasp? "

I rush off to the S.P.T. to get a permit to allow me to use their ' bases ' in Turkestan. But the director says:

" Does the leader of your expedition accept full responsibility for taking you with him? "

" Why, yes, I think so. I have just come from his house. We have arranged to meet on the train."

" Hullo! Auguste Letaviet? So your departure for the Tien Shan is all arranged then? Do I understand you accept responsibility for this young foreigner who is travelling with you? "

.   .   .   .

" Right! Thanks! "

I feel a bludgeon is about to descend upon my head.

" Letaviet tells me he is not prepared to give any undertaking in regard to you. I cannot therefore provide you with a permit."

How am I to interpret it? Can my new friends really be

so double-faced? No! With time for reflection, they had evidently begun to waver at the thought of encumbering themselves with someone they hardly knew, in the face of difficulties they could not foresee. I know that personally, in their place, I should not have taken the risk.

Still, it is best to have one's conscience clear. Before giving up, I had better go and have things out.

The same honest, but this time expressionless faces, look up as I go in.

" Ella, it's difficult! You must realize! We don't ourselves know what dangers we may have to face. We're not even sure whether we shall be allowed to enter a region so near the Chinese border. Besides, though we are hoping to get four horses in a Sovkhoz near Lake Issik, all sorts of complications might arise. . . ."

" Yes, yes, I see. . . . I'm awfully sorry. Good-bye! "

My throat contracts. I summon up all my resolution. I dare not look at the eyes that follow me.

Back in my room I go to bed in blank despair. But night brings counsel. Obviously, if it had been merely a question of joining some facile picnic in the Bois de Boulogne, I should certainly not have been so wild to go.

And it was July already, the very last moment to get something done.

Full Speed Ahead

But first I must get out of Moscow. As for later, that could take care of itself. Then, too, I was anxious to visit certain political exiles in Alma Ata, Frunze, and Tashkent, whose addresses I had.

Ah, an inspiration!

Immediately I wake, I telephone Auguste.

" You remember I told you that I already have my ticket for to-night. Well I've decided to go in any case. But I should like to ask whether I may accompany you as far as the stud-farm you mentioned near Issik-Köl. Then, while you were away in the mountains, I could stay and study how collectivization is working."

A deliberation follows. The others agree. We arrange to meet on the train. Oh, the relief! All that remains now is to straighten things out, for I have to get the railway ticket and mountaineering outfit that I pretended I had already. I know it's hopeless to get them at the Sovtourist shop. I did that once before, and in the Caucasus the points of the Russian crampons bent like rubber against the rock.

At the Tajik bureau, Comrade Krausch, every whit as amiable as I had guessed her, provides me with a certificate in writing, to the effect that I am taking part in an expedition, and therefore entitled to purchase ice-axe, rope, and crampons of German manufacture.

But at the shop I find everything sold out. However, I am sent on to the S.P.T.'s general depot, a vast courtyard, surrounded by arcades, in which at the moment hundreds of mattresses are being unloaded. Very deliberately, a cashier clicking away at the traditional abacus, works out a bill in duplicate for a hundred and ten roubles, and hands me what I want, with the words:

"The very last we have in stock."

So far so good. Luck is on my side.

Then, betaking myself to 'Intourist,' the travel agency for foreigners, I go straight to the office of the Chief. I explain how the expedition I am joining leaves that very night, and try to convey how terribly important it is for me to have a railway ticket.

"But it's too late. It's midday already, and we book up all the places we want by ten!"

Catastrophe! Final, irrevocable!

"Well, anyhow, come with me!" he adds.

He says a few words to a clerk behind a wicket, and motions me to wait my turn.

I know that Letaviet has taken his tickets for Frunze, the capital of the Kirghiz Republic, and, to be tactful and not embarrass his party with my presence on the long journey,

I book to Alma Ata on the same line. In that way I can be certain I shall not be travelling in the same compartment.

"Hard Class, with platzkarte[1] will cost you eighty-seven roubles fifty kopeks," says the clerk. "Come back at four, we shall have had a reply by then. It is impossible to guarantee anything earlier."

There is not a moment to lose. My temporary *visa* must be converted into one permitting me to stay six months. But at the offices on the Sukharevskaya they tell me I shall have to wait three days, owing to my having neglected (entirely voluntarily, I may say) to hand my passport over to the House Committee where I lodge. But then experience had taught me that one's papers never were returned by the time one wanted them. Anxiety seizes me. . . .

Nevertheless, I feel within me a force capable of overturning mountains. How wonderful it is to feel that miraculous potency flood one through and through. From one office to another, I charge straight at the multitudes provided with consecutive numbers to show the order of their arrival before me. But what avail their indignant protests against the armour of my will? Finally, I take the office of the Chief by storm, and the impression of his rubber stamp recompenses my temerity.

Then, with a rush, I find myself at 'Insnab,'[2] on whose books I have managed to get myself inscribed as a journalist. Thirty tins of 'bully,' ten pounds of sugar, twelve slabs of chocolate, two pounds of bacon, two packets of tea, two cakes of soap, dried fruits, two loaves, and candles: total one hundred and twenty roubles. In Berlin I had loaded up with soup cubes, rice, oatmeal, butter in tins, and cocoa.

I must find a taxi, I shall succumb otherwise, and so miss the train. But in Moscow disengaged taxis are practically non-existent.

---

[1] Which gives one the right to a wooden bunk on which one can stretch out.

[2] Provision stores for foreigners working in Moscow where roubles are taken in payment. The Torgsin shops only accept currencies based on gold.

Yes, over there, by the petrol pump, I see one with his flag up.

" No, Citizeness! Impossible to pick you up here. Against regulations. Try at the rank. It's only a couple of hundred yards."

But at the rank, nothing! Whatever happens, that taxi must not escape me. I manage to catch it once more, and win the driver over by promising him a dollar.

In a flash I am at ' Intourist ' again. Victory! I've got a ticket. It is four-fifty. Five minutes still to get my permit from the S.P.T.

But the Chief has been gone some time, and so has his secretary. I'm done for!

I knock at every door, on every flight, then run into an elegantly dressed gentleman with a black moustache, to whom I pour out all my woes.

" I know about you," he says. " You're leaving for the Tien Shan. Some friends of mine were talking about you last night. There must be a typist about still. We'll give you some sort of permit that will do."

Much later I heard that this gentleman, whose providential appearance meant so much to me, had brought down on himself all the thunders of his Chief in coming so generously to my aid.

CHAPTER III

Six Days on Board

I'M OFF. The worst is over.

At last I am in the train leaving Moscow, though with shattered nerves and muscles broken with fatigue.

I spend the first thirty-six hours asleep, lying on my sleeping-bag in an upper bunk which I have chosen in the hope the bugs will circulate less freely there than on the lower story. When we get to a station, however, I am forced to wake in spite of myself ; then joining the other passengers, I rush out on the platform, to size up whatever eatables the natives may be proffering.

Always, one expects the prices to have dropped, or some bargain one would be sorry to have missed, yet practically always all one finds are the same things at the same prices. For a rouble there is the choice of an egg, three tomatoes, four onions, two apples, a glass of milk, two slices of bread, a herring, or three salt cucumbers.

Women offer their goods in hands stretched over the station palings, or else they stand behind the trestles of some tiny market-place. A whole cold chicken is priced at fifteen to twenty roubles, and finds no takers.

At the end of the platform a jostling crowd of passengers gathers round the boiling-water supply, each trying to get his teapot first under the tap. By explaining that all I have is an aluminium canteen and that it takes no time to fill, I nearly always manage to get to the 'kipetok' in front of my turn ; so that, however short the stop, there is still time to find out how the market prices run.

Even the first day of all, my eyes were charmed by the sight of two women standing on a station platform, their lovely faces like full moons, yet definitely Nordic with their fine-cut noses, thin lips, and calm, limpid eyes. They belonged, I was told, to the Mordvin race. They were wearing round black turbans on their heads, and scarlet overalls with long sleeves which, gathered at the breast and fitting tightly round the neck, ended half-way down the thigh in three white rows of Russian braid. Beneath this overall and reaching to the knee, appeared a white crash dress trimmed with red galloon, and lower still, above the large bare feet, showed a bright strip of pantaloons caught close around the ankle.

They were holding their sickles by the blades which had been wrapped in rags, and were trying to sell some scraps of bread out of a wooden bowl.

An interval elapses, then the vast gleaming horizon of the Volga appears.

I see an immense raft of floating tree-trunks moored close to the shore. Men live on this vast wooden plain in huts with glittering roofs which they have themselves set up.

Isolated, a white church with cupolas the colour of verdigris seems like an ark at anchor among storm-tossed clouds.

"A bridge! All windows shut!" cries the conductor as he passes through the carriages.

We cross the bridge, but why the strange injunction: is it a warning against some possible bomb?

The train jogs slowly on: it is very hot. July! The scrap of fat bacon among my provisions melts and begins to seep out of its sack. Yet on and on we must go, over two thousand five hundred miles, on board for five times twenty-four hours.

Samara! A huge station, motley crowds; and we draw up by a train about to leave for Magnitogorsk.

"The new giant of the Ural Mountains," proudly exclaims my neighbour, a Kazak from Alma Ata answering to the name of Said Achmet.

He has screwed-up eyes and a round head, and is leaving Moscow, having completed a course in pedagogics at the University there. 'Kazak' means vagabond, and is the name given nowadays to those who dwell in the steppes of Turkestan. Their cousins-german, the Kirghiz, are of Turki-Mongol origin too, and live among the mountains which stretch from the Pamirs to Mongolia.

Solitude!

I seize the opportunity to commune with myself for the last time. Soon this tranquillity will have vanished, it will be impossible to withdraw into myself. Like a recording drum, I shall be turned completely outwards, while every faculty, keenly stimulated, will be concentrated on capturing all that surrounds me.

I remember what someone had said to me: " Once I get back I am at home, no matter where I go. I speak all the dialects, and could travel three months on end without spending a penny. As for the frontier, I need no passport to cross that: all I need is time to grow a beard. Now if I were to give you introductions to the chieftains that I know, it might make as much difficulty for you as them; they would be quite unable to conceive what sort of person you were. I should have to be there. But if you really mean to risk it, go ahead, you'll see for yourself how my compatriots live."

He had veiled the fire that flashed from his eyes behind two swollen lids that all but met, as though the brightness of a Berlin sun in June was all too fierce for eyes to which the Asian plains had given birth. He was short, and his black jacket gave him a professorial look, but I preferred to think of him untrammelled, wrapped in the wide ' khalat,' astride a galloping horse. All his knowledge had been gained while working with his hands at rude and humble European tasks, yet he remained simple and direct. He had also said:

" Suppose you do spend six months or a year, and end up with a book. Where will that have got you? You are clearly not one of those degenerates who have to be always on the move, with no idea what they want. I feel there's strength in you, and that the things you do, you do well. Bear children, and see them grow into strong, real men; that's what the world needs."

"Yes, but that takes two, and a sedentary life at that! No . . . the rude earthborn faces of the steppe call powerfully to me. Civilized life is too remote from life. . . . And let me tell you, I want to earn my bread in a way that satisfies me."

To learn how to deal with life!

And above all, make it real, by reducing it, morally and physically, to simple terms. For only so can its robust savour be known.

Everything must be relearnt again, before life can be truly gauged. What life is worth is a conception we have all lost, more or less. But in contact with primitive, simple peoples, mountain-dwellers, nomads, and sailors, it is impossible to ignore the elemental laws. Life finds its equilibrium again.

My way leads towards desolate lands, treeless and empty of habitations. I shall pass months in a solitude as old as the hills, but then I shall be able to judge what crowds mean to me. With all the weight of the heavens over my sleeping body, I shall learn what a roof is, and cooking over a fire of dung I shall learn the true worth of wood.

But for the moment ' bread *ad lib.*' daily assumes connotations of a richness and depth I had not hitherto suspected.

We stop. The station is Emba. Vast naphtha reservoirs! The eyes of the natives screw up, their skins are yellower than before. Hands proffer piles of ' lipiotchka,' flat pancakes, and cakes of flour baked in the oven. Green, rosy-fleshed water-melons are being gutted by dozens, the juice dribbling from the chins that are busy devouring them.

" Why don't you come and talk to us? " says Volodya, his hands full of fruit.

Both he and Auguste are in canvas shorts tight at the knee. Skilfully, the two women begin making a Russian salad. When it comes to eating, all draw spoons out of their pockets. Then they stretch out to sleep, or read the *Life of Balzac* and Giraudoux' *Susanne and the Pacific*, both in Russian translations.

The heat remains constant. Sweat oozes stickily from

immobile bodies. Once the train is in motion it becomes impossible to open the double windows, for a whirlwind of sand is sucked up by our passage. On all sides the same flatness, the same desert.

Profiled against the south a camel appears, like an ancient skinny bird pecking away at something. A wave of feeling floods through me. I have never seen one before in its natural surroundings.

Late that night we stop at Aralskoie More, a port on the Aral Sea. Shell necklaces and many kinds of fish, both dried and fried, are on sale here, but we find the prices too high for us.

Mila buys a lovely sweater of camel-hair for herself for fifty roubles, from a woman of the steppes. It is shearing time, and all the women carry bundles of the natural hair in their arms. I pay four roubles for a pound for myself, with which to line my sleeping-bag when we get to the mountains.

Parallel with us, suddenly with deep emotion I see the track that leads into Turkestan, and on it slow beasts that barely seem to move. In the dry, clayey earth the innumerable pads of the camels have hollowed out the trail that is so characteristic of them: a narrow, flat-bedded, steep-sided track.

Who sang the flaming colours of the East? Far from being intensely bright, the landscape on the contrary is dust coloured, grey, monotonous; and the unbroken horizon is circular as at sea. Now I understand why the nomads have such narrow eyes. Dazzled, only the narrowest slit is permitted to remain open between eyelids so clenched that they form a parallel line. There is nothing around them on which to rest their gaze, but horizontal infinities of sand that tremble in the heat; flat sea, unending steppe, and disappearing rails. . . . Nowhere the vertical line of a building or a tree.

And at the close of day, when the colours revive, it is never at full strength, but only in exquisite shades, as the beige sand and patches of rosy lichen, and far away, between two monticules, the blue-black streak that denotes the Aral Sea. A smell of wormwood hangs over the burnt-up earth.

SIX DAYS ON BOARD

Little did I then think that six months later I should be back here again, arriving on camelback from the south, after fifteen days in the desert, with the thermometer minus 25°C.

Far from a station in the midst of the sandy desert the train stops. While the engine fills up with water, crouching Kazak women, with ancient, leathery faces, and the flowered cotton of their chemise-like dresses caught in by long black waistcoats, sell water from their ' boils-itself ' (which is what samovar means).

An acrid smell of valerian and wormwood comes from the few rare bushes; cut, their branches serve to sweep out the carriage floors, black with melon seeds.

Birds with flat beaks perch on the telegraph wires. They look like rooks, but their plumage is scarlet and buff. They look extraordinarily comic with their large tails as they struggle to balance themselves in the high wind.

"Nane, Nane," tiny, all but naked, beggars are crying, stretching out empty meat tins in which to catch the crusts of bread or melon rinds that are thrown to them. Like their remote Mongolian ancestors, they permit one solitary tuft of hair to dangle from the top of the otherwise shaven head.

' Nane! ' means bread, my Kazak friend informs me, and begins to help me to compile a glossary of Russian and Kirghiz words. The Turki-jagatai languages of the region bear the same Ural-altaic origin and have much in common with each other. Even while his chin is being shaved by his soldier neighbour, he manages to find an application for the words he happens to be teaching me.

' Iakchi.' (All right! Fine! that was a nice clean sweep of the razor.)

' Iamane.' (Bad! for the blade has caught on an unruly patch.)

Late at night we stop at Turkestan. We unload our rucksacks, while numerous young men surround a bearded wise-acre, head of an expedition setting out to explore some lead mines newly discovered in the small mountain range to our left.

35

Morning comes, and the Moscow aeroplane lands close to the railway line. It is flying via Tashkent and Samarkand to Duschambe-Stalinabad in the Pamirs of Tajikistan. Perhaps Krylenko is on board, for it was by this route he had intended proceeding to his base camp at Garm.

Birds are playing at being fish. Three short strokes with their fins, followed by a sinuous, effortless glide, which when it spends itself is followed by the repetition of the same three short strokes. But there are others, perched and motionless, their plumage cockatoo-green.

Hope at Last

To-day my book did me signal service . . . much more use in fact than stuffing my medicine box in my sack. . . . I had taken a copy with me, thinking that in some town or other it might prove a credential, since I had no others. Mila and Volodya, who knew French, had read it, and doubtless Auguste had been told about it, for with a smile that quite transfixed me with delight, he said:

" We're going to see whether something can't be done: perhaps it will be possible for you to join us after all."

Instinctively my first thought is: " If they do take me I must make sure they never regret it, so I'll volunteer for every task, however tired, hungry, or ill I may be feeling." By the extravagance of this vow I realize just how intense has been my desire to journey with them into the legendary mountains.

Then Mila remarks:

" I envy you being able to write, for then one has to be observant when one travels, and so one remembers better what one sees."

No one can say they were not excellently placed to judge of how I wrote, having visited Suanetia themselves.

At Aris the railway line[1] branches off, and one line passes southwards to Tashkent, while that on which we are travelling

[1] Built in 1906.

continues eastwards, later linking up with the Turk-Sib which eventually joins the Trans-Siberian Railway.

Our train begins a skirt a cloud-capped mountain to our right. We have reached the foothills of the Tien Shan, the Celestial Mountains, an immense range buttressing the Pamirs on the north, whose culminating peak is Khan Tengri in the region where our destination lies. To the east it stretches into Mongolia's very heart.

Zigzagging frequently, the train continues to pick its way round vast patches of yellowish earth which mask the quicksands underneath.

Then a tiny canyon opens beneath a bridge, and to our astonishment reveals masses of foliage, intensely green, held in by double bluffs of sand.

Finally our train stops high in a pass, to which with some difficulty two engines have dragged us.

" This is a historic site," Volodya says. " Jenghiz Khan and his army always passed this way." And he begins to recite a poem on the subject, impressive and sonorous.

The sun now sets behind us, over the red plains we have just left. It is an impressive moment, and I seize the opportunity to take a photograph. But hardly have I got back into my carriage when an O.G.P.U. soldier starts questioning me.

" Did you take a photograph? "

" Yes! "

" It's prohibited. I must confiscate your camera."

" My Leica? But what will happen to it? " Neither menaces, prayers, nor showing him my papers makes the slightest difference to him: just as at La Maddalena, where the unrelenting Italian officers impounded our ' Bonita.'

Then, realizing my anxiety, the man gives me his cap to hold in ransom.

" I might as well have my head cut off as lose that cap," he says, " so I'll be bound to return, you may be sure."

At Aulie Ata he seeks me out again. Twilight; clean platforms! At the O.G.P.U. office he telephones his superior, who shows not the least interest in my case . . . and my camera is returned to me. I recover from my fright, eating some excellent soup at the buffet for sixty-five kopeks. Volodya comments:

"They are no doubt watching the railway line because it runs so close to the Chinese border."

I change compartments before we get to Lougovoe; and we switch off on to the branch line which terminates at Frunze. Every Kirghiz I see wears a white-pointed felt hat, with the brim slit into sections lined with black velvet. From a distance only the tip of the nose, the cheek-bones, and the lower lip catches the light, the rest vanishes into the shadow cast by the hat and the hairs of the beard.

Where the land is irrigated, the grassy plains give place to immense green gardens dotted with tiny white houses as in the Ukraine. Maize, cereals, and vegetables are framed by poplar and willow.

CHAPTER IV

FRUNZE

IT IS MORNING when we arrive. Avenues, dust, crowds, walls, gardens, half-built warehouses! The word Frunze appears on the station façade both in Russian and the new Latin Kirghiz characters. On the ground are two huge bundles composed of folded squares of felt, reed mats, smoke-blackened stakes, cauldrons, blankets, topped by a large wooden circlet which forms the dome of the yurt: a collapsible homestead is ready to move off.

As our luggage is being loaded into a light cart, I seize the opportunity to 'snap' a compact group of some forty Kirghiz, whose headgear looks like so many white dots.

"What are you up to?" Volodya cries, "don't you see they have soldiers guarding them?"

And so they have. Fortunately no one has seen me, and again my camera has a lucky escape.

We follow our cart as it bumps over stones and tilts into deep ruts in the brown earth, seeking a roof under which to install ourselves. Clear mountain water is running in the 'ariks,' narrow channels on either side of the wide avenues bordered by poplars. They run at right angles to each other, and at every corner we have to overstep the rushing water.

The footpaths are flanked by pisé walls pierced every fifty yards by tall double doors: they mark the entry into the native houses which we cannot see. Occasionally, however, we see a Russian house with symmetrical windows and three steps leading up to the pented doorway.

It is a garden city we find ourselves in, with a few scattered public buildings such as a bank, a school, some restaurants. Originally its name was Pichpek, but one of its sons—who died in 1925—being made Commissar for War, the town was

39

rechristened Frunze after him. It is the capital of the Kirghiz autonomous Soviet Republic and claims forty thousand of the total of roughly one million inhabitants.

Eventually we land up at a native ' chai-kana,' or tea-house, comprising a first room containing tables and benches, a second vast sleeping chamber, the floors of both of which are beaten earth, and beyond them, a walled-in courtyard, sheltering a few horses, and containing a cistern, supplying water in the merest driblets, and the closets. We take possession of two rooms on the first story, unfurnished save for some benches. Everyone, however, travels with his own blankets. A woman is washing the floor in a smell of lysol. Our rooms give on to a gallery embellished by a rusty and deafening loud-speaker.

Our balconies, however, provide an enthralling spectacle. To our right the horizon is bounded by lofty snow-capped mountains, the middle distance is verdant with foliage, while below at our feet is the main square of the city, in which the bazaar is being held. The ground swarms with people, tumble-down houses, booths, open-air eating-places, and carts bringing in fruit, vegetables, and forage, drawn by pairs of camels, wearing a harness of coarse woven wool which fits closely over the forehump. The reins are attached to a rope muzzle fastened round the jaw.

Kneeling, they seem like enormous swans whose necks are adorned with ruffles, while the two humps on their backs look like small and downy offspring. As they ruminate, the flaccid skin of the vast pendulous lips reveals a spinach-looking mass of what had once been clover. The bulging eye is fascinating. Its glittering polished surface is brown and seems to recede into unfathomable depths, fringed by long, dull eyelashes that one feels must be as silky as the hairs of the wild silkworm.

It seems as if everyone lives squatting on their heels. The woman watching over her beasts, the twelve-plaited girl gnawing her slice of melon, the Uzbek wearing a bowler hat (where on earth can he have got such a hat?), bartering with

a comrade in a peaked leather cap, the Kirghiz offering rugs
for sale, and his Kazak cousin merely doing nothing at all. . . .

The Russian women, not supple enough to squat, perch on
the sides of their cart. For a cup of honey the price is five
roubles, for 'lipiotchkas' one rouble each, for a kilogram of
horse-meat sausage twelve roubles. Mila seizes the opportunity and buys great quantities, before it is sold out shortly
afterwards. Even the bowl of soup we eat at the Chinaman's
on the corner costs a rouble.

Smells of frying, dung, mud! Then it begins to pour in
torrents, adding a smell of new-mown hay.

All the same, men go on standing in a queue, pushing and
elbowing for first place before the window of the 'Centro-
spirt' Trust's depot, where vodka is on sale after five p.m.
Suddenly the pushing becomes more vicious. . . . What in-
stinctive curiosity lies concealed in us, to make a fight with
bare fists excite us so? A shirt tears off, the man rolls over in
the mud, then lies still; and his opponent seizing a bottle full
of a transparent fluid, smashes it against the wheel of a cart.

Our men return worn out with their many errands. We
need a lorry to get us to our first stop, the stud-farm near the
shore of Lake Issik. The postal lorry is held up till further
orders, for the road is flooded, and it would be sure to stick in
the mud. Three other possible lorries have been requisitioned
by the Pograbetzki expedition, whose thirty members are still
camping out in a railway coach.

As for the S.P.T. 'base,' that simply does not exist. The
two lads in charge of it have nowhere to stay themselves;
they are unable to help us as to provisions, and they cannot
even say if there is a 'base' at Kara Kol.

The engineer in charge of the Meteorological Station is
himself living under a tent.

The officer in charge of the O.G.P.U. base is away.
Auguste insists on being given a general permit covering the
rest of our journey, and gets it, and lucky it was for him he
did so.

This morning, getting up, I find myself staggering: extreme thirst and difficulty in swallowing point to fever and angina. But thirty-six hours spent gargling and swallowing aspirin turn it into a heavy cold. It was then or never, for my comrades' faces said clearly:

"Don't think we're taking you with typhoid coming on."

Besides, we had managed to procure a lorry for the following day. Before leaving, however, I meant to get a bath, to rid myself of my lice, a desire which had turned into a veritable obsession since leaving the stifling train. It is in places like this, centres of latent epidemics, that it is so supremely important to keep one's body and hair as clean as one possibly can.

I find the 'bania' by a mountain stream where it is bridged by the main road. For one rouble fifty kopeks, in a room surrounded by superheated bricks, I am able to give myself and my clothes a thorough washing in two great vats, fed by taps, one running hot, the other cold.

A Visit to an Exile

After which I determine at all costs to visit a Trotskyist exile whose address I have taken care to memorize. My intention must be kept secret from my companions, however, for they might not like it. They do not know I have no political convictions whatever, and that curiosity merely is my motive. Also they might be afraid of possible accusations of having taken a politically unsound person with them. . . .

I pretend I feel much better and that I want to take a solitary walk. And so I start off, inquiring my way, and trying to seem as Russian as I can, not too difficult a task, thanks to my Nordic ancestors . . . who at last are standing me in some stead.

What had Vassily Ivanovitch done? What is he still doing perhaps? If he is under observation I shall be caught, and my journey will end abruptly, then and there. . . .

But I am determined to risk it. The risk spurs me on. I

must go forward in spite of the bitterness of the quinine in my mouth and the depressing effect it has on me. My ears buzz, fever hammers at my temples, everything in the evening air looks strange. I remember suddenly how in Berlin, to break the monotony of my existence and not lose the habit of taking risks, I would arrange to meet him on a certain day in a 'bus for which I had no ticket.

I cross from corner to corner, with a feeling of inevitable approach. Women are taking advantage of the last rays of the setting sun to wash their cauldrons in the ' ariks.' Men are squatting in circles, beginning to uncork their phials of powdered tobacco.

I knock. A voice asks me to go in. A group is at supper round an oil lamp. " Vassily Ivanovitch has moved," they tell me, giving me his new address.

In front of another Russian house I knock at a padded door. There is no reply. I go in. A Primus hisses away in the anteroom which is full of the smell of paraffin. I call out.

" Yes, here I am ; come in. Who is it ? "

" It's Ella. Good evening ! "

A spate of exclamations. Who is it ? But where do you come from ? What are you doing here ? How did you get the address ? Where did you learn Russian ? You've come from Paris ? Incredible ! I must kiss you. What's happening over there apart from world conferences, Fascism, and unemployment ? What do they think about Russia ? Where is Trotsky ? How much influence has he ? What are conditions like in Moscow ?

The room is whitewashed, lit by electricity. A bed, three chairs, a trunk, a table. Tea is offered me, and bread and cheese to accompany it, with the words :

" Don't stand on ceremony, there's plenty more ! "

In front of me stands a tall, thick-set man dressed in a blouse of Russian crash, with regular features, lofty forehead, abundant chestnut hair, and beetling brows above two deep blue eyes which seem extraordinarily vital and open : it is a magnificent head. He is one of a group of persons which

43

meets here nightly, all of whom have been exiled for periods of three or six years, mainly because they openly criticized certain measures of the Government for which they absolutely refused to accept responsibility. Vassily's wife would be returning soon from Tashkent. A young Georgian woman, with black hair and dressed in red, lies on the bed wrestling with a bout of malaria.

Then a man enters with a pointed beard, sparkling eyes behind pince-nez, and a bald head.

" But where have I seen you before? Was it you who called just now while we were at supper? "

" Yes, it was. I recognize you! "

" Well I'm blessed! And after coming four to five thousand miles from Paris. Do you know who we took you for?— the washerwoman. . . ."

I am incapable of answering all the questions that are put to me, nor have I ever regretted so deeply the little interest I take in political questions.

Vassily Ivanovitch explains:

" I scribble away in an office here, and so I earn my keep. But if I do any work of a more complicated nature, even after hours, I am immediately posted to another job. My papers have to be regularly endorsed at the police office. Apart from that I am free enough. Patient? Oh, yes, we are, and it isn't difficult for us; but it's impossible to find out where the others are, whether they have been exiled or not, or whether they are able to organize. . . . Where is the country going? If Stalin doesn't slow down soon, it's all up with us. He'll never be able to get the peasants back again. Then what will happen to us?

" In this place, of course, the Nationals (which is the name the natives go by) detest the Russians who are colonizing them. They've had it impressed on them that the post-revolution Russians are altogether different, but they themselves so far have had little say in the government. The positions to which they are appointed are purely honorary ones, or else they are allowed to act as liaison officers and in-

terpreters between the Kirghiz people and the State. Those
sufficiently educated to occupy more responsible positions,
would, of course, be capable of intelligent criticism. . . . Yes,
I know they have their newspapers, their language, schools;
but they can never, never depart from the line laid down by
Moscow."

"And such mistakes were made; though they were all so
glad to see the end of that Tsarism which was responsible for
so many abuses."[1]

"But it's almost eleven," they remind me, "and you're at
least three kilometres from your 'chai-kana.' And it's to
dark a night for anyone to venture out; we'll make a bed up
for you on the floor."

But my comrades must already have begun to feel anxious
about me, and we are due to leave Frunze at dawn. So the
'washerwoman,' as they call me, summons up the last rem-
nants of her resolution to take her departure, nevertheless.

I have been asked so many questions I found myself unable
to answer that my head is swimming, and seems as empty
as a newborn child's looking at the things of earth for the
very first time! Vassily goes with me. The poplars are indistinguishable in the black night. We guess our way by the
noises of the hurrying 'ariks' that we jump at hazard.

Finally, after many a foot-bath, I take possession of my
bunk again in the dark hostelry.

On awaking, I find I have let myself in for a serious scold-
ing from Capa, which reveals the general feeling about my
escapade—my own included too.

Luckily, strange sounds create a diversion just as they are
about to question me. It is the noise of bells, whose deep
muffled tones, slowly swung, evoke in some inexplicable
manner, danger and solitude. We rush towards the sound and
see an imposing string of camels passing by, each laden with

[1] The reporter that I am notes objectively what was said to me. It goes
without saying that I do not personally take any side in these differences
of opinion between contending Soviet factions. The fact that I report the
replies evoked by my questions does not mean that I identify myself in any
way with the tendencies they express.

two square bales of wool. So deliberately do they move, that it makes one think of the ' slow motion ' of a film.

A Kirghiz guide, sitting astride a minute ass, tows the first beast by a halter made of plaited wool, stuck with double and triple hanging tassels, making a very decorative effect. Beneath its muzzle hung two bells, and from the jaw strap on the nose a plume of stiffened wool rose into the air. The nostrils of each succeeding animal were linked to the pack-saddle of the one in front by a cord. Thus they passed, all moving with the same boneless step. Other bells, cylindrical in form, hung from the beasts' necks; and the sound that issued forth from them was moving in the extreme.

They had come from Kashgar in China.

CHAPTER V

TOKMAK

AT EVERY HOLE in the road our lorry gives an enormous bump, and shoots us into the air, as well as our packages, two spare wheels, and three gallon cans. Then we fall again, helter-skelter, to lie in a confused heap. More than once I begin to fear for the contents of my medicine-box. The cameras run no risk, for they, like Capa's water-bottle, are hanging at our backs.

Capa, unlike us, is not wearing a sun-bonnet; she uses instead a leather helmet, with ear-lappets which produces a most explorer-ish effect. The effect, however, is somewhat spoilt by the brown wool climbing shorts she is wearing, which, neither close-fitting enough, nor loose enough, end somewhere round her knees. Mila is wearing a good pair of riding breeches. I personally still cling to my blue mechanic's suit, one leg of which still shows the bite taken out of it by the dog in the Caucasus two years before.

Volodya is the nicest neighbour to have, because he doesn't weigh much, and has the knack of arranging his seat so that it doesn't fly away every other minute. Whenever we start off again, I try and get as near him as I can.

Five thousand roubles, it appears, has recently been spent remetalling this so-called road, though no one would guess the fact. Actually it is a mere track. It appears that the foundations lie on a bog, the cause of many difficulties in the construction of the railway line. Nevertheless, it now reaches to Tokmak and eventually will link up Kara Kol.

But really our chauffeur drives like a lunatic. He has merely to see a mud crater a few yards in front to lose his head completely, and charge it at full speed. I find my simplest remedy is to stick my head between my shoulders, and ballast myself inside with juicy apples.

47

At Tokmak we come to a standstill in the main street. The one-story thatched roof houses touch. In front of each is a wooden platform shaded by projecting eaves which gives on to the street. Here the inhabitants, with one eye on what is going on outside, exercise their several trades, making slippers, wheels, or ' lipiotchka ' buns.

Close to the vast saucepans of the cook, we make a meal of Siberian ' pelmeny's,' a kind of ravioli swimming in burning red-pepper sauce. All round us, garlands of red peppers are drying under the eaves.

They are wonderful for creating a thirst, and so we make a move to a near-by Soviet ' chai-kana,' where, with crossed legs, we squat on a platform covered with Turkish carpets that have seen much wear. A china teapot is handed each of us, and a bowl called ' piala.' Surrounded by quantities of teapots, an ancient greybeard keeps a sharp eye on the glowing charcoal in his samovar, while another, hunched over a table with a drawer, looks after the cash. The waiter, his dirty feet pushed into ancient rubber goloshes, quite the most common form of footwear in the Soviet Union, shuffles about over the carpets, on which we now recline on our elbows, having quickly tired of sitting with bent knees.

Out on the street a crowd of curious urchins stares in at us.

But what seems very strange is the Communist atmosphere by which we are surrounded, for the ceiling is practically covered with garlands of small red banners, while on a single wall I count no fewer than fifteen portraits of Soviet leaders: Stalin from every angle, Voroshilov, Budyenny, Kalinine, Gorky.

Simple as they are, the latrines of the Mussulman village of Tokmak are the cleanest and most pleasant I have ever encountered. Situated near the mosque surmounted by its crescent, at the end of a garden of swaying poplars, a house rises, standing on piles. Partitions make a dozen doorless cells of it, each with two planks for the feet on either side of a hole in the flooring. . . .

The climate of the country desiccates everything, reduces

it to a powder. At the same time it sterilizes it, and air being able to circulate freely, there is no odour. On the other hand, the Russians are determined at all costs to go on digging holes over which to erect closets with shut doors: with the result that the clayey earth turns into so foul a cesspool that one would rather soil the ground anywhere than have to use them.

Our lorry drives on again, among fields that stretch across the plain to far hills stripped bare and worn into ravines by erosion. Lorries pass laden with merchandise and passengers atop of it. Our savagely hooting lorry drives the ox carts from our path. Slowly they plod along in the shade of their round straw roofs, carts of the migrations of the past, very sisters to the 'covered wagon' of the American trail. . . .

A hole, a bump, a grinding crash! Breakdown! I take myself off. The little cubical shanties are eminently photographic, a perfect match for their surroundings since they are made of the same clay. There are no windows to the exterior, only to the yard. Fodder for the animals is stored on the roof. Bricks are drying in the sun, simple rectangles of pressed mud.

Three Kirghiz are building a wall: two mix chopped straw into the wet earth; the third, perched on the wall, rams the stuff into the log shuttering. The white, many-pleated seat of his trousers makes me think of the Cretan 'vraka.' And the dark turned-up brim of the felt hat he wears seems like a cocked hat made of bronze.

The breakdown turning out to be serious, a broken part, we are forced to return to Tokmak. Twenty-three miles gone out of the fifty-six covered in the day. We find ourselves lodged in the Communal Centre, comprising restaurant, schoolroom, and Workers' Club-room. The "Red Corner" falls to us, but it is night. Only at morning do we see the posters with which the walls are decorated, including huge diagrams revealing the mysteries of the interior of the petrol engine. The long table is strewn with magazines of an educational nature, higgledy-piggledy, and very dirty.

Time and again workers throw open our door, only to withdraw, surprised by our presence. One of the servants, a tall, thin woman, her health undermined by malaria, tells us all her woes: she has finally settled down here after fleeing from the famine in Siberia.

There are a hundred lorries attached to this station, but only about twenty are capable of functioning. Another machine is provided us, and we go along to the offices of the Tokmak branch of 'Soyustrans,' where we are charged three hundred and twenty roubles for transportation to the stud-farm at Chulpan Ata. They insist, however, that we return to the garage to pick up four tyres meant for someone else. . . . Long arguments, time wasted, the discussion begins to turn acrimonious. . . .

We have barely covered another twelve miles when a tyre-burst brings us to a stop.

The atmosphere, as evening falls, is translucent, as though it had been varnished almost. The setting sun casts the slow, lengthening shadows of poplars, whose heads glow luminous in the light, across a wide swathe of grass. That avenue leads towards the sharp outlines of the mountains whose crests stand out against the illimitable sky.

The Life of the Past

The Plain of Tokmak. . . . An historic site, once the capital of the Western Turks. In the year 630, under the great Khan T'ong, the Empire was at its zenith, and all the hordes were gathered together in this region.

The pilgrim Hiuan tsang, on his way from China into India by way of Issik-Köl, came upon them, and was amazed by what he saw.

" The horses of these barbarians were exceedingly numerous. The Khan dwelt in a vast tent ornamented with flowers of gold, so bright they dazzled the eyes of the beholder. In front of his tent long mats had been stretched by order of his officers, and there they were seated in two rows, all clad in glittering habits of brocade. Behind them stood the Khan's own guard. And though it was a barbarian prince whose habitation was a tent of felt, it was impossible to gaze on him otherwise than with respect and admiration." It is strange, as one reads these lines, to think of the pages in which, in almost identical terms, the western voyagers of the thirteenth and fourteenth centuries described the aspect of majesty produced on them by the princes of the house of Jenghiz.

"The Khan wore a mantle of green satin, and all his hair could be seen, except that round his forehead was bound a silken scarf, ten feet long, which after a few turns fell loose upon his back. Some two hundred of his officers surrounded him clad in mantles of brocade, and all with plaited hair. The remainder of his forces was made up of cavalry mounted on camels or on horse, dressed in furs or fine wool, and bearing long lances, banners, and tall bows. So vast was their multitude they stretched far out of sight."

The vision the Chinese pilgrim evoked in these lines is part of history in the making, for what he had thus come upon were the immense reserves of the barbarian forces.

"Have we any conception really what those assembled hordes meant, awaiting the signal to sweep off? The site? This savage region of Issik-Köl, situated high in a fold of the Tien Shan, one slope of which looks at the world of China and the other at the Iranian world? And the historic moment? That decisive moment in the destiny of Asia, that seventh century, in which the Turkish Empire is doomed to break up; the ancient Empire 'T'ou-Kiue,' as the Chinese called it. A few years more and the T'ai tsong, having subjugated their Mongolian brothers, will humble the Turks of Turkestan as well. The 'Kuriltai' witnessed by Hiuan tsang in 630, was the last roll-call of the Turks, still united on the soil that gave them birth, before dispersing to meet all destinies and every epic endeavour. Remember, that for the last time of all, Hiuan tsang saw gathered together the grandparents of Seljuk, of Ghazan Mahmud, and of Mohammed of Kharezm, of the Turkish armies belonging to the immense family of Jenghiz Khan: and those of Timur and of

Mahomet II. Even to-day, the menace of those terrible hidden squadrons, gathered together in a fold of the Ala Tau, can thrill us with something of the awe and breathless expectation that makes the pilgrim's story touch us so close.[1]

Six centuries later, Temudjin, who deep in the heart of Asia had been consecrated Emperor Inflexible, Jenghiz Khan came to grips at Tokmak with Gutchluk, his enemy who had fled out of Kashgar, and utterly routed him. It was in 1207 that the process of Mongol unification began which was to stretch from Pekin to the Danube. Commercial routes came into operation again across the continent, and caravans could start for China knowing the way secure.

It was from the Khan of Kipchak, grandson of Jenghiz Khan, that Genoese merchants sought and obtained commercial concessions in the Crimea, whence their merchandise could set out for the Far East.

We hear also of the Italian monk, Plano Carpini, journeying at no great distance from Tokmak. It is in 1246, and he is on a mission from Innocent IV to the Great Khan Meungke, who succeeded the grandson of Jenghiz.

Another monk, a cordelier, William of Rubruk by name, passes through Tokmak the following year. He has journeyed from the Holy Land, under the orders of Saint Louis, to negotiate a treaty with the Khan of Kipchak. After which he will proceed to Karakorum, where there exists already a colony of French under a Norman bishop.

A little later, Kubla Khan, brother of Meungke, will be reigning over China: in 1269 he commissions the uncles of Marco Polo to beg the Pope to send him a hundred learned men. When the Polos return to China for the second time, by way of Kashgar, they take with them Marco and two Dominican friars, but the latter turn back before they reach their destination. Even by this date Christianity has its converts everywhere. Tokmak is the seat of a Nestorian archbishopric.

Turakina, the lovely daughter of Jenghiz, was a Christian

[1] René Grousset, *Sur les Traces du Buddha.*

of the sect of " Prester John." The mother of the Great Khan Meungke, of Kubla of China, and of Hulagu of Persia was Serkuteni, the Christian. There was great tolerance, an intense eagerness to welcome new ideas, but Europe was in the throes of utter disorganization, with the Pope captive to the King of France. It was the Great Schism, there was either no Pope at all or there were two.

This was the moment. Afterwards it was too late.

By 1339 the Franciscan Richard of Burgundy, Bishop of Iliski to the east of Alma Ata, had been martyred, and the few Franciscans dispatched on a mission by Benoit XII in 1388 might as well never have been sent, for Tamerlane had reigned as Great Khan for nineteen years, all Islamized Turkestan had been ravaged by him, the Pax Mongolica and transcontinental routes had been wiped out for five centuries to come and commerce was forced to discover maritime routes.

And in our own time numberless difficulties again beset the wanderer. Even our own little party cannot be sure whether it will be allowed to proceed beyond Kara Kol. It was in Mongolia that the Citroën expedition into Central Asia was thrown into prison. China is delivered up to bandits, and explorers like Sven Hedin and Sir Aurel Stein no longer have the right to journey where they will.

Is it possible to claim, other than ironically, that communication between nations has never been so facile as in the twentieth century? Even in the fifth century we read that Attila was treating with the Emperor of China as equal with equal, and in that case it can be assumed that intercourse between the two countries must already have been of long standing.

In 1921 it took a month on horseback to reach Kara Kol from Aris, which was where the railway line stopped; and it begins to look as if our automobile will take equally long, if our breakdowns go on occurring with the same frequency.

We manage another twenty miles, but then an inner tube

needs patching, which gives us time for an alfresco supper by the roadside. A Doungan, with simmering pans, happens to have set up near by. A dusty carpet is spread on the earth, and we take our places on it, squatting in Turkish fashion, while an ' arik ' from which we draw the water for our tea runs at our feet. Juggling with a grey, pasty mass, the skilful cook pulls, folds, and twists it several times, with the result that soon he has a skein of supple macaroni in his hands, which he draws out for the last time before plunging it into the boiling soup. Three minutes later the dish is cooked, spiced hot enough to burn your mouth out.

A tiny chick, seeking shelter from the chill of evening, takes me for its refuge. Its chirrupings are simply heartrending as it cowers under my knee, then in the hollow of my elbow. Only by confiding it to Mila do I succeed in mastering my macaroni, which goes by the name of ' lapcha.'

A lorry which we had overtaken now passes us in its turn with piercing triumphant outcries on its horn.

Night is beginning to fall as we bump off again in the direction of a gorge cleft in the Alexander Mountains.

Then one of our double back tyres bursts. Nevertheless, we continue on the good one. It does not, however, hold out long against the sideways thrust of the innumerable ruts, which eventually tears off the metal disk that, riveted in place, clamps tight the gaping edges of the outer cover.

Scattering over the pebbles of an arid slope, each of us works himself into a sleeping-bag.

First unforgettable night passed on Asia's very soil.

Profound communion with the unyielding earth that bruises every angle of my body, with the sky at last an immense uninterrupted dome stretching illimitable above my insatiable gaze, with the wind, the vast primal element that sweeps from over a whole continent.

At last I can yield myself, undistracted, to the unending saga of its many voices. Striding the mountains, and issuing from their wild clefts, weighted with all the immensity mown down in its path, it roars like a furnace filling the valley, and

54

mutters like a torrent. Like a spate of waters it sweeps bellowing down, it is a vast rushing flood that pours over me, turning and twisting me, as though whirlpools were dragging at my hip and shoulder. . . .

With difficulty and with cunning, at last I find a position in which I can get air enough to breathe. . . .

CHAPTER VI

ALONG THE IRON WAY

WE WAKE TO a fine morning. Passing through the gorge
of Boam[1] and skirting the grey waters of the Chou,
we climb slowly to about five thousand feet. The rocky walls
of the ravine are first a brownish purple, then verdigris.

Three oxen draw an immense McCormick combine after
them; then I see that quite a procession of the strange
vehicles is on its way to the heights of Kirghizstan. Passing
an island green with reeds and willows, I think I am looking
at dust-covered giraffes, invisible save for their heads. Closer
scrutiny, however, reveals them as pasturing camels, unloaded,
though their backs still bear the heavily padded, rag-stuffed
saddles.

Then our conveyance stops near a hut, a compulsory halt,
where our papers have to be checked. Later, our conveyance,
passing another at too close quarters, tears a hole in a sack
from which an endless stream of hard grain begins to flow.
A magnificent volley of oaths succeeds the accident, and in
the momentary storm the protagonists come almost to blows.
Our chauffeur, however, helps to repair the accident. He is
black with grease and dust, as is his mate: sixteen hours out
of the twenty-four they spend at work, and have long since
passed the stage when one rebels against the blows of fate or
mechanical defects.

The valley opens out. A long way in front of us we behold
lofty ranges dotted with white glaciers. Close at hand the
mountains open out in a sudden revelation of a vast sun-
flooded plain.

[1] Probably identical with the place known as Kastek in the seventh
century. It is mentioned by Gardisi, an eleventh-century historian, under
the name of the Djil pass.

Reeds, then sandy shores, and Lake Issik-Köl appears. It is deep and vast, and has no outlet.

In 1916 grave revolts took place among the Kirghiz peoples who were being conscripted by force for the armies of the Tsar. There had, it is true, been an earlier nationalist awakening in 1905, at the time of the publication of the newspaper called *The Kazak*, but that was on a small scale. In 1916, however, the whole country was involved. Banding together, the natives began to dig a canal with the object of diverting its waters into that of the Chou, and thus drowning out the Russians inhabiting Tokmak and Frunze-Pichpek. But the insurrection was suppressed by Cossacks under General Anienkof, and the moving spirits were exterminated.

The road straightens out again, widens; tumbledown houses begin to appear to right and left, then a clump of trees, dust, camels, and a three-masted schooner at the end of a jetty; we have reached Ribatchi.

We stop for an hour. The workmen we have given lifts to take their leave, hoping to find a freight leaving for Kara Kol. It is important while in the village to keep an eye on our belongings, and so we take it in turns to eat at the restaurant, a branch of the General Provisions Trust. When Capa and I have done eating, an old man begins to pick up our crumbs, and the sauce left from our highly seasoned 'goulash,' with his fingers.

Down by the water a Kirghiz woman, with Mongolian eyes that look strangely in this Mediterranean landscape, leans against the sturdy schooner, holding a baby on her arm. The water is salt, and as I am nursing a cold I do not join Capa, bathing ecstatically in the vicinity of three astonishingly fair children.

" What is your name? " I say to the smallest.

All I get is a bored expression.

" And what is your father? "

" Ich verstehe kein Russisch."

They are German children belonging to the Mennonite

57

colony in Aulie Ata, whose parents art trying their luck yet once more in a new land.

Armed men are guarding a depot surrounded by barbed wire: loads are being weighed, then lifted on to the backs of camels. Untying themselves in two jerks, they rise and stalk off, borne by their "X"-looking legs, making a fine fresco against the background of water and mountains. But a deep sadness has overtaken me, for our jolting conveyance had flung me between two packing-cases, knocking out one of the lenses of my camera sight, so that I could not find it again, however carefully I searched in the dust and straw or among the crevices in the floor-boards.

I could have wept for vexation. All I was seeing and all I had been hoping to see, and the pictures I had come such distances to hunt for! There was no way of profiting by them because I could not tell what I was focusing on. All I could do was to trust to luck, and that was as bad as having one's eyes shut.

I was cleaning my teeth in front of a little hut where we had drunk tea when Volodya came up, looking as though he were going to tease me.

" What would you say if I told you I had found your lens? "

" It's impossible," I reply, for I had not yet learnt that Volodya is too kindly by nature to make a mock of the misfortunes of others. His eyes are curiously uneven, for an asymmetrical black pupil encroaches on the blue iris of the right eye and, like a target, its dark centre is shot through by two adjoining holes.

" Well, here it is. I found it while I was waiting for you."

And there in his fingers is the tiny glass square which makes life worth living again. No words can express my gratitude, and the depth of my feeling takes the path of tears: tears and toothpaste mingle on my cheeks as I hasten to clasp him by the hand.

We start off again, watched by a crowd of patient travellers squatting in the shade of white walls, and begin to make some headway after the hundred miles covered in the last three days.

There can certainly be no doubt about our driver being a moron. He has no idea how much farther we have to go, nor even the name of the place we are going to.

The gently sloping plain over which we bump runs parallel to the lake and leads down from the Kungei Ala Tau by a road which the mountain streams have worn into ravines at intervals. A new obstacle, down goes the accelerator, and once more a tyre bursts.

We are furious with Auguste. Why could we not have taken the schooner and gone gliding over the gentle waters of the lake, rather than this frantic rush to sure perdition?

"How many days is it going to take us getting there?" Capa asks.

"Seychass," the chauffeur replies, with unruffled mien.

This " immediately " is as elastic a term on Russian lips as is the *mañana of* the Spaniard.

And we spend another night by the roadside, while the single telegraph wire zooms over us in the sky.

Although Issik-Köl is twenty times larger than Lake Leman, with the setting sun I seem to find a likeness in the western extremities of both lakes and the country about them. Ribatchi, some twenty-five miles away at the end of the lake, would be an unspoilt Geneva barely born. The majestic Tereskei evoke the Savoy ranges, and like them end up at the water's edge with a large flat-topped mound which reminds me of Salève. Finally, the Kungei, on whose last slopes we now compose ourselves to sleep, recall the Juras and their unbroken line.

The most vital difference, however, is that only solitude surrounds the metallic-looking flowers of the immense thistles. Europe and its capital of World Congresses in truth is immeasurably remote. . . .

When in 1375 Tamerlane passed this spot leading his savage hordes, the lake of Issik bore the Mongol name of Temurtu nor, or Iron Lake.

And while the mountain peaks cast at each other, like a ball, the storm whose iron-grey clouds are seared by lightning flashes, one thought pierces me through as with an awl of steel. Tamerlane, from Timur, meaning iron. Attila, in Hungarian Aitzel, meaning blacksmith. And in Moscow to-day Dugashvilli calls himself Stalin, man of steel! His reign extends over Turkestan, a just reprisal for what once happened here, when the fourteenth and fifteenth centuries saw Russia held in the Mongol yoke.

The ancient Turks adored both fire and iron . . . and it can be claimed, I know, that Stalin in no way belongs to them, being Georgian-born: nevertheless, his succession is to a most impressive line of chiefs. . . .

And we ourselves; are we not continually moving nearer to the same stern ideal? If Guglielmo Ferrero is right, it is the age of iron we are now about to enter on: a call to heroism, sacrifice. . . . Liberty is ended, Fascism takes its place. Ended is the age of gold, the mines are giving out. . . .

Last hours of travel. . . . And another two villages passed. Storm and rain! At our backs a tin bursts, and the oil flows over the floor and our sacks. Capa asks:

" But what is there in these cans? "

" Oh, one is full of petrol, the other of oil, and the third simply dances round," is Mila's response.

Our ill-humour suddenly disperses in a gust of laughter, the description is so true. And it is on foot we set off to look for a cart to take us on to Chulpan Ata (meaning ' Father of Shepherds '), for now the engine has completely given out. But I suspect the chauffeur of having a plan entirely of his own of making something on the sly, for he shoots off as by enchantment the moment our backs are turned.

Chulpan Ata

We spend some days in this village with the lovely resounding name. A sparely furnished room at the stud-farm is reserved for visitors. Not only are the meals excellent, but the little collective kitchen out under the trees regales us with cream, milk, and honey from the local collective farm, which employs some eight hundred pairs of hands, native and Russian. A couple of pigs have littered to such an extent that in three years they and their generations now muster two hundred and seventy all told. The sows, enormous and swollen to bursting-point, look as horribly repulsive as that egg-laying mechanism, the Queen of the Termite Ant.

A calf sucks at a mother even smaller than itself. It has its work cut out, and the way its neck curves suddenly makes me feel I have seen that scene before. Then I remember. There is, in the museum at Candia, a coloured Minoan tile of a goat sucking milk which repeats the same harmonious lines. Our calf was a cross; its father being a Schwytz and its mother a tiny Kirghiz cow.

The manager of the farm, named Karl Martin Riss, had left his native Lithuania at the age of seventeen. Now he made us free of all the hospitality of his dried-earth house.

But there was no chance of getting horses for ourselves in this place. They were too good and too dear, worth at least a thousand roubles apiece. All but myself have permits to purchase horses, for our expedition can claim to have utilitarian objects, both in the service of science (Mila in her leisure is learning to draft maps and draw glaciers) and the charting of the country for possible future tours. We put our trust in Kara Kol.

Enormous antlers of mountain sheep, black and grooved like the under-surface of a motor steering-wheel, are nailed to the walls of some of the cottages.

Twice a day we go down to the sandy shore for a swim in the Alpine sea, nothing but clear space in front of us for fifty miles, with snowy ramparts in the distance rising twenty thousand feet into the air.

Magnificent horses with Cossack saddles are lent us, and we spend a day cantering over the surrounding pasture grounds; a first general rehearsal which leaves us with aching knees and raw thighs. A most critical day for me, for I was totally at the mercy of my beast and its good pleasure in regard to me. True, I did not get myself thrown off, but that was merely a relative success. And I found it quite impossible to resolve the great problem as to whether to use a whip or not. Those who managed without seemed to make as good progress as those who did not. . . .

A boat was due to put into the creek of Chulpan Ata the following day, we were told. Prudence warned us, however, to be on the spot, according to the custom of the country, some time in advance. Leaning against our rucksacks, Mila and Auguste played chess, while the mountains on either side the lake played shuttlecock with a storm. Tarpaulins were being stretched over the sacks of grain piled close to us. And that, apart from two wretched fishermen's hovels, plagued by the cold wind, is all that constitutes the port.

As night was falling two tiny masts doubled the farthest cape. Could that be the *Pioneer*, a large boat with accommodation for one hundred and twenty first- and third-class passengers? It turned out to be the *Progress* instead, a motor freighter, its decks black with people.

The *Progress* drew inshore, a plank was laid on board, and we embarked with all our equipment, forcing a way through for ourselves with ice-axes and rucksacks. Volodya, after arguing with the captain, obtained for us the right to install ourselves on the narrow bridge, the only part of the ship not yet encumbered by bodies or limbs stacked in all directions.

I find it much too cold up there, with not even room to put out my sleeping-bag, and therefore prefer to spend the night crouching in a corner under the iron stairway leading to the upper deck. Feet mount and descend a couple of inches from my face, strewing me with sand and the husks of sunflower seeds (all Russians of all the Russias are perpetually cracking them open with their teeth). Using my oilskin to cover my head, however, I nevertheless manage to get some sleep.

In the morning we touch at the 'Kurort' of Koi Sara, a

spa situated in a desolate plain, whose whole extent consists of numerous yurts and a long building of new wood.

Near this spot various utensils have been dragged up from the lake, and in particular some ancient cauldrons. Legend tells that the Ossounes, a people issuing in the dim past from the region of the Yenesei, as later the Kirghiz did in the sixth century, had for their ruler a good king, immensely rich, who lived only for the happiness of his people. He dwelt in a splendid palace, and lavished hospitality on all and sundry. But, strangely enough, he demanded a new barber every day, so that in the end there was but one barber left in the whole country. He, too, like the others, came to the court, and strangely enough survived. But then he began to fade away, so deeply did he feel tormented. At last he went to see a hermit in the mountains, and told him what tormented him so. To rid him of the secret that so weighed him down, the hermit counselled him to whisper it down a well when the sun had sunk to rest: then carefully to shut it after him. This the barber did. He went to the well, and three times in succession cried into it, " Our good king has an ass's ears," after which he fled hastily, but forgot to shut the lid. Then the water in the well rose and rose and drowned the splendid palace and inundated the whole land, becoming the great lake, the Issik-Köl, which never freezes in spite of the altitude at which it lies. Over two thousand feet deep, it is one hundred and fourteen miles long and thirty-six miles wide. Yes, indeed, King Midas must have had his origin in the East!

CHAPTER VII

KARA KOL

A WOODED INLET of the lake does service at the port of
Kara Kol. The *Soviet Kirghizia*, a large steamer, flying
the Red Flag, lay moored to one of the jetties. Further out
two schooners stood anchored, their masts taller than the trees
on shore. There was no trace of docks.

The crowd of disembarking immigrants, each with his load,
began rapidly to mount the ascent that led ashore, the smart-
est of them managing to hire their conveyances almost before
one had time to look round. There were many who thus, day
after day, were leaving the cities to come and settle in these
distant regions. While hoping for a bargain to come our way,
we passed the time chewing raw peas; then we discovered an
open-air kitchen with a few remaining boiled potatoes and
some water-melons, which helped us to appease our hunger.

Seen from this spot, a mile or so away, Kara Kol seemed a
forest of verdure surrounded by fields of grain, lying at the
foot of lofty mountains.

Then our handsome driver, who looked Ukrainian, con-
ducted us to the Leninskaya, where we found the Tourist
' base.' As in Frunze, the avenues were wide, bordered by
running water, and planted with splendid poplars.

There was a courtyard with a shelter for the horses, and
in front of the house two large tents. Inside there was a
dormitory containing some fifteen bunks, with a geological
expedition, spending the summer in the region, intermittently
in possession.

The following days were spent in all sorts of discouraging
errands, the exact significance of which remain hidden from
me; from hour to hour, however, the information we receive
is so contradictory that at one moment we are in the skies,

and the next precipitated into the sombre gulfs of depression. It seems we shall never get away. Merely to have quitted Frunze, and have got so far, seems a veritable triumph.

The State stables, run by a tiny fat Armenian, have only three horses left, everything else having been bought by expeditions preceding ours. But after a day spent thinking it over, this personage decides to bring three mounts down from the mountains to make up the number that we need. When Auguste gets back however, imagining that at last everything has been settled, all he finds is one solitary horse, and lame at that. Can the Armenian have been making a mock of us?

At the horse market Volodya happens on a ' dziguite ' who has come from a near-by village especially on our account; but as this cavalier, who aspires to be our guide, knows no Russian, he goes off to the bazaar to find an acquaintance who can act as interpreter. But neither one nor the other turn up again, and it appears that the ' dziguite ' has retired in confusion. The other horses that we had heard were available, though only on hire, disappear in their turn.

All this does not prevent us making our preparations as though we really are going to leave. First we go to the food bureau to get our vouchers for butter, cheese, corn, bread; for without them nothing can be bought. Then on to the ' Raikom ' (the District Committee) whose president, a Kirghiz with a desk dominated by a portrait of Lenin, provides us with information, and reads the documents we submit with frightful slowness. The violet velvet curtains, the tables covered with red cloth, and the two glittering telephones look most impressive.

It is puzzling in the extreme to unravel the various departments and their particular functions. There are our vouchers which have to be stamped, then the corn which has to be taken to the mill four miles away to be ground. Then at the ' Brinzetrust ' a man plunges a long, sharp sound into a barrel, and draws out a sample of yellow butter like a shaving. Brinze is a cream cheese, heavily salted and cheap. Then off for the twenty pounds of bread which have been allocated us. We find the bakery at the end of a field used by the horsemen of the O.G.P.U. to exercise their fine horses. While we wait for the return of the manager we watch the bakers at work, kneading the heavy, sticky, and flaccid masses in wooden troughs. We pay two roubles twenty-five kopeks, and each of us leaves with a warmly glowing brown, heavy ball under his arm.

At the bazaar we buy four roubles' worth of faggots, then salt; and Volodya, having returned with the flour, two Kirghiz women who live in the earthen cube in the middle of our courtyard set to work.

A fire is lit in the great dried-earth oven which backs on one of the walls. To the flour the younger of the women adds salt, water, yeast, three ladles of melted butter, and then begins to knead it with closed fists and all the power of her muscular arms in their silver bracelets. She kneels on a scrap of felt. Her dress, fastened across the breasts by a safety-pin, has been patched so often that no one could tell which stuff was the original one. Then she stops to suckle her infant. We have no words in which to talk to each other, but the infant wails feverishly, and the mother smiles wanly at me. Her simple, swollen face is beautiful after a fashion, and of the colour of the wood it seems to have been carved from. Her forehead is high and her eyes are flat to her face. Her nose is small, clean-cut with a flattened bridge, and her widely separated eyes have turned-up corners and puffy eyelids. . . . With the pink kerchief of crocheted cotton on her head, there is something of a tired Madonna about her appearance.

The mother strips away the cloths with which the dough is covered, rolls it into balls which she flattens with her palm, and then stamps each centre with an instrument garnished with five nails. Then the oven being hot, the unburnt wood is raked out, and the cakes stuck round the inside walls of the oven chamber. At moments when the glowing embers shows signs of causing them to burn, she sprinkles them with water; after which she picks them out, done to a turn. That

66

was how we were able to take with us two sacks of 'toukatch' that would keep throughout our journey.

Bazaar

Wherever we were going, looking for fruit (three apples one rouble), for vegetables, or saddles and harness, our way led always through the bazaar, the heart of the city. It was a fascinating spectacle to watch the ground piled with the strangest assemblage of all the diverse objects to be found only in rag-fairs, while the variety of types of human beings would have ravished lovers of the picturesque with delight.

There were Kirghiz of noble birth—all honour where it is due—with straggly pointed beards, piercing eyes, and velvet bonnets on their heads which, with their grey or black astrakhan brims, seemed like large round crowns. Certain of the bonnets had only tiny bands of fur round them, a sort of toque whipped round the edge. They were always to be seen sitting astride their little mounts, their stirrups hanging low and with thick blankets hiding the wooden saddles. These are the 'Manaps,' or patriarchs, chiefs of their tribes, on whom often hundreds of yurts depend. Their wives wear enormous turbans, dazzling white, the material wound in close and narrow spirals—not crossing as in the south—which are made to pass below the chin, providing a most impressive bandage for the head!

Others were still wearing the summer headgear of white felt, which rises to a pagoda point, the brim being split into quarters, each worn at whatever angle the proprietor desires, with a black velvet binding to the edges. For garments, a number of loose, ill-fitting robes are worn. Among them mingled Chinese Doungans, bonier than the Kirghiz, with hairless faces and yellow-greenish skins.

Every type of Russian was to be seen. Some with fair beards, some without beards at all; in hard hats or in soft, made of leather or of cloth; in knee-boots, or bare-footed; in

Russian blouses or modern shirts; while the women, with large round faces and kerchiefs on their heads, wandered about with baskets on their arms.

The Uzbeks have thick, jet-black eyebrows and wear embroidered skull caps on their heads. Here, their women do not go veiled, though the ' paranja ' is still worn—a robe which hangs from the head, leaving the false sleeves hemmed with braid to dangle at the back. The older women appear to have but one functioning eye, the other being hidden behind a second fold of the robe.

As for the baby Kirghiz, they sometimes wear a tuft of eagledown rising from their velvet bonnets, with the most elegant effect.

All are vendors, selling whatever comes to hand. Someone appears, squats down, and spreads on the earth whatever he may have; old iron, knives, slippers, stuffs, glasses, cooking-pots. One Kirghiz sits by his squares of felt that go by the name of ' koshmous,' and with absorbed attention plucks his moustache, with a mirror in his hand. At his side a boy is working a sewing machine to see what condition it is in. A specialist in empty bottles has for neighbour a vendor of second-hand footwear, where a prospective buyer is testing the quality of a leather boot by stretching it in all directions. Skis lie on a samovar, and a noble Kirghiz with enormous yellow Chinese spectacles on his nose is buying a dagger for himself.

Eyes scrutinize each other wondering how much they dare ask. When some prospective buyer appears, the first price asked is beyond all reason, and one retreats shocked and disdainful, to return with a lower offer later. But, like a spider in his web, the vendor will not budge. I have to pay a hundred roubles for a saddle and its appurtenances.

Mila is wonderful. She knows a few words of the language picked up the year before in the Pamirs, and so she bargains for a large red and blue screen with geometrical designs, made out of willow wands, each of which is wrapped in woollen threads: this frail partition lines the felt walls of the yurts, and is the present a mother makes for the marriage of her daughter.

Farther off are the open-air cookshops, ' pelmenys ' cooking in their cauldrons, or frying ' pirojkis ' in the shade of some roof of thatch. . . . Then there is a sudden commotion, shouts of thief, the dust flies. . . .

Numbers of strolling vendors are offering their odds and ends at arm's-length : fine ladles of white willow, shirts, old field-glasses, lamp glasses, hunting falcons, ancient Primus stoves, and empty canvas sacks. Should the vendor not happen to have the article you want, a word to a friend, and in half an hour the desired object is in front of you.

Standing before a backcloth depicting a colonnade, a photographer with an engaging gesture strives to bring a smile to the faces of a whole family with Mongolian eyes, frozen stiff where it stands by the immensity of the occasion.

A lugubrious trio wanders among the carts in the vegetable market, questing for alms in a metal basin : a man and woman, blind and pallid, led by a young girl, all three singing aloud, uninterruptedly, in ear-splitting voices.

Filthy and half-starved, a dervish passes with his calabash hanging from a bandolier. Sitting by the edge of the running water, an old man turns down his ragged trousers and starts on a big game hunt after his insatiable lice and fleas.

Barbers abound who, according to Mussulman custom, shave the heads of their numerous clients. In Russian their signs read ' Parikmakherskaya,' and in Turki-jagatai ' Sastar-ass.' A great number of horses with ' koumiss ' skins hanging at the saddle wait for their masters in front of a caravanserai in the main street. To shoe his horses, the blacksmith fastens the beast by a band under the stomach to a transverse bar between two uprights, which makes it look as if suspended.

When our feet begin to give way under us we do as the natives do, and seat ourselves on the platform of the ' chaikana,' where we drink green, unsugared tea as we gaze into the street. First the bowl is heated with tea, which is then poured back into the teapot, and when one has drunk the last drops are always flung overboard. . . .

The baker is at work next door, crouching on his heels over his earthen oven. He lays the round of raw dough on a pad of stuff, then leaning over sticks his arm into the interior and smacks the ' lipiotchka ' on to the wall. In front of him rises a mound of the cooked scones. When a rider stops, there is never any need for him to get out of the saddle, for some gamin or other is always sure to be present to hand him his purchases.

His neighbour, an Armenian, is preparing ' shashlik ' over an oblong brazier. The meat splutters: three skewers cost one rouble. A camel trots past dragging a light cart after it.

How I should like to be able to look at it all without anxiety, but there is always the thought of the future. Horses being so difficult to come by, my companions suggest that, instead of accompanying them, I go off to Karkara and visit the great fair there.

To-day I happen to pay a visit with Volodya to the editor of *The Tuoussu Kolkhoz*, a local newspaper published in Kirghiz, appearing every three days, with a three thousand circulation and selling at five kopeks. The editor, a man of intelligence, provides us with information concerning the region and tells us how almost completely collectivized it is.

" Comrade Ella here would very much like to come with us into the high mountains. But as the region is practically uninhabited, don't you think she would get a better idea of the Kirghiz by remaining down in the plain? "

" But nothing prevents me doing that on the way back," I cry.

" She simply must not miss the chance of seeing the Syrt where the nomads live," replies the editor: " then she really will have some idea of what has been accomplished in transforming the lives of this people."

"But," added Volodya, "her equipment isn't warm enough."

"That's a mere detail. I can get some fur to line my sleeping-bag in a moment. As for clothing, I'm absolutely all right."

I am soon in the throes of bargaining, and for fifteen roubles acquire a long, black-haired goatskin. When I get it back to the 'base,' I give it a good beating, brush it, then shake it out well, after which I hurry off to the O.G.P.U., which controls the Tien Shan frontier region to which we are going and, producing my passport, ask the chief whether I am allowed to accompany my comrades.

"Why certainly!" he replies. "And so you're all ready to start."

"No, alas! There seem to be no horses available. We are put off day after day. As for our Auguste, he's actually beginning to talk of hanging himself."

"What! what's that you say? I'll go along to the horse market myself and see what's happening!"

Can my instrumentality have helped? In any case, next day Volodya arrives riding bareback, and wearing a modest air of satisfaction that really suits him to perfection, and makes his eyes, under the limp cotton *piqué* hat, gleam as brightly as his nose scorched and peeling from the sun. Later, noses of both Volodya and Auguste are to be objects of the most touching solicitude, which will even extend to the nostrils of Matkerim's horse.

Matkerim is our sly, garrulous interpreter, who wears a caracul toque, and helps us to outwit Jocubai, our taciturn guide.

Now each of us has a horse, with a pack-horse in addition. We take them to be shod with crampons, to help negotiate the glaciers and rocks. It seems I have everything to learn from these beasts: if one approaches them from behind they rear, and if one takes them by the bridle they bite you in the forearm. Lord, what is going to become of me?

Life at the Base

We began to laugh like lunatics. Our horses, for which we had paid on an average the low price of four hundred roubles each, turn out to be all mares, and in foal by asses. That no doubt will help us to resell them at a profit, not mentioning the ass of course, on our arrival in Alma Ata. But think of the surprise for the purchasers when the hoped-for foals turn out to be mules.

Auguste and Volodya have to put up with a great deal of teasing, for we keep on telling them they are starting at the head of a harem.

There is nothing frightening about a mare, I tell myself in the courtyard of our base as I practise trying to leap into the saddle. But instead I seem to make a slow-motion dive and find I am lying on the ground, having turned round on myself in the process. I had left the halter tied to the rope drawn across the courtyard, thinking in that way to keep my horse in position. But the animal had moved forward, and the rope tripped me up. I don't know whether anyone saw me, but I felt very foolish.

Follows a visit to the prison, the men there being organized into an artel (a community of artisans), to have our boots studded with nails and one of our Primuses resoldered, it having melted the night before in our room while we were cooking a fine cauliflower—a delicacy we had been promising ourselves for a week at least.

Our lives are spent under a chromolithograph of Lenin, across which battalions of flies march, as they do over the red cotton curtains, the windows, and the table at which we eat.

Our group of five gets on well, nor do we stand on ceremony with each other. Auguste, fortune's favourite, has a pocket electric lamp, and at night I can hear him switch it on to track down some flea that is harassing him under the blankets. As for me, I have to wait for daylight before

undertaking a similar hunt. At times we say to the men,
" Look out of the window for two or three minutes," and
in that way manage to dress the sores caused by our wild
gallop over the Chulpan Ata pastures. Every day starts off
with the same refrain:

" Plokho spala, blokha koussala! " (Bad night, fleas bite.)

We wash at the edge of the rivulet of water which every
house borrows for a few yards from the adjacent ' arik.' The
inhabitants of Kara Kol number twenty thousand, and a
large proportion of them live upstream from us and have
already used the water before we get it. Spitting and
emptying the rinsings of our pots and pans far from the
stream, we hope and pray the others have done likewise.
Then we give no more thought to the matter. The transparent water looks innocence itself.

Nevertheless, Capa has not been well for some time past,
and is now running a high temperature. We put her on a
diet: dysentery, typhoid, typhus, all are possible. She even
began to sing aloud in her bunk this evening, while the
worried Mila skilfully cut herself out a waterproof jacket
and hood, the seams of which she stuck together with rubber
solution. One has to know how to manage for oneself when
the shops can't sell you what you need. . . .

Returning from the bazaar, I fall in with a procession of
' October ' children, brown-skinned nationals and blond
Russians mingling, clad solely in blue cotton shorts, and led
by an energetic young girl. A tiny Kirghiz is extraordinarily
comic. He is the only one wearing stockings, and has them
pulled up over his trousers and held in place by a woman's
belt and suspenders. It seems there are eight thousand
pioneers in the district. Wanting to get some information
about the Komsomol movement, and having been present
at their very first congress, I walk towards their club-room
through the park, passing on my way a ' kamenniy baba,' a
large upright stone on which, vaguely sculptured, appears
a human face which somewhat reminds me of the pointed
heads of the figures from Easter Island. Such stones are

very ancient, prehistoric possibly, and are met with only in Mongolia, where they would seem to perpetuate the memory of some hero. What theories will be propounded, I thought, when ten thousand years hence masses of bronze Lenins come to light, little by little, over the extent of this vast continent. I must really mention it to H. G. Wells. He omitted to provide for this contingency in his book on the future. . . . But all this is a parenthesis, of no importance. . . .

The Chief of the Komsomols had asked me to call on him at his office, but though I went there several times I never found him in. The place was like a railway station. I stayed a couple of hours, putting my notes in order. All the time people were coming in and, mistaking me for a secretary, would ask me questions in Kirghiz for which, of course, I had no answer.

CHAPTER VIII

On To The Syrt

CAPA IS WELL again and at last our caravan sets forth. We say farewell to our base, and for the last time eat at the 'Technicians' restaurant,' where we had regularly taken our meals. A smallish place, with green plants on the tables, and the voucher for the meal costing only a rouble and a half. Kara Kol was a paradise. And, height of luxury, there was even at times a little honey with which to sweeten our tea, or a couple of sweets (konfett) to be eaten as we drank. But what irritated me was seeing the lethargic way the servant wandered aimlessly about, leaving the room empty handed when the tables remained littered with dirty crocks.

"But what good do your sharp remarks do?" a stranger at my side asks. "Send your comments to the newspaper: then they will be published, and in that manner social amelioration will be achieved by way of self-criticism."

Jocubai trots in front of us, his pointed hat on his head, his musket over his shoulder, and leading the pack-horse whose load is framed in the tent poles. We follow as best we may, trying to keep out of the way of the dust raised by the other horses. Over the cruppers of our mounts are our sleeping-bags, while at their sides hang the sacks containing our belongings and provisions, fastened to each other by a throng passing under the saddle. If they are not of equal weight they slip and bang against one's foot at every step. . . . But what does that matter when we are off at last?

"Auguste! I must confess I never really believed we should get off till this moment."

"But why so pessimistic? Is it because of the way you were brought up? If we hadn't been determined to succeed,

75

do you think we should ever have achieved anything in this country?"

Can one possibly change one's mentality? A last anxiety continues to gnaw at me: shall I have money enough?[1] Auguste had told me in Moscow that I should need a thousand roubles for the trip. And as I had about that sum at the time, everything seemed all right. But I had not taken into account the fact that my last hectic day in Moscow would cost me three hundred roubles to complete my equipment, purchase food, and buy a railway ticket. Then there was my share of the lorry fifty roubles, the boat ten roubles, food on the journey forty-seven roubles, my horse four hundred roubles, my lodging at the base twenty roubles, my primitive saddle fifty roubles, and my fifth of the general expense of hiring a guide and laying in provisions one hundred roubles, so that practically all I had started with was spent. And we had still two mountain ranges to cross before we could reach Alma Ata, where I should try and get a *visa* for Sin Kiang.

I therefore telegraphed to Moscow asking to have five hundred roubles transmitted to me at Kara Kol, and meanwhile trust to my comrades to advance me what I need. But what am I to do if by some mischance the money fails to arrive, or if we are unable to sell our horses at a profit?

It is a lovely day. Huge sunflowers, their centres packed black with seeds, stand to attention, and tractors throb among lush fields of rye.

If only Jocubai would not outdistance us all the time. As though glued to his saddle he trots along (is that what the 'trapatka' is?) and we must canter to catch up with him. Our beasts seem starved; they are always wanting to stop and browse, and we have continually to urge them on in an attempt to circumvent their efforts.

The road crosses a river, flowing over a bed of round

---

[1] I must apologize for attaching so much importance to this matter. But my journey lasted some six months, from July 1932 to January 1933, and all the money I had available was francs to an amount equivalent to rather less than £75.

pebbles, which makes me anxious as to the best way of dealing with my mount. . . . I do nothing, however. But in the very middle of the stream it stumbles, lurches over to the near side, lurches still further, and at the very moment when the water is slapping against my stirrups and the sack on the cruppers, rights itself. Phew! That was a close shave, and I shall never feel the same about fords again.

"When we were in the Pamirs," Mila said, "there were times when we would have to do this fifteen or twenty times a day. . . ."

"Yes, I know, that's where you have to cross the River Panj on blown-up bladders, and where you land a couple of miles down-stream from the point you started at, that is if you've not been sucked under by the whirlpools."

"Oh! That's the sort of story Pilnyak writes. You won't find that any more."

Kirghiz Settlers

The sun is sinking into the remotest portion of the unseen lake, when a group of poplars tells us we have reached Chalba, the village in which we are to sleep. We shall thus be spared the necessity of guarding our horses through the night, in order to prevent them straying into the corn.

Our guide having palavered with various men, we enter a courtyard, tie up our horses under a shed, and carry our belongings into one of the rooms whose floor and walls and roof are all of earth, and in which there is only one tiny window.

By the light of an oil lamp we see the woman of the house unfolding some blankets, the only furniture in the room. To give them some idea of what a useful person I am, I go out into the darkness again with the object of unsaddling my mount that has been sweating hard.

"No, never!" Jocubai explains by signs. "It would catch cold. Wait an hour. . . ."

Then a boiling samovar is brought, on which our tea is already brewing, and adding some bread and cheese, we eat our supper. Staggering with fatigue after our first day of eleven miles covered at a trot, we blow out the lamp. I have to go into the courtyard for a moment, and as I glance into the mud-framed window of the adjacent house I see a whole family stretched on the ground and wrapped in blankets. Only the mother remains awake as she looks some clothes out of a chest.

In the morning we make our toilet by a stream where ducks are paddling in the mud; an attractive little girl watches us as we brush our teeth, then using the contents of her round teapot, rinses her own mouth out and rubs a finger on her teeth.

We cook our eggs at the bottom of the samovar, pay two roubles per horse for hay consumed, and start off once more full of enthusiasm, though stiff all over.

For once our yellow spectacles are no use to us, the sun being at our backs. In the fields the delicate tints of the giant poppies seem fresher than ever. But most of them have faded already, exposing the spheroid capsules full of tiny seeds which, surmounted by starry crowns, stand at the apex of rigid stems. Some we eat, and they taste like dust, so dried up are they; others have a subtle flavour of ground nuts.

The sides of the seed pod show dark scars, where six or eight parallel cuts about a millimeter apart have been made. The brown, bitter sap that oozes out is collected by men with spoons. The petals of the flower serve to wrap the opium round once it has gone hard. As pills it yields sweet sleep or pours a dread oblivion with its spluttering grains.

We pass carts and hurrying riders: and an ancient turbaned dame, ambling along with what looks like the immense cover of a cheese-dish, but which in reality is the wooden crown that forms the tracery of the yurt roof.

As we pass through the small Kirghiz villages, I notice a semicircular brown yurt standing by every house. By no means all the natives have taken to a sedentary life. They stifle between four walls. Sometimes they pierce large holes in the ceiling over their hearths, or else they stable their animals in the house while they themselves live in the tent.

Since 1916 many attempts have been made to wean them from their nomadic lives and settle them in colonies founded by Russians. But they show little interest in cultivating the earth. On the other hand, they do at times enrol themselves in some collective farm, but as a rule they soon leave to resume their old nomadic lives, complaining they have not received all the benefits they were promised.

It is estimated that under the Tsarist regime about a hundred million acres of the immense Kirghiz-Kazak territory was distributed to Russians. In 1868 Kolpakovski, founder and first Military Governor of the fortress of Kara Kol, offered various inducements to his countrymen to come and settle in Syemiryetchi, or Seven Rivers, as the region was called, promising them exemption from taxes and military service, as well as subsidies for a period of fifteen years, or alternatively twenty-five acres of land.

Enough of the Kirghiz people took advantage of his offer to found a total of twenty-nine villages, while seven thousand of them went to live in the towns. In 1891 all further immigration was prohibited: nevertheless, it still goes on. By 1911 Syemiryetchi numbered one hundred and seventy-five thousand Russians, and one hundred and twenty-three exceedingly prosperous peasant villages, in addition to thirty-two villages of Cossacks, every Cossack having received some ninety acres of land.

Then came the Revolution, and in its name the Government promised the natives to restore the lands that had been taken from them.

A delegate of the Moscow Communist Party, George Safarov, at the Tenth Party Congress in 1921, declared that within two years from the date of the Bolshevik Revolution Russian-owned property had increased from 35 per cent to 70 per cent, to the detriment of the population of Seven Rivers.

Safarov then embarked on various agrarian reforms. Seventeen Russian villages, established after the Revolution, were

restored to the Kirghiz nation, while all the compensation
that the owners received was merely a concession permitting
them to buy cheaply the wood with which to build new
houses for themselves. In the end, however, Safarov and the
local Government officials were accused of counter-revolu-
tionary and chauvinistic tendencies, and were deprived of
their positions.

On the other hand, if I understand it rightly, it may well
be that one of the objects in punishing them was to reassure
such of the Kirghiz people as still retained their nomadic
habits, and to lead them to assume that, apart from Government decrees, no one had the right to inaugurate agrarian
reforms with the object of compelling them to settle down.
Later, in 1923 and 1924, there was an official partition of
the land among the Kazak-Kirghiz peoples. Russians and
Kirghiz from then on possessed their fields according to the
law. It was a reform based on moral considerations, which
sought to efface what Safarov had done.

But then in 1925, and only in Kazakstan, it is true, an
edict was proclaimed to the effect that all Russians who
elected to settle in the country after August 31st, would be
condemned either to leave the country or to hire their land
from the State. Forty thousand families would have been
affected by this measure had it not been annulled in 1927,
in spite of the decision of the Party Congress.

Now one reads that the Five-Year Plan provides for
settling four hundred thousand Russian peasants in this same
Kazakstan, in the wake of the new Turk-Sib Railway.

The country is exceedingly rich. They tell me that during
the Great War, the Imperialist War as they call it here, the
Governor of Kara Kol was served with an order to furnish
over one hundred and fifty tons of grain within three days.
Numerous requisitions having been made already, it was a
matter of some anxiety where the grain was to come from.
The head of a neighbouring village happened, however, to
visit him, and, learning what the trouble was, said at once:

" Don't let that disturb you, please! What's a mere hundred and fifty tons? It will be a pleasure to me to lend it to you. You shall have it to-morrow."

Noon! We have reached Pokrovskoe, the last village on our route. The market is crammed with bustling people. We are probably too late, and there will be nothing left but melons and sunflower seeds. We go into a little restaurant, the walls decorated with political portraits, and are brought chopsticks with which to eat our peppery raviolipelmenys.

On a platform in the shade, with a rivulet under his feet, squats the flatbread vendor. We take our permits, allowing us to continue to the frontier, to the office of the O.G.P.U., and pass a pigsty containing a bear cub caught in the mountains only two days before.

Leaving the plains and the heat, and turning our backs to the lake, we begin the almost insensible climb to the Tereskei range. A last turbaned woman passes us, astride a little beast as curly as a spaniel. Although the heat is stifling—my legs are bare—she wears a thick velvet mantle with the sleeve dangling at her side, which, as custom demands, is long enough to hide her whole hand and half her whip.

" Towards the Syrt? " she asks.

A grassy plain succeeds the millet fields. We enter the mouth of a valley, then rest awhile to let our horses feed. I see an unbroken dyke, and find it masks a swift flowing stream. In a moment a cake of soap is found. I strip, and it is purest joy, in the great heat, to feel the icy, limpid water from the near-by peaks flow over my body.

In spite of the distance I can see Jocubai first wash his feet and then his bosom.

A number of tombs rise at the foot of the mountain, bright splashes of colour, cubes festooned about their upper surfaces . . . one of them looks like a tall hay-stack with a square porch stuck on.

The telephone wire ends abruptly in a guard-house of the S.T.O. (Soviet of Labour and Defence) with a watch-tower surmounted by a flag. And here begin the trails that lead by four different passes into the region of Kashgar in China.

The Valley of the Chuguchak

Now the mountain reveals itself between two cliff-like faces of ruddy rock built up of obliquely running strata. Abandoning the main river we continue to the left, and enter a ravine whose red escarpments are studded with bright green vegetation.

Very vivid is the green of leafy willows by the river. The transparent water flows over a bed of ruddy sand. Steep slopes surround the valley. To our left is a sunlit rocky wall; to our right steep slopes, clad in Tien Shan firs. Out of the light each slim and towering tree-trunk seems a cathedral spire. How on earth are we ever to get through?

Our precipitous trail rises straight out of the ravine, tracing a zigzag path through a rock fall. We reach a pasture ground and begin to work round its edge. Below us, on a trail parallel to our own, two riders, a Kirghiz and his wife holding an infant in her arms, pass in front and disappear, descending vertically into the depths of the ravine. Where can they have gone? And shall we have to follow that same road?

Yes, for we round a bend, then begin to descend ourselves, while our mounts drop from rock to rock at the risk of breaking their legs. Jocubai, however, remains in the saddle, his stirrups on a level with the eyes of his chestnut mare, skilfully dodging the low overhanging branches of the firs. My own mount's bumpings has begun to shake loose its load, and the saddle and all the rest begins to slip over towards its round barrel.

When it comes to crossing a torrent, fearing a ducking, I hastily slip my Leica into its waterproof case. Then the trail glides among fir-trees with gnarled roots. There is no more strength left in my knees, as a result of continually digging my heels into my horse's belly, which is the only way I can get it to move on.

"No," says Mila, "gather your reins, pull his head up, click your tongue, and hit him with your whip!"

ON TO THE SYRT

When the ascent is particularly steep, I am forced to hold
with both hands to the pommel of my saddle. And whenever
I get a chance I rest my legs by letting them dangle outside
the stirrups. When there is only rock on one side of the trail
and sheer void on the other, I have to keep a careful watch
lest my swollen sack catch against the rock and make my
horse lose its balance.

Roasted by the sun, my face seems on fire, but the evening
air is damp and cold. A snowy peak blocks the valley. Auguste
is shivering and puts several coats on. A penetrating odour
comes from the pine-trees, and I chew at the young and
tender needles. Night has all but fallen. Matkerim has stayed
behind at Kara Kol to buy more cartridges and gunpowder,
and Jocubai is unable to answer our questions as to how far
we are going and how much longer we have to grit our
teeth.

" How high up are we now, Auguste ? "

" The altimeter has gone on strike."

Which renders exactly what I myself feel. And they say
that mechanisms have no soul! And we had passed through
a couple of clearings just right for camping. I had seen an
eagle, too, caught in a net, at the door of a hut.

Raging inwardly I go on climbing, dragging my brute after
me, punctuating my ' Khaidas '—come on—with every curse
I have ever known, in every language. Not yet being
acquainted with Arabic, exceedingly helpful in such cases I am
told, German-Swiss seems at the moment endowed with remarkable properties.

Without a word our guide comes over, and, passing the
leading rope of the pack-horse to me, by a sign invites me
to get on his sturdy nag. How refreshing the rest is! Without
the least jolting, my squat little bay goes on climbing, picking
our trail through steep and age-old undergrowth, while its
saddle, padded much more thoroughly than my own, seems
like a veritable arm-chair.

8

CHAPTER IX

THE FIRST AUL

FIERCE BARKING! Above us appear fires: and luminous points through the latticed doorways of the yurts. I feel we have made port at last, that warmth and rest await us.

As the convention demands, we wait at a distance, while our guide palavers with the headman of the aul (the cluster of Kirghiz dwellings), explaining who we are and what our destination is. Then the Chief invites us to enter his yurt, and shakes our hands by taking them in both his. Our horses are led away to be hobbled: a lad will take them to the pastures.

The chieftain raises the door-flap, after making sure the women are ready for us. A low fire burns on the earth in the middle of the hut. Quilts are laid out in the place of honour, facing the door, and Auguste takes his seat on them.

Matkerim has caught up with us at last, and tells our host that all we want is hot water for our tea, whereupon our large-bellied kettle is set down in the embers. The woman of the house, who has gone on squatting in that part of the yurt which serves as kitchen, gets up and goes to a sheepskin-covered stool on which stands a square-bottomed, largish water-skin, down the sides of which run four vertical seams and from which projects a wooden handle. The woman shakes the handle energetically and a liquid is heard slapping against the sides: then she takes hold of the supple neck and crushes it against the paunch, whereupon milk flows into a bowl. Our host tastes it, then passes it on to Matkerim, who tosses it off.

It is 'koumiss,' fermented mares' milk, the favourite Kirghiz beverage, so health-giving and medicinal that it enters into the anti-tuberculous treatments of the Kazakstan sanatoria. I had tasted it before at our inn in Frunze, but then it was bitter and seemed very strong.

Now, however, I must drink it like the others, according to the ritual, while our Kirghiz hosts break wind with the best of grace. My face begins to prepare for the grimace that will follow, but instead discovers it has the agreeable fresh taste of a light white wine, and nothing at all in common with the Frunze liquid.

The woman cleans out the bowl by running her finger round the inside, after which she licks her finger clean.

We stretch our legs out blissfully as we warm our hands. Auguste is immediately asleep. The whole family observes us with calm, grave faces. The young woman wears a scrap of stuff on her head, with her hair dressed in plaits from which coins are hung to the tails by bits of cord. The plaits fall below the woman's buttocks, outlining them when she bends, and the weights prevent the plaits from falling into the cauldron. When I look more closely at these ornaments, Matkerim says to me:

" The coins are Chinese, because when there was silver money, the Russian authorities thought it unseemly for the Tsar's effigy to go wandering over the buttocks of the women."

The old mother has nothing but a key at the tail of her plaits. Though wrinkled as a witch, she presides over our tea-drinking with such dignity that I cannot take my eyes off her, and envy her aristocratic poise. A loose, dark gown under a patched black velvet waistcot, permits her brown and bony breast-bone to be seen.

We all drink quantities of tea, handling our ' pialas '—bowls—in silence to the lady of the house who fills them, after which we drink, holding them between the third finger and the thumb. When we finish we turn the bowl upside down in front of us and someone else immediately makes use of it. These bowls, and the stuffs in which the women dress, are often the only factory-made objects in the yurt.

The man of the house has a scanty beard, narrow eyes, a

white felt hat, and feet in lambskin boots: the wool inside and laced at the ankles. Under his instep he wears iron crampons with four studs.

" No, they are not Russian," he says in answer to my question. " They are not very common round here, but our hunters have always worn them. In the winter I take old horseshoes to the blacksmith at Pokrovskoe and he refashions them for me."

A man with one eye, half-witted, comes in from watching the sheep and a girl goes out to take his place. The breeches he is wearing are of thick, natural sheepskin with an ample seat, and the thigh on which he wipes his knife is bare and shining with filth, like the gleaming skin breeches of the Tyrolese.

Numbers of utensils, leather buckets with teapot spouts, weapons, head-dresses, hang on the wooden lattice-work which forms the inside wall of the yurt.

The neighbours succeed each other, coming to gaze at us, and squat in two or three rows near the double *portière* of straw and felt. Though curious, they keep their distance.

The bread and brinze we offer them is tasted first by the woman. Like most peoples who live on the ground, she is sitting on her right foot, the other knee being upright and supporting her left arm. Her youngest baby is asleep against her hip; the squatting other two are determined to miss nothing: nevertheless, their eyes begin to close in spite of themselves.

Just as I am about to throw an egg-shell into the fire the woman puts out her hand. What does she want to do with it? I pass it to her, but she still looks dissatisfied. How irritating it is not to be able to understand each other.

" Bother! " says Mila, " it's an egg she wants, and there aren't any left."

THE FIRST AUL

A Night in a Yurt

We begin to unpack, whereupon everyone wants to finger the rubber outer lining of our sleeping-bags. To explain what the material is, Volodya points to the goloshes Jocubai is wearing in place of shoes. Most of the men in fact are wearing rubbers over their boots. Then they examine our shoes, and lavish praises on the triangular nails with which they are studded. At last, however, we are allowed to prepare for sleep.

I hang my trousers and socks on the lattice-work. Our baggage has all been stacked in the tent near a baby calf brought in for the night. The double door-flap is dropped, and the double door of carved wood shut after it. The Kirghiz take off their boots, but retain their ample shirts and underpants. Rarely does a screen divide a yurt in two, and then only for a time, when the eldest son, having married, brings his wife beneath the paternal roof. Only when the second son marries will the first have a yurt of his own.

It is cold. Only the embers still remain awake.

The dogs are howling wolf !

From outside the felt walls come bleatings and the stamping of horses.

Here at last is a roof as it ought to be, through which the glittering stars can be admired before one drops off to sleep. Remote and encircled by the yurt, they lie at the bottom of some fabulous well. . . .

If they could only tell all they have seen enacted here in the very heart of Asia, this empire of the Turki-Mongol nomads!

For how much longer will their descendants go on living as they lived a thousand and ten thousand years ago? Now the Bolsheviks are trying to settle them, collectivize them . . . .

It may be that the nomad will continue to exist as long as there are flocks to lead to pasture in the great plains of the world. . . . And are we not perpetually, in Europe itself, meeting the untamable nomads that are called gipsies or tziganes.

A New Life

A loud beating and the sound of clacking koumiss wakes me. In the six yurts that compose our aul the women have finished milking the mares and are now vigorously churning. The door frames a long tail and the gleaming cruppers of a horse, a green sloping pasturage, and the opposite slope of the valley; scree and mist-veiled firs.

Whereupon we give ourselves up to acrobatic antics in an attempt to get into our trousers inside the sleeping-bags, lest we should shock our hostess by appearing half-dressed.

At breakfast I am almost responsible for a tragedy. Volodya asks me to pass him a slice of bread which is kept in a napkin with the sausage Mila had had such pride in buying at Frunze. I am just about to hand him the package, when his terrified eyes strike me motionless: sausages made with pork are impure in Mussulman eyes.

" When we were in the Caucasus," Capa relates, " one of our porters discovered there was sausage in his pack. When later he told his family about it, they refused to have anything more to do with him."

So it is in secret that we have to eat it in order to add some extra calories to our buttered tea. Later we told our men that the sausages were made of horseflesh and were being kept for Tartar consumption.

The mute keeps us well under observation, and frequently bursts out laughing while making long speeches in guttural tones. He seems a butt for teasing, and at times they hustle him about, but it is all friendly enough. Our young hostess puts a small willow screen in front of her cooking pots, dons an ample coat of violet velvet, and unhooking a short leather whip sets off for the town.

We put our own tent up and Auguste stretches out under it.

" How are you? " I ask.

" He's got a temperature of 103°," Capa explains as she draws me away; " quite out of the question to try and get him over the Chuguchak pass, which is our next stage. Why, it's nearly fourteen thousand feet! "

I could almost offer thanksgivings for the forced stop; there are so many things my curiosity urges me to discover in this strange camp.

Matkerim regrets that we have forced our mounts so hard; they are almost too tired to eat.

Squatting in front of a neighbouring yurt, four women, with all their might and with wands that whistle in their hands, beat smartly on some camel-wool scattered over a sheet. Rhythmically the arms rise and fall, the elbows are pulled sharply back, and the sticks automatically release themselves from the flocculent mass.

It is the first process in preparing the felt, and only the summer wool is used, as giving the best wear.

The children scrutinize us, their plump cheeks smeared with scarlet from the berries they have gathered and passed from dirty hand to hand. The long shirts they wear are nothing but patches, and they wear soft leather boots, though the youngest go barefoot. For ear-rings they have red and yellow bobbles, and better still, there is a young girl who swings a triangle of silver wire with every movement of her head. A tuft of feathers rises over her fur-edged hat.

While I am mending a thick strap, this gamin takes my wrist-watch off, listens as it ticks, expects me to give it her; then tries all my pockets and calmly takes their contents out, after which she throws her arms around my neck, perfectly convinced her attentions cannot but fill me with delight. Worthy offspring of her Mongolian forbears, she has but one unique lock hanging over an ear: the rest will be allowed to grow when she is married. With much surprise she runs her hands through my hair and amuses herself by pulling at it. What a find this well-covered head must be to her!

The locks of the children are not destined to haul them up

to Paradise should they die. Their mothers cut them off and hang them, it appears, as votive offerings on the tombs of Saints. As for Mongols, they have always kept their long plaits, and made the wearing of them compulsory among the Chinese whom they conquered. Thus in 1911, when the last Emperor was overthrown, pigtails disappeared from Chinese heads to bear witness to their liberation.

A Visit to Patma

Each yurt has a contrivance for varying the diameter. In the construction the first operation is to set up, end to end and in a circle, six or eight pieces of lattice-work some four feet six inches high, which makes a kind of palisade fastened together by thongs.

This lattice-work consists of laths placed obliquely to each other to form lozenges. At every intersection they are pierced through and tied together with a small thong, thus forming a sort of scaffolding which can be given whatever dimension is desired. It is in some sort the walls of the dwelling, round which straps are tightly bound.

Then a woman stands in the middle of the yurt, and with a forked prop raises the dome of the roof, while other women insert the points of long poles into the holes provided for them. The poles arch, and so take the weight of the felt walls. Then the lower ends of the poles are fastened to the tops of the lattices, and the carcase of the dwelling is complete.

After which a low hurdle of willow wands is placed around the lattices, and felt squares—'koshmou'—are fastened to the frame and pegged down in all directions. A felt lid covers the hole in the roof, and a running cord enables it to be opened or shut at will.

" Aman zisba ! " I say, going into the smallest of the yurts.

" Aman," a woman with regular features answers gently. She has the immense wing of an eagle in her hand, and is using it to sweep the koshmou on the floor.

Our conversation is carried on by gestures. Her name is Patma, and she offers me koumiss and then sour milk. She is intelligent: she does not ask the same incomprehensible question five times running and always on a louder note, like the rest of her compatriots.

Then her four children arrive wanting a meal. Out of the embers she takes a copper jug and pours some boiling water on a dark square of stuff which makes a thick liquid that looks like coffee. It is an extract made with a mixture of tea and clotted cream. Then she takes some millet seed flour, mixes it in a wooden bowl with milk and the 'tea' extract, and makes an appetizing-looking mess that they greedily lap up. Only the baby puts on airs.

More marked than in the parents, the Mongolian type persists in the children, whose bulging cheeks squeeze up the eyes and reduce them to a single line.

With her forefinger Patma cleans out the bowls. A hat hanging by its chin-strap makes a nest for a china teapot, and the pile of quilts over the place of honour is but low. Patma is poorer than our hosts. She takes out a needle and thread with which to repair a thick koshmour. Her thimble is worn on the first finger and looks like a signet ring. A silken loop is attached to it, which has a running knot passing round the middle finger. To push the needle forward the flat of the ring is used. Laughingly I try to imitate her, then go in search of my own thimble to demonstrate how it is used.

We hear shouts of laugher outside and find one of the children bumping round on a calf.

Capa, Mila, and I go off in search of a bathroom in which to wash ourselves and our shirts, and in the next ravine, source of our drinking supply, find a spot that quite enchants us. It is a gorge, surrounded by bushes and great pines, in the midst of which a limpid torrent bounds from rock to rock. Under the cascades great ferns arch, and the whole scene is impregnated with a crystalline virgin atmosphere such as enraptured Melville when he discovered the valley of Typee.

Children searching for berries pass immediately above us:

what will they think, seeing our white bodies plunge in the natural pool?

Throughout the morning Jocubai and Matkerim have sat in front of the tent manufacturing vast quantities of cartridges, enough almost to make one think we were preparing for a siege.

A hunter returns with a marmot and the trap it was caught in. With hands protrected by felt gloves he pulls apart the iron teeth, and the close-furred creature, whose skin seems too large for its well-fed carcase, drops to the ground still warm. The man wears boots of soft leather, coarsely stitched by hand, drawn over stockings of koshmou. Planting a foot on either paw, he slits up the pale furred belly, which ends in two short velvety paws like those of a bear.

A youngster, with an impressive piece of lambskin on his head and a protuberant stomach pushing out his shirt, looks on with knitted brows, both curious and disturbed at one and the same moment.

Some sudden detonations make me jump. Two Kirghiz are practising firing with our men. The apex of a fir-tree has been taken as a mark. One of the Kirghiz, whose cheekbones stand out with unusual prominence, uses a forked prop stuck in the earth with which to steady his musket while he takes aim. Matkerim sitting, rests his arm upon a knee. His is the one moustache among all the beards. The spent cartridge cases are collected afterwards.

The smiling Patma will not interrupt her work for so little. Using one booted foot, she stretches the hair-cord she is making, plaiting the strings one within the other. Her youngest and her darling, with a running nose, tries her blandishments in vain to make her come and play.

Looking utterly out of place in this Alpine landscape, the camel is its dominating feature. Peeled and worn, its knees look like ancient stones in contrast to the feet covered with close, dark fur in which thick toe-nails are embedded. The massy foot, soft-fleshed and webbed, spreads wide at every step. The fore quarters are adorned with enormous dark bulging ruffs that exaggerate the lower portion of the silhouette, while the long neck disappears into a wiry-looking ruff that dies away beneath the chin.

In youth its chaps do not hang down, but ruminating, express complete disdain for everything around. Above the slits of nostrils, almond-shaped, a plaited cord passes through the septum of the nose, its other end being fastened to a peg stuck in the earth. It must surely be this halter in the nose that is responsible for the expression of noble indignation that it bears.

The eye stands prominently out from the steeply jutting arch of the socket. There is no forehead, and then comes sprouting hair in crinkled waves, a veritable negroid skull which flows on to a scanty mane that, as it descends, unexpectedly reveals ears like a dog's.

After which follows the monstrous poem of the back: two fleshy waves, in line, whose tufted crests tilt over the same way. In themselves they are hard, but in comparison with the animal soft, and seem the continuation of the belly walls. But the relation of the second hump to the hind quarters looks all wrong, for the monumental back thins suddenly away into narrow quarters with no rump, a scrap of triangular tail, and long and skinny thighs.

The Lamb

Matkerim has suggested that we buy half a lamb for thirty roubles, which will enable us to take some of the cooked meat away with us. Preparations for the approaching banquet are put in hand to the accompaniment of great local rejoicing.

I arrive at the principal yurt as everything is already simmering in an enormous hemispherical cauldron resting on a tripod. The men understand a few words of Russian and realize where we come from, but all conversation has to be carried on through the intermediary of Matkerim. They all want to know where my husband is?

"In Frunze," says Mila, before I have time to answer, "where he is awaiting our return. He was ill and so unable to leave with us."

"You must remember," says Mila to me in French, "that these men are unable to conceive of a woman travelling without her husband."

They all listen intently to the strange sounds that pass between us. Jocubai explains to them that I am a foreigner, 'farangui.' They begin to laugh, talking among themselves, and Volodya says:

"They are commenting on the absence of your husband and the rarity of fair women. I think it would be advisable for you not to wander about alone at any distance from the aul."

My reaction is a strange one. If it were not myself that was in question, I should have said, "it might be worth wandering off alone, if one could count on something out of the ordinary happening." But I know I shall not run the risk, even though I have already taken the risk into consideration, and preparing for the worst packed some neosalvarsan with my other medicaments.

The children are playing about with our empty tins, which they have turned into buckets with pieces of string.

The old mother takes some of the broth in a ladle, pours it into a bowl, and tastes. Is it strong enough? She passes it to the head man, who considers it satisfactory. Then a child takes a jug of warm water from near the fire and goes round, pouring it on our hands. These latter are held well forward to make sure the water falls into the zone of dead ashes. Then a towel is past round, the state of which had better be left undescribed, and a light cloth is unfolded in front of the seat of honour to serve as the tablecloth.

Then from the cauldron out comes the liver, which is cut into slices, in addition to chunks of fat—all their sheep have fat tails—and the table is laid. The meal is eaten with the fingers, by making small sandwiches of liver and fat which are plunged into a bowl containing salt passed from hand to

THE FIRST AUL

hand. The delicate flavour is delicious: I would willingly
have made it my main sustenance.

The woman then takes the pieces of meat from the
cauldron and begins to sort them out, the head and joints
going into a wooden platter, which is passed to Auguste, who
is still too ill to be able to eat any. Whereupon our host takes
up the head, gouges the eyes out, and eats the points of the
ears on the end of his knife. After this the platter is passed
to us. The meat is delicious, and comes away of itself from
the bone, so tender and succulent, that even when we are full
we go on energetically chewing for the pleasure of having the
feel of the firm, sweet-tasting flesh in our mouths.

When I come to a stop at last, my knife, cheeks, and all
ten fingers swimming in grease, I begin to observe my Kirghiz
neighbours. They are still eating, slowly and scrupulously;
masticating the very tendons even. One would think they
had not had a decent meal for ages. But, as Karutz writes,
" To realize how they give themselves up to the pleasure of
eating, one must have witnessed it oneself. Anybody who
wants to know how the mounds composed of the débris of
past feasts built themselves up in prehistoric caves, needs only
to eat one sheep among the Kirghiz people. He will then
realize what a ' clean sweep ' really means. Only then will he
divine the zeal, the understanding, and success with which a
mutton bone can be handled, the persistent and ingenious art
with which it can be gnawed, scraped, bitten, crushed, broken,
sucked; and how without the aid of the least instrument it
can be scraped so irreproachably clean."

When the guests have finished, the dish is passed to the
other men, then to the children, and finally to the women.

Thus a child can be seen to pass a practically gnawed-clean
bone to his father. The gesture might seem ironic, but quite
the contrary, for the marrow is considered a great delicacy,
and the father sucks mightily away.

The fragments of meat that have come away in the cooking have been put on one side. Now two boys take them, and
seizing the meat firmly between the thumb and left forefinger,

95

so that it projects slightly beyond the hand, begin rapidly slicing and, cutting towards themselves, make a hash of it. The fat is treated in the same way, after which a little of the boiling broth is added, and the third course goes round, the 'bish barmak.'

We each help ourselves, filling our bowls, and this, too, is eaten with the fingers, and that needs courage, for if one attempts to grasp the mixture, it is so greasy that it slips away at once, and it is impossible to get a decent mouthful. The Kirghiz are wonderful, for with one hand they take up a handful of the hash, gather it in their palms, and neatly compress it in their shut fingers; then, at the very moment they open their mouths, the fingers are released, so that the food is carried into the lips and sucked up in one breath, leaving the hand absolutely clean.

Try it! It's a trick worthy of a conjuror.

Neighbours keep coming in, depositing their goloshes to one side of the doorway before squatting down, and odd relics of the feast are presented to them. For the last course a bowl of broth goes round again, very greasy and hot, because it comes straight out of the cauldron. It does one good. Though I have filled up in every meaning of the term, I drink the velvety, fragrant liquid with delight.

The cloth containing the débris is then gathered up, water is poured over our hands, and the same towel is called into service again. Instinctively I have used the rich white fat that has solidified on my hands to grease my shoes, and lo and behold! our host does the same.

Then everyone stretches out, takes a siesta, and breaks wind. How Matkerim is still able to swallow a few more bowls of koumiss is a mystery to me. Noting my utter astonishment, the temperate Jocubai says to me:

"Cheitan!" (Satan) and winks in his direction.

He takes out a little bottle, his inseparable companion, full of a spinach green powder. By reversing it once, a small heap of the powder is left in the hollow of his palm, which he then casts into his mouth. He passes the bottle to his neighbours, and for some moments remains with the inside of his mouth paralysed, before beginning to spit at regular intervals.

It is powdered tobacco, which stings fiercely, because it is mixed with ashes, as betel is in Indo-China, I am told. I have also read that the South American Indians mix their coca-leaves with lime. This custom doubtless prevails wherever the natural aliment is not rich enough in lime. A 'doumbra,' a sort of squeaking violin, provides a background to my thoughts.

Soviets, Iakchi?

For days the skin of our lamb has been lying in the sun, stretched out flat on the cropped grass: the old Kirghiz woman is tanning it by rubbing a whitish paste of flour and sour milk into it.

I pay a visit to the worthy Patma. I have grown fond of her resigned face whose gentle features I have watched, now illumined from above by the white rays of the sun through the hole in the roof, now from below by the flickering fire.

Her cordial, likeable husband, a few odd hairs to his chin, naturally asks me where my husband is. Whenever he addresses me he taps me on the shoulder, convinced, no doubt, that in that way it will penetrate my understanding quicker. He knows a few words of Russian, and we converse in a horrible jargon. The winters he spends in Pokrovskoe working as a bootmaker.

Patma brushes her teeth with one finger, then rinses her mouth out and spits into the ashes: earnestly she asks me to give her a toothbrush. I have plenty of knives, scissors, watches to give away, but devil take me if it ever occurred to me to take some extra toothbrushes.

There is a leather satchet fastened to the lapel of her waistcoat, held in place by a safety-pin. It is triangular in shape, and contains an amulet, some relic from a tomb, or verses from the Koran.

Patma repeats the word ' Ukraine ' several times. Yes, I

know what it means. But she wants me to understand that she has a brother living there. And yet again they ask me where my 'kibitka' (dwelling or family) is. Of course they have never heard of my country, so I explain:

"Ukraine, ten days' journey. France another ten days by the railway." Nevertheless, they have travelled. In 1916, during the great uprising, they crossed the passes on their way into China.

From beneath the unwrinkled eyelids the man's eyes look out, youthful and frank. He has been melting lead and is now pouring it into a wooden mould for making bullets. I take the opportunity to ask a question that has long been on my tongue:

"Soviet, iakchi?" (Good).

"Iamane. . . . Oh, iamane. At, koï, djok! Francia, koï bar?" (Bad, oh bad. Horses, sheep, none at all! France, are there sheep?)

Obviously, to them, the efforts and objects of the Soviet Government must be quite incomprehensible. All that can be done is to wait until their children can explain to them what is happening.

And because I say yes, their eyes glitter enviously. Here money means nothing at all, the only currency is sheep, and it is into sheep that all their savings go. The Kirghiz editor in Kara Kol had told me how in 1918 his first wife had cost him twenty horses. And I think how in Latin, pecunia—money—derives from pecus, herds, and that in the Iliad the value of a shield is expressed in terms of so many head of oxen.

CHAPTER X

To the Source of the Iaxartes

WITH AUGUSTE WELL AGAIN, we set off. Our pots and pans go back into each other and our tin spoons on top.

The horses run round in circles as though mad: we are absolutely winded by the time they are caught. Then we are in a quandary. Our pack-horse, rubbed raw along the spine, has an immense lump on its withers. Matkerim takes his knife, cuts crosswise into the swelling as though it were butter, and presses on the edges with all his might; yellow matter mingled with blood begins to flow. There is a kettle at his side still containig hot tea, and this he pours into the wound, whereupon steam rises and the operation is over. . . .

A dressing for the wound is made of a piece of koshmou shredded into a large pad, and the saddle is put back. Now we are all ready. We go from yurt to yurt shaking hands and drinking the yoghourt and koumiss of farewell as we say:

" Kosh! Rachmatt! " (Farewell. Thanks!)

The women teasingly try to snatch my beret. Then they give my mount a great smack.

The black earth trail begins to climb up under the firs.

Climbing, we pass a last three yurts, with poles, fifteen to eighteen feet in length, planted before each door. Then the trees come to an end, giving place to straggling, stunted cypresses.

To our right a stupendous wall of rock rises sheer into the air: in front is an immense and very steep moraine: high up and to our left a tongue of glacier descends towards us. Immense eagles are soaring in the air with every feather of their vast wings silhouetted against the sky: others stand perched on rocks at no great distance from our trail. The Kirghiz protect their eagles, for they drive away the crows and magpies which settle on their beasts and, pecking the raw places, turn them into incurable sores.

It makes hard going to rise above the rocky mass, dotted with whitened bones, arching ribs, and massy femurs. Suddenly below, I see the carcase of a horse in a disagreeable state of decomposition. Its unkempt coat is still round it, and a desiccated head droops from the bent neck; but behind white bones and the tracery of the pelvic basin appear.

Then we reach the glacier, an endless saddle rising to the very sky. Long rifts, too narrow to be called crevasses, startle our beasts. The coarse crystalline snow shows traces of ancient scattered tracks, those which descend taking the shortest cut. Zigzagging always, we go on climbing. Suddenly an icy wind springs up.

Blinding sun! 'Ware eyes! It is out of the question to think of unfastening the load in which my snow spectacles are packed. I tie a silk handkerchief, worn transparent, round my head, and this enables me to see my way. At the pass the glacier branches right and left and rises into the mountains. In front, eastwards, the eye sweep onwards to a lake dark blue in the plain, and beyond appears the Ak Chiriak range, with here and there a snowy peak.

At fourteen thousand feet the eternal snows begin, and we are through the Chuguchak. This is the pass that leads most speedily to the Syrt. The Jukka, to the south, takes twice as long, though easier for the big caravans. The transport of forty thousand tons of goods yields Gostorg (the Import and Export Trust) an annual profit of a million and a half roubles. As a result, the possibility of cutting roads wherever possible is now under discussion.

Between our position and the Jukka two other passes exist, Ittishti and Kashkassu, but the latter is impracticable because heavy rains have flooded the lake round which the trail winds.

The descent is easy: the last pebbles are negotiated and our horses break into a trot on the moth-eaten plains of the Syrt. The wind has dropped again. The light is lovely near the lake, from which wild geese and duck fly up with outstretched necks. Matkerim, tremendously excited, takes aim much too late.

" Ella," says Volodya in a thrilled voice, " that trickle you saw flowing out of the glacier we crossed is the source of the Syr Daria, the great Iaxartes of the Ancients, which pours its waters in the Sea of Aral after watering the cotton fields of Ferghana, Tashkent and its five hundred thousand inhabitants, and the plain where boars and tigers still live hidden in the reeds. Here it is called the Narin."

Joy! We take the descent at a gallop, landing at every bound on tufts of edelweiss springing out of the black earth.

Some sugar, loose in an aluminium tin somewhere in Mila's load, tinkles with every movement of her mount, a musical accompaniment that will link itself inseparably with the memory of these unforgettable moments.

In the midst of the Ak Chiriak a snowy pyramid rises, gilt by the setting sun, and the harmony of its proportions makes me think of the summit of Mont Blanc.

"No one has yet climbed to the summit," says Auguste meditatively, his health miraculously restored it seems, and his blue eyes sparkling in his scarlet face.

A cube of stone set in the midst of the broad valley, whose altitude is some twelve thousand feet, increases by degrees to the proportions of a house: it is the Glacier Observatory of the Tien Shan, where we are to stay overnight.

Now and again our horses' hoofs, proceeding over the spongy boglands, strike a sharp sound from some pebble. And then, half a mile from the building, my eyes fall on a human skull, a white cup with black eye-sockets.

The Tien Shan Observatory

Surrounded by barbed wire—protection from wolves or brigands?—the rain-gauge, wind-gauge, hygrometers, and thermometers are connected with the building by duckboards stuck fast in mud. We hear dogs barking, but no one appears. Then we turn the corner, and see a yard bounded by low sheds, and the front door, which gives access on the left to the kitchen, and on the right to an ante-room leading into the living-room. A round stove, a large table, bookshelves containing scientific works and dictionaries, and dry batteries for the emission of wireless messages, since there is a meteorological bulletin to be transmitted daily to Tashkent, nearly six hundred miles away as the crow flies.

We find eight people, each putting in a year, on this desolate plain, where the mean average temperature is 43° F., approximately that of Franz Josef Land. They know each other so well, the Superintendent, his wife, the students, and Maria Feodorovna on whom the catering and cooking depend, that they have all but stopped conversing with each other.

Some Russian Alpine climbers had preceded us two months earlier. The best of them was in training to join the Pograbetzki expedition, but he had fallen ill with typhus, and now they were nursing him as best they could, a rider going regularly to fetch milk for him from the nearest aul, twenty-five miles away. But the invalid got no better, and could not even keep liquids down. Volodya, who among other things, had a medical degree in his scientific baggage, visited him several times.

For the night Maria Feodorovna invites us to share her room, and it is on her floor we spread out our things.

With morning the world looks like an Arctic plain. The black earth has disappeared and snow covers everything; we are in the centre of a white world which scintillates in the sun. Close to the palisade wide tracks reveal the passage of a lynx. On the hillside the black spots are our hobbled mounts trying to find something to eat. In winter it would be too dangerous to leave them to themselves in this manner; but the wolves are not hungry in summer, there being plenty of marmots for them to eat.

" Ella! take your temperature," Capa bids me thoughtfully. " You don't look yourself at all."

" Of course not. There's no need! I'm hot because it's so stuffy in here."

But she insists. Results a reading of 102.5°! Devil take it, what can it mean? Is there something wrong with my health? I presume to set out on an expedition, and am I to find myself on my back?

In the rainy season, Chinese coming from Turfan by way of the Jukka make a détour to stop at the observatory. The wireless terrifies them, they call it the ' pig,' the demon of the mountain. They dare not touch the front door, so devoutly do they believe that the building is possessed.

One of the students—they all drag about in immense felt top-boots—tells us about a bear which not so long before amused itself by standing on a glacier and throwing stones at the riders passing by.

As far as meteorological observations go, the position of the station might have been better chosen. But its main purpose is to observe the glaciers from which the Narin issues, since the irrigation of the whole plain depends on it. This was the object for which the grant was made, and a million roubles has been spent on the place.

When the foundations were dug, the ground at a depth of five feet was found to be tundra, frozen solid. Below there was only ice to an unknown depth.

" We may possibly be on a glacier that is in imperciptible motion," remarks the hairiest of the students.

The upkeep of the station costs two hundred thousand roubles a year, thirty thousand roubles of which is spent merely on wood for heating and transportation.

Our hosts tell us that owing to the rarefaction of the air, work that demands sustained mental effort is found to be difficult and exhausting.

The wind, so icy it pierces through us like something solid, is blowing the clouds away, and Auguste can resist no longer the call of Sari Tor, immense and impassive.

" I hardly know from which direction it would be best to attack it," he says, putting his binoculars down. " Whether from right or left. But we can see when we reach the glacier."

Volodya and Capa go with him. They will have to bivouac in the open, so they take the little storm tent, the rope, ice-axes and crampons, warm clothing, and provisions.

I admire them terrifically for starting off in the icy cold, without turning a hair, to spend a night on a glacier. Capa betrays her excitement by the abruptness of her questions.

They start off on horseback to traverse the plain as far as the foot of the glacier. Matkerim brings back the animals.

During the night the noise made by the wind turns shriller. It howls all round us. Can I be feverish? I think I am afloat, in harbour: and keep on wanting to jump up on deck to drop a second anchor! And the others are still off-shore, hove-to in the gale under their tiny tent.

" Why are you getting up, Marie Feodorovna? "

" To put the last batch in to bake," she replies.

Then one of the young men on the night watch breaks in, very pleased with himself indeed.

" At last I've got Berlin for you on the wireless. Come quick! You know our time is five hours ahead of theirs."

I haven't the least desire to follow him, but he is so positive I shall enjoy it that I cannot find it in my heart to undeceive him.

We go into the common workroom where laboratory apparatus jostles scattered papers and a pair of felt gloves. I put the receivers to my ears and listen to a dim tango that is all but inaudible. The bewitching rhythm, broadcast from the intoxicating atmosphere of some Germanic ' Eden,' with scintillating glasses, and flowers glowing against white napery, tinkling in the fastnesses of this desolate mountain nearly four thousand miles away, sounds unreal, ridiculous. There is only one thing true at this moment, and that is the wind rushing across the snow, which drives the howling wolves away.

In the morning we try in vain to see our mountaineering party with the binoculars.

Mila and I go fishing with the Superintendent's wife. A branch of the Narin idles between banks of earth as black as peat. On the river-bed the weeds sway all in the same direction. There the fish sleep, and are caught with a cleft stick, as in the Mediterranean. We find the stick, but broken. . . .

In the afternoon I pick out three dots moving along the glacier.

" Matkerim: the horses! "

But our garrulous guide is nowhere to be found. He has gone off for a drink of koumiss at the nearest yurt, twenty or twenty-five miles away. That to a Kirghiz, who has no settled home, is hardly worth bothering about.

At last, however, we succeed in capturing and saddling the beasts, and set off to meet our Alpine climbers.

Victory on Sari Tor

" Couldn't you even get the horses to us in time? " demands Capa the minute she gets in.

The combined effect of wind, cold, and sun has been to turn their faces scarlet in spite of liberal applications of cold cream. But they are happy, for the summit was reached. Auguste relates.

" We attacked it from the left. Slept very well, but weren't able to eat. The crampons were useless, the snow is powdery right up to the top."

" Ella, it's just made for you," Volodya says. " A perfect mountain for ski-ing."

The atmosphere at supper is cordial to a degree. The stove purrs behind me. We share the meteorologists' repast: a piece of boiled beef in our plates of ' bortsch ' and three duck shot from our very windows. The flasks of vodka are brought into service. I produce some excellent kirsch, fragrant and lingering in the mouth. Auguste is most surprised.

" Did you find that at the Torgsin Store? "

" No, but before leaving Switzerland, way back in Zürich, I was able at the very last moment to get my flask filled at the station restaurant."

But kirsch and vodka can go hang for all I care. One of the men has found some skis which he sets down on the floor. I choose the two least warped, and manufacture fastenings for them out of copper wire.

I have made up my mind to get some exercise on the slopes of Sari Tor next day while the others are away studying the approaches to the Petrov glacier. I have still, however, to wax my skis, for I shall meet with varying snow conditions. In the shed I find a liquid containing tar, kept for painting the roof. That serves as an excellent substitute for ' klister.' . . .

Skis

Next morning Matkerim goes with me. He does not seem in the least to appreciate the honour of having my sticky skis confided to his keeping. He puts them crosswise over his saddlebows.

After crossing the transparent waters of the Narin, we reach a lateral moraine on our right, which we follow as high as we can. Here and there I notice the forked track of steinbock.

Then the Kirghiz departs with the horses to lead them to pasture.

" Come back for me towards evening! " I say to him.

I hack a few steps in the slippery wall of the glacier, after which the rest follows easily. I hardly notice the gradient, and work my way on my skis towards the centre moraine, over the still frozen snow. Straight in front of me I see a black spot moving over the surrounding whiteness. It must be a bear! What does one do in such a case? Surely I have read adventure books enough to know by now. When it's an Asiatic dog, one crouches down, of course. And when it's a bear, the thing is to lie down and feign death? Several times I am frightened in the same way, my heart jumping into my throat. But each time it is some solitary rock, shaped like an animal . . .

For two hours I have been advancing rapidly. Then the

glacier turns left, becomes steeper: and in front of me I have the wall of seracs which forms the face of Sari Tor, an immense surface powdered with fresh snow which the wind sweeps up in wild confusion round the ridge.

About me the slopes covered with fallen rock are not deep enough under snow to permit me to ski. I therefore embark on the upper portion of the long, monotonous glacier, which reminds me of Trélatête, and which turns into a veritable Turkish bath immediately the sun appears.

I see the deep tracks made the day before by my comrades and the place where they have camped. From time to time I feel a need to stop, take deeper breaths. I go on for two hours more, and the perspective begins to open out. I reach a pass which continues to the left towards the massif that dominates the Petrov glacier. To the right rises the arête leading to Sari Tor. The peak seems near: it would be a pity not to reach it, now I've got so far.

There is only one thing that bothers me, and that is the tearing wind that turns icy cold whenever a cloud passes. Fortunately, the sun always breaks out again, for I find it impossible so high up—it is so difficult to breathe—to hurry my pace and keep warm. The wind razes the powdery white snow, sweeping it clear away in places, and reveals the underlying hardened snow. The frozen tracks of my comrades fill up with greyish hail.

I take off a ski to flatten the fastening out and put my foot casually down. Immediately I find I have sunk thigh-deep. "Brave little Capa, you must have worked like a Trojan to do all this on foot yesterday."

Another squall stings my face with icy needles. Shall I turn back? No, it's only mist, I feel sure. Give up now I have got so near my object? Likely! This is just when it begins to get interesting!

I had calculated it would take me an hour and a half to conquer this arête, but it proves deceptive, made up as it is of successive stages. My sticks too are a nuisance in the thick snow, for though I was using two of the three theodolite supports with a string passed through the screw holes, I had omitted to supply them with circular pieces to take the weight off the spikes, so that they sank in deep every time I put my weight on them.

Rarely have I lived through such a wild, impetuous hour. I vowed I would succeed, that I had all but got there, the feeling of my total isolation increasing all my forces tenfold. To get my breath I rest a moment every two hundred yards, and then at intervals of only a hundred yards. I am not overloaded, for all I have is a haversack.

To turn the spool of my Leica, I have to take one of my thick gloves off, whereupon my fingers stick fast to the burning metal. It makes me cry with pain . . . and those were not the only tears those negatives were to cost me. . . .

The cold strikes between one's eyebrows, paralysing them; then descends on either side of the completely insensitive nose to freeze the muscles of the mouth. Then it affects the jaw. The quivering muscles contract and the shoulders hunch themselves to protect the neck. The rest of one's body is kept warm by the movement.

The mountains around me diminish by degrees, transform themselves to hills. A last effort: a few more steps. . . .

I am on top, in the lee of an inaccessible cornice which puts the overhanging summit less than twenty feet above me: an immense frozen wave whose crest curls in the clouds. Sitting on a block of ice, I gaze at what I have come so high to seek: a sea of motionless peaks sheathed in ice. To the east a compact pile of black clouds surrounds the twenty-three thousand feet of Khan Tengri, that giant mountain the whole of whose south-easterly slope is still ' unexplored territory.' The magic in those words! To the north, through a break in the clouds, I see the near-by Tereskei range, and behind a vast luminous void with the pale line of the Kungei chain beyond the invisible lake. The ledge shuts out what remains of the panorama. Sari Tor, hitherto measured only in ' sagines,' rises nearly sixteen thousand feet, and I think of it with affection as ' my sixteen thousander.'

Now I have to descend as fast as I may, battling against the cold. No! I decide not to undertake the impossible task of taking a ski off to knock away the thick snow with which it is caked.

I rush down warmthwards . . . and at what a speed! But I am going too fast. I brake, and immediately plunge head foremost into a snowy mass. The deep snow is packed so lightly that it seems as if I am struggling with feathers to get out. I had forgotten my fastening was far from being obedient to my foot. I must change my technique to 'safety first.' Were I to break a leg, it would hardly be the luge of some 'Hôtel Palace' that would come to look for me.

Nevertheless, unforgettable swoops punctuate my descent, doubtless to leave their tracks upon this ridge for all time.

Sheltering below the pass, I stop in the sun to munch some mutton-fat and chocolate, the bread and meat being too dry for my taste.

The upper glacier provides a superb and uneventful glissade. But the dense and melting snow of the lower section makes heavy going. Three-quarters of an hour after beginning my descent I am in the saddle again. The others took fourteen hours, if my memory serves me, whereas it took me only seven.

Crossing the Narin is an altogether different business from what it was at morning: now it is a powerful river, swollen by the muddy waters of the glaciers melted by the heat.

Slow return as the light fades! We join up with our comrades who are themselves returning. Proud of myself, I want to yell out and tell them where I have been, but I wait for Auguste's intensely interested questions.

" It isn't possible in so short a time," says Capa.

Mila laughs as she looks at me, and winks in Capa's direction. You can read her like an open book. She is disappointed not to have been the only woman to have scaled Sari Tor.

Volodya congratulates me and shakes me by the hand, adding, " Tell me what I can do for you! "

" What a pity we weren't there to photograph you as you were coming down," says Mila.

" When Pograbetzki hears of it, he'll regret not having taken you with him. You would have come in useful for his film."

A fine day's work: full of interest. I eat enough for four . . . and my fever has left me!

CHAPTER XI

Ak Bel, or the Desolate Valleys

EVERYWHERE THE BLACK earth has swallowed up the snow. Each clump of grass is tufted with woolly edelweiss. Our horses' hoofs pull away from the ground with loud sucking noises. A wide horizon stretches before us as we descend into the vast, denuded plain of the Narin.

Where the road, leaving the river, begins to climb to our left we come upon the great trail that leads to the Bedel pass, a score or so of parallel ruts, a foot deep, which our horses do their utmost to avoid.

Every hundred yards we come across small heaps of stones: these are not, however, sacred 'obos' as in Mongolia, destined to appease the anger of the gods. Their only purpose is to protect the pickets stuck in the earth, which mark the line of the projected route, from being trampled down by the horses.

The nearest peaks are round, covered with immense snow-fields which the thaws have worn into deep grooves that make them look like inverted pastry-tins. My ears are full of the din of the mighty wind that sweeps the whole sky in front of it, for we have reached the most exposed point on Ak Bel —the White Saddle, a pass open to the four cardinal points. The grass is covered with tiny flattened blue and yellow flowers.

Matkerim utters a cry. On the ground below us, in a ravine, stands an eagle beating its wings. We continue on our way to keep out of sight, and Matkerim sets off at a gallop to take it from behind, fires, and returns crestfallen.

As I am looking at the enormous white carcase of a camel, my horse stumbles, falls on its knees, and I describe a slow somersault over its head.

"Ella, you should hold your horse's head up, going down hill."

To our right, in the foreground, rises an enormous dark sugar loaf, like a huge slag heap in some Dantesque landscape: the Kara Saï. To the left, in the middle distance, is the long spine of a low mountain, which at regular intervals thrusts in our direction rugged spurs covered with artificial-looking pink earth.

The summit of Borkoldoi, a rocky mass crushed under an immense flat plain of snow, is straight in front of us at a fair distance. Succeeding it comes the famous Bedel, and after it the descent into Uch Turfan. Matkerim pronounces the name like us, but Jocubai makes it Tourp'han, aspirating the 'p' strongly. Hearing it thus, I realize that this is the manner in which the Germanic 'f' and 'v' becomes 'p' and 'b' in Latin. At last I understand why the young woman we met in the first aul was not called Fatma, and why on the Frunze railway station the Kirghiz spelling reads 'Prunze.' For Voroshiloff, the Kazaks would say Boroshilop, and for that reason it appears the populace cannot understand the newspapers.

Hiuan tsang, journeying from Kucha, followed this same route after passing by the foot of Khan Tengri. His feet may even have walked over the very spot where I bit the dust. During the crossing his caravan lost thirteen men. He says, speaking of the Tien Shan, the Celestial Mountains: "This mountain of ice forms the northern angle of the Pamirs. It is exceedingly dangerous and its peak rises into the very sky. Since the beginning of creation the snow has been accumulating on it, turning into blocks of ice which do not melt even in spring or summer. The hard, glittering expanses stretch endlessly, finally merging with the clouds. To gaze at them is to be dazzled by their brightness. Then there are sudden faults in the steep icy slopes, some as much as a hundred feet in lenght, others dozens of feet across, so that the latter cannot be crossed without difficulty nor the former surmounted without peril. Add to that the sudden gusts of wind

and whirling snow that assail one at every moment, so that
even with fur-lined clothes and boots one cannot help but
tremble with cold. When we desire to eat or sleep, no dry
spot can be found on which to rest. There is no resource
left us but to suspend the cooking-pot in which we prepare
our food, and stretch our mats out on the ice." (René
Grousset.)

We begin to skirt the first of the pink-sloped humps. At our
feet, parallel to that in which the Narin flows, stretches a wide
valley. Carefully scrutinizing the smooth, almost unbroken
surface of the slopes, we discern the pale spots of a few yurts
gleaming in the sun like the eggs of flies in the crevices of
a piece of meat. . . .

We do not descend towards them.

For many days we travel thus, proceeding from valley to
valley, from Teuz to the Ak Tach. I am always thinking
something new is going to turn up: a landscape, aul, some
new person. . . .

The desolation is superb! As at sea, the monotony throws
into extraordinary relief the slightest happenings.

Halt! Matkerim has lost one of his rubbers. He has to
go back and look for it.

From time to time, hugging the ground, a sort of small
pulpy plant appears, bearing scarlet protuberances like
veritable drops of blood.

Whenever the sun goes in, it gets so cold that I have to
protect my ears with a scarf. An ancient sprain begins to
hurt my ankle, as a result of having to bear my weight in the
stirrups in the descents. But what troubles me most is one of
my molars which broke on a piece of bread, so that when I
chew it feels as if a needle were being pushed into the gum.
An abscess might gather there at any time: that would be
comforting!

We continue to advance, eyes glued to the play of muscles
in the buttocks of the horse in front.

Troublesome thoughts take possession of one towards the
end of the day, when one is tired and overcome by cold,

hunger, and sleep all at the same time. At every little combe where there is grass and water for the beasts I wait expectantly for the signal to halt. But we have first to find an abandoned camp and traces of yurts, large pale circles of down-trodden grass. It is only there our fuel is to be found—horse and cow dung dried by the sun: ' kisiak.'

The men put up the tents while we pile up the cakes of dried dung in our arms. Before collecting them we turn them over with a foot to make sure they are dry beneath. We build an open hearth. They burn well, like embers, without flame, but throwing out a good deal of heat. The acrid odour of the kisiak permeates one's clothes, and it is that odour which came from every nomad that I met. One soon gets used to it, and welcomes it with pleasure when it announces the animation of an aul. Only some tourist in a hurry could have taken it for the smell of filth. . . .

It freezes in the night. Luckily I have lined my flea-bag with my skirt, and the camel-hair bought in Aralskoie More.

During these nights under the tent, I come at last to a full realization of the fact that the monkeys are my brethren, in spite of all the sacrifices my parents imposed on themselves to perfect my education.

Imagine yourself comfortably settled in the dark tent, warm in your sleeping-bag, between two companions whom you touch whenever you move at all. Half asleep, you feel something worrying you, pressing into your skin like a crumb. Is it a flea or merely an old bite that still itches? No, it moves, gets under your sleeve, and then stops: another one that means to make a meal of you. But you know just where it is, in the middle of your wrist. So with the utmost caution the other hand approaches stealthily and a finger pounces on the prey, knocks it senseless, rolls it about, and seizes it with the thumb's help.

But the only way of making sure you have killed it is to cut it in two. Yet, imprisoned as you are in your bag, you cannot at every capture waken your neighbours by switching on a light. I challenge anybody in darkness to divide the hard little creature, hardly the size of a peppercorn, in two. Picture yourself alone, with the man-eater at your mercy ... wondering as the moments pass what tactics should best be employed. All things considered, you decide the tongue and the teeth are a good deal more handy than the nails: and lo and behold! there is no longer anything to bother about: it was all very simple; the tongue seized the creature, the teeth bit it in two, and then it was spat out. Rid at last of the enemy, sleep becomes possible again.

But also we hunt in good earnest. There are pigeons which make a welcome addition to our soup, and Mila plucks them, tiny objects, soft and grey, as we ride along. Matkerim has the eyes of a lynx, and can see a possible shot from immense distances, but in his excitement he roars in a way altogether contrary to the most elementary rules of the hunting art.

'Arrkharr! Tam na prava!' (Argali over there to the right.) The flock having descended into the valley, their retreat must be cut off. Jocubai relinquishes his pack-horse, and gallops to the crest of a rise dominated by a wall of rock. Hardly a moment elapses before the two Kirghiz have dwindled to mere marionettes of riders. The argali, a large animal standing four feet to the shoulder, live up to altitudes of twenty thousand feet, in the winter finding their grazing under the snow, and frequenting slopes swept clear by the wind. To sleep, they mount into regions quite inaccessible to man.

These mouflons are exceedingly difficult to sight. Minute rectangles, they hardly show up against their background.

Pa ... ha! A shot. Paa ... a second, leaping from rocky wall to wall. ... The entire herd, with its whitish buttocks, goes galloping off into the mountain, opening out along some scree, and is soon but a cloud of dust swept up by the wind.

No luck!

Valleys with dried-up water-courses! Hillsides riddled with marmot holes! Some frontier guards catch up with us at the gallop. A maze of deep canyons hollowed out of the rock: the 'Five Slashes,' the work of devils, according to the legend! Hillocks of fine gravel on which nothing grows! Then innumerable combes, identical, succeed each other, the 'mainaks' whose floors are strewn with bones: the skulls of argali, the spread of whose horns covered with parallel ridges astonishes us by its width, and the two roots of which cover the whole forehead. It would have been an easy matter to have gathered dozens for anyone who wanted to boast of epic huntings.

When we meet with Kirghiz, we stop and drink koumiss with them. The skin hangs behind the saddle, the yielding neck is bent over, and the fluid, almost transparent milk, flows into our aluminium canteen. They are always armed, and the wind tanning their faces makes veritable Karakirghiz out of them.

Then there are hurried plunges in icy rivulets from which we issue uttering 'ughs,' as though resuscitated.

The Eagles

Suddenly rounding a bend, we meet the most impressive sight of all: three Kirghiz riders with eagles on their fists.

The first is wearing large, dark snow spectacles. The others gaze at us and at our mute astonishment. The birds of prey are enormous, it is the only possible word for them, so mighty that I cannot imagine what other bird could better deserve the title 'king of birds.'

From the jutting shoulder the wings hang, their dark, shining plumes like an armour of overlapping plates. The heads of the birds are covered with leather hoods through which they cannot see. The cries they utter sound as though ten doors were screeching on their hinges. The hooked beak is on a level with the man's forehead. The black talons are enormous, and issue from a grey, scaly sheath of skin to grasp the leather glove which, in order that the reins may be held, is cut for only one finger and a thumb. The bird tries to tear a piece off with its beak. A slip-knot fastens a long thong to one foot. The man's fist rests on a wooden fork socketed in the saddle.

The nape of the eagle's neck is a tuft of white disordered feathers. The hood removed, the implacable eye appears, glittering like a jewel.

From the cruppers of a pack-horse the stiffened skins of wolves, ibex, and marmots hang in quantities.

We sight a marmot, and track it down. The bird, released from its noose, is cast off after it. It does not rise very high, then it swoops down towards the marmot, and cuts off its retreat by settling in front of the warren. The marmot, disturbed by the noise, seeks its hole for refuge, and falls into the fatal talons. The Kirghiz comes up, finishes it off, ties up the eagle again, and gives it the entrails to eat.

The marmot will end up in our soup, and Capa stakes a claim to the skin.

" It is the beginning of my fur coat," she says, as she fastens it to her saddle.

The men are finely bred. They have straggling beards, drooping moustaches, small straight noses without much bridge, prominent cheek-bones, and the sun has made deep crow's-feet at the corners of the eyes.

We learn that even a young eagle is able, four or five days after its first flight and accompanied by its mother, to catch a hare. At the end of a month it will attack a fox. To capture an eagle in a net, the trap is baited with a pigeon.

Then for forty days and forty nights it is worn down by being carried about always hooded. Meat is given it once a day, cut up in a dish, to which water is added. Then its eyes are uncovered so that it may see its food. When the forty days are over, the meat is fastened to a goat's shoulder, which is removed ten paces at feeding-time. On the second occasion the goat is removed twenty paces, and on the third fifty. . . . Thus by degrees the eagle is trained and grows accustomed to the voice of man. It is never allowed to eat its fill, so that it shall hunt better. They tell me that a well-trained eagle is worth several horses.

Falconry, art of the Middle Ages, this land was its cradle! I think of Attila, whose banners bore a falcon for device.

Occasionally at evening we light upon a few yurts, smoke rising lazily from their roofs. An exchange of visits procures us sparkling koumiss and sour milk.

Several times we start herds of argali, but do not succeed in tracking them down. . . .

Matkerim mechanically chants the same refrain the whole day through. On waking, his is the first voice we hear. He is barely up before he is spitting noisily and frequently. The mornings start fine, but there is never a day without a flurry of snow. We keep our oilskins always at hand and never take our woollen gloves off.

CHAPTER XII

ISOLATED LIVES

WE FIND TEN or fifteen yurts set up in the Ak Chiriak
pastures. The water that runs at our feet will die away
in the sands of China, once it has met the Yarkand Daria or
Tarim.

One of the yurts does duty as a Co-operative Stores, and
there bear-meat is on sale at fifty kopeks a kilogram. The
meat, however, is by no means fresh and it finds no buyers,
for the hunter, in the hope of selling it himself, waited too
long before turning it over. The store seems to have sold out
of everything, possibly because the new season's stocks have
not come in.

A number of Kirghiz live here throughout the year, the
snowfall being negligible on account of the dry atmosphere.

Another yurt is in charge of a ' feldcher ' or field surgeon
and does duty as a clearing station. Every day natives visit
it, sometimes coming from great distances. The feldcher
follows the camp as it moves about. He must find it no slight
effort to pack up all his bottles which, lined up on a table,
make the inside of the yurt look like a novel cocktail bar.

Cases of syphilis are rare, I am told. Chiefly abscesses and
affections of the eye—one-eyed people are numerous—
because the acrid smoke of the kisiak is a predisposing cause
toophthalmia, even though the natives live as close to the
earth as they can in order to keep out of the smoke's way.
There is no tuberculosis. The feldcher gives us an ointment
for the thigh of Capa's horse.

The broad, tanned faces of the women have a laughing
expression. They are always spinning, even when walking
about, and make the spindle revolve against their thighs with
a skilful movement of the hand. One of them wears a chased

silver ring, in addition to a Chinese brooch comprising a tooth-pick, an ear-pick the size of a small spoon, and a nail pick, all beautifully chased.

They much enjoy watching us bathe in the stream where we wash our heads. Incomparable moment! The silvery water wooing one's skin while the eyes feast on snowy summits. . . .

A youngster bumps about on a small grey yak with an opulent tail; a strange, humped creature that makes one think of hairy bisons. The milk they give is rich in fat and very thick, but there is not much of it.

Two frontier-guards stationed at a near-by O.G.P.U. base pay us a visit in our tent. In exchange for numbers of shot argali, they have recently acquired goods generally reserved for export, such as a gramophone, an accordion, a balalaika, and cigarettes which fill us with delight. For a long time now we have been reduced, like all Russians, to rolling our tobacco in scraps of newspaper.

" But why do you have a ' base ' in the mountains here? "

" We have to keep watch as well on the less-frequented passes that lead into China. The opium smuggling season should be beginning soon, now the harvest is over."

" Can there possibly be carts in this region? I saw wheel-tracks in the dust," I add.

" No, those were beams we have recently been transporting, to be used in constructing our new quarters. There were a thousand and thirty-four all told, and they had to be dragged all the way from Barskaul by strong camels."

They disappear at a gallop, the chin-straps of their pointed bonnets floating behind them.

Kneeling near a yurt, a group of natives at regular intervals bow their heads down till they touch the ground. I hurry up to take a photograph of devout Mussulmans at prayer, as I imagine, but instead see damp felt being subjected to repeated pressure by rolling under the wrists and forearms. In this way the felt is given a second working after passing through a woolly state, when, wrapped in a straw mat, it is dragged about and stamped under foot.

ISOLATED LIVES

Just as I am about to turn away, I realize I have mislaid the yellow filter of my camera. I look about, and suddenly behold an ancient dame gazing through it at the sun.

At the upper camp I find an immense loom set up. Secured at both ends, the double threads of the warp stretch all of thirty yards. A woman, her knees on a level with her shoulders, squats astride a buff-coloured band of camel-hair and casts her shuttle from side to side. Hanging from three poles fastened together at the top, is a rope suspending the headle which raises the warp and permits the interweaving of the strands. At regular intervals she pulls over the worn, smooth comb and tightens the weft.

The narrow band becomes a close-textured waterproof gabardine, similar to that which goes to make the ample ' chapan ' of the men, a sort of raglan overcoat they all wear.

The weaver has a crony at her side, spinning her thread from a mass of raw wool fastened to the back of her hand.

It makes me smile to think how this material would be all the rage at home, where hand-woven stuffs are the last word in chic.

They observe me in friendly fashion. A little boy with bandy legs and a few sparse hairs straggling from under a skull cap comes to me, wanting to play. He has at least a couple of dozen mother-o'-pearl buttons down the front of his clothes.

He seems determined at all costs to finger my gold-fillings, whereupon all the other members of the family hasten to admire the handiwork of my dentist.

The woman who was spinning looks into my camera sight, and, realizing what has happened, makes a gesture with her hands to signify everything has been reduced. In a twinkling dozens have glued it to their eyes. Some discover at once how to deal with it, others persist in holding it too far; all, however, are astonished by the unusual object.

The men, of course stay where they are, looking on with smiles on their faces.

Mourning

Some calamity must have happened in one of the yurts; loud cries resound and lamentations. A rider has come up from the plain: and even as he drinks his koumiss his mount continues to pour with sweat. He announces a death in the family, Zahissa's brother. The news spreads like a contagion. From every yurt loud cries of distress, which continue a full ten minutes, pierce the air. The exhausted rider throws himself down on his stomach, and his back and loins are trampled on by a child, an ingenious remedy for complete exhaustion, which I can well see myself putting into practice at the end of a hockey match for example, or after a race on skis.

The man goes into the yurt again, turns to the south-west, kneels, passes his hands over his face, prays in silence, and touches the earth with his brow. It is the only time, in all my sojourn in the mountains, that I saw anyone at prayer.

Twilight is falling, and, carrying the pail with its embossed leather spout, I go out with the Chinese-looking Madam Issil Khan to help round up the mares and bring them back to the foals. We find the foals roped to pickets in the middle of a field. My companion steals adroitly up to a mare and suddenly flings a halter over its neck, a loop of which serves to secure one of the hind hoofs in the air, thus preventing all further movement. First the foal takes a suck at the udder, then the woman milks it with one knee on the ground. Afterwards the mother is restored to her baby.

The art of preparing koumiss is of Mongolian origin. Skin is an ideal recipient in which to store fermenting liquids. The hide has been smoke-tanned, and the beverage fizzes like a new Swiss wine. A third of yesterday's milk is always mixed with the new milk: then it is allowed to settle in the warm temperature of the yurt before it is churned.

Mare's milk is the only milk that does not clot during fermentation. During the first six hours koumiss is alcoholic and then it turns into lactic acid.

ISOLATED LIVES

The Last Manap

While my face roasts at the fire and my back in comparison freezes painfully, I listen to the story of the Manap Kendeur, the last of the Patriarchs.

This sage, whom nowadays the people revere as a saint, was elected chief of all Kirghiz, and before the great insurrection of 1916, about which I have written already, was visited by a delegation anxious to hear his opinion in the matter.

"Bring me a bucketful of sand!" he said.

When the bucket was in front of him he took a handful up, and then, letting it fall immediately, said:

"Now find the grains that were in my hand."

The plain significance of which was: "The Russians completely submerge us, and we can do nothing against them or without them."

Then, before the revolt broke out, gathering his people, a total of many families—for under his protection were all his poor and weaker relations—the Manap made his way into China. Sarabaguich, for instance, the richest of all the Manaps, numbered seven hundred yurts in his tribe.

Later, Kendeur returned again to Aksu, his region, but no attempt was made to visit his defection upon him. When he died in 1927, untold multitudes flocked to the funeral, among them five thousand Russians come to render a last homage.

The main function of the more powerful Manaps, of whom there were some one hundred and fifty in the region of Kara Kol, was to preserve the general order. The boundaries of the Syrt were familiar to all, defined by custom from the most ancient times, so that year after year the nomads could return to the same pasture grounds. Grass being much less abundant here than in the Alps, the necessity for moving to new pastures assumes an infinitely greater importance than in Switzerland, although subject to the same laws. If we wish to keep strictly to the truth, we must stop thinking of the nomad as untrammelled, moving always onward according to his mood.

123

To-day the Syrt is the property of the State, and new boundaries, though not always practical ones, delimit it. The men in charge of the Collective farms are not yet expert enough to know the best moment for changing over the pasture grounds, and though Kirghiz are employed to take charge of the live-stock, it seems to them they are being exploited, and so they neglect their duties, to the impoverishment of the herds.

Many errors must have been committed, for it is estimated that the total live-stock is only a third of what it was. When the great division of live-stock took place, animals on occasion were handed over to families so poverty stricken that they did not know how to care for them, with the result that they perished or were turned into butcher's meat to realize an immediate profit.

Then there were the requisitions which, with a view to stocking the State farms, rounded the animals up before there were stock-men or stables to deal with them, thus creating further losses.

Again, the utilization of tractors displaced draft animals in the field. Since the machine did the work, the retention of horses laid one open to the charge of being a kulak, and so they were got rid of. Then if the motor broken down the work could not go forward. When I quoted these indictments of the malcontents, the new officials that I questioned answered that they were passing through a period of experimentation and that a certain amount of trial and error was inevitable; but that also, by degrees, the people were beginning to adapt themselves.

Those in authority realize the danger of the situation, and have now launched an extensive propaganda campaign to encourage the breeding of horses, sheep, and oxen.

A Rein Under the Tail ...

" No! Ella's medicine box must be left behind! " says Capa.

" Right! We can leave my Primus too. . . ."

" No, that would be stupid of course! There's no kisiak where we are going," Capa retorts sharply.

" Ought I to leave some slabs of chocolate behind as well? "

" Not, on your life. We shall need it all. Who's been at it already? Auguste, pull your stockings up, your impossible. . . ." Capa explodes, though no one seems to bother.

" If you had only mended the elastic it wouldn't have happened," says Auguste, smiling.

" Whose upset a packet of tea in the rice? "

I glanced anxiously at Mila, but she whispers:

" Capa has a rein under her tail, as we say. She'll have forgotten all about it in five minutes."

We are departing for the uninhabited frontier to spend a week exploring the unknown. Capa mounts the pack-horse, since her own is still lame, for we are only taking the absolute minimum with us.

Through a sudden squall of snow we gain the hollow of the valley in which the O.G.P.U. outpost rises.

An inner yard, ducks and cackling geese, and a dining-room with tables covered with American cloth. Comfort! The new bread we have been promised is not yet out of the oven. As it is noon we are offered a bowl of cabbage soup and a sort of porridge, ' gritchnivoie kasha.'

In charge of the ' base ' is a cool young man with sympathetic blue eyes set in a face burnt brown by the sun.

" Maybe I'll come and visit you! " he says as we depart.

CHAPTER XIII

Exploring "The White Bull"

A STEEP SLOPE which we descend by a crumbling trail. A considerable river which we ford tentatively, our ears deafened by the noise of turbulent water, and with the terror communicated by opaque waters which at any moment may turn out to be deep. . . .

To the east, a straight road towards China and the Kok Chal range delimiting the frontier; an area which till recently remained unoccupied territory, belonging to no one.

We penetrate into the Kaiche gorge and proceed upstream, passing incessantly from one bank to the other. Our horses refusing to cross a rocky ledge midstream, surrounded by running water, we abandon them to Matkerim, who takes them over one by one, up to the chest in water, while we work perilously round against the steep, rocky walls.

The valley falls away. On a pebbly slope my marvelling eyes discover a sort of wild rose, whose flowers, a deep red, shut up for the night, look like tiny tulips budding on many-branched candlesticks.

Our tent is hardly up in a small meadow when the rain begins to drum down on it. Capa stretches out with appendicitis pains. But the Primuses get going and soon we have the tent warm.

"You're a soft one," says Mila, seeing me tear away a handful of grass from under my sleeping-bag. "One ought to be able to sleep on anything."

A shot awakens us! Have we been attacked by 'Bass-matchi'? No, it's morning, and Jocubai is returning from the chase, having wounded a mountain goat in vain. But in reality I think he must have gone to reconnoitre our future route, for he has never been here before.

A lofty mountain, steep, pyramidal, and with a glacier atop, bars the valley. We should have borne off to the left towards the Jengart pass, but Jocubai in error gets us into a ravine, and we have to return to the main valley.

There we strike a circular patch of grass, very green, still flattened by some weight that only recently must have left it.

"That's where a bear has slept," says Matkerim, who has already noted the excrement of the beast.

Great excitement! Every hole in the rock seems a lair worth investigating. . . . Tracks lead from one to another, evidently made by steinbock.

Finally, we find the valley we are seeking, and begin climbing rapidly. The trail we have just left continues between two stupendous rocky walls, and soon after reaches the Kaiche pass, the gateway to Sin Kiang. A little farther, a bare twelve miles and to the left, is the first Chinese post. How magical are words! In my unconscious I was ready, I know, to follow anyone we had met then, going towards the East.

Matkerim is full of solicitude for the pink nostrils of his mount, which are one mass of cracks owing to exposure to the sun. He covers them with a black ointment containing ichthyol given him by the feldcher, and as a last precaution sticks a piece of paper over the lot.

Now we have left the last grass behind. Two slopes meet, and we follow the line where they join. To our left the mountain is of black, gravelly schist, to our right is a glacier which neatly caps the invisible peak with dazzling snow.

Jengart Pass

Where Kaiche ought to be, twin icy points surge upwards in audacious flight. It must be they, the two sharp blades from which it takes its name, Kaiche—the Scissors pass.

At the summit of the Jengart pass our altitude is nearly sixteen thousand feet. To the north our gaze plunges into a valley, mountain-locked, secret, and uninhabited. To the left are vertical sweeps of red, then blue, and then the yellow of the gigantic pebbly slopes on which our horses slip. To the right is a screen of majestic rocky walls at whose foot a glacier-river issues from a summit as isolated as the Cervin, and winds and breaks into *séracs*.

We have to descend on foot, for our horses' legs are trembling. Crossing the moraine of the great glacier their hoofs crunch through ice-bound pools.

Matkerim brings down two mountain cocks, large, plump birds with speckled plumes. The descent continues unendingly, exhausting to the knees. A breach appears opposite us in the rocky wall, and reveals a glacier hanging into the void, threatening the grey valley below.

We set up camp, and with some difficulty collect a little horse dung for a fire: very occasionally do hunters pass this way, and then only with special permits.

" When I get back to Moscow, I'm sure that instinctively I shall pick up all the well-dried dung I see," Volodya remarks.

Snow squalls, our daily interlude, send us hurrying into the tent.

Although we do not know it, we are under observation. We hear of it later, when offering hospitality to Osman the Kirghiz, who carries a ' vintovka,' a matchlock resting on a wooden stand.

" I hid when I saw you coming down. I took your poles for many guns and thought you were ' Bassmatchi.' But when I saw your fire and tent, that reassured me."

" Are there any round here? "

" You never know! Would you like some meat? There's half a steinbock hidden under that big square stone. . . ."

Reconnoitring

A succession of grassy slopes, then a towering wall of rock dominates our camp.

" To-day we'll try and climb to the top," Auguste declares.

" I think it will help us to work out the best way of attacking the peaks of the Kok Chal range there in front of us."

Volodya and I follow our leader in a stiff, difficult, breath-taking climb An unforgettable sunrise rewards us for our pains. High in the still sky, the planet of day, burning hot already, issues in silence from behind a range of savage needles. Against the light the mountain is black, and black is the minute valley in shadow at our feet; red are the bright-lit rocks, and white the glacier on Jengart's peak; while over the perfect outlines of this new created world floats the purity of an Italian sky.

On all fours, I drag myself up a rock-fall, hunting the best spot from which to take some photographs. Auguste goes off in an attempt to rediscover the Mount Cervin we have already glimpsed. We are high enough to see, towards China, the middle of the great Ak Oguz glacier.

I rejoin Auguste, who says a little later:

" I startled a steinbock a minute ago, which disappeared into that chimney there, straight over us. He can't have come down yet, for I heard a stone rattle. His horns are bigger than a chamois' ! "

At once I begin to scale the fine, solid rock. The animal is trapped and I shall take it by surprise. There seems a chance of sidling round. I'll try it. I hear the creature move. A ledge, then a small chimney, and I am still climbing, with every muscle functioning perfectly and obedient to my will: then a vertical flat wall rapidly traversed, too rapidly, for . . . phew . . . how do I go on?

Devil take it! The rock in front of me, worn down by some cascade in the past, is smooth as polished marble. Yet there is nothing for it but to go on, for I am hanging on with one toe on a jutting point. . . . It is impossible to turn, I shall never succeed in flattening my shoulder out against the rocky wall. My leg begins to tire, the knee trembles more and more. . . . I shall drop off. There is a fall the height of a house between me and the scree-covered slope. It's all up with me! Fear sends icy waves through all my limbs, I must act that very second, otherwise . . . With my free hand and foot I grope back towards the last holds. It is impossible to see what I am doing. At last, however, I hold fast, half crucified, with the void sucking at my back. And now if only my fingers do not slip while I risk changing the position of my foot!

Success! I'm saved. I can see what I'm doing. Auguste is watching me. But only when I am safe again and after some moments have passed, do I find the strength to say:

" That's better. Better than up there! "

An undercurrent of rancour hangs over the camp: no one knows our next step. Capa dissipates the tension by crying:

" Go on, you men! Off to the river with you and take some soap. Aren't you ashamed of yourselves, not washing for over a week. They look like ' Bassmatchi ' with their half-inch beards."

As we plunge under the water to rinse off the suds, snowflakes begin to whirl round us, blotting out the dreary sun.

Later, the Comrade-Chief from the fort arrives accompanied by four young men, the shortest of whom has a scrap of black paper stuck over his cracked lip. It is the moment to go hunting, and we set off in two parties to attack the cliff.

In vain I try to keep up with the Chief, who climbs at racing speed. Three shots are wasted on a mountain cock. Then we lie in wait, scrutinizing the rocky slope with our binoculars. The imagination creates the profile of a beast and walks it over the rocks until it hits against something real.

But there! Three animals are moving under the point.

A mad race follows. The Chief leaps forward like a gazelle in spite of his enormous felt boots, then skids thirty yards down a steep gulley on his heels. Three shots ring out sharply against the magnificent walls of rock; but we return despondent.

What magnificent lives they lead, these frontier guards, coursing in epic fashion over this boundless land.

EXPLORING "THE WHITE BULL"

China

Dawn finds us in battle-order. There is a reconnaissance to be made to the east towards the Ak Oguz pass that leads into Sin Kiang.

We cross the river mounted, and follow a moraine, rising by slow degrees from one gradient to the next. At every traverse we cross the flat bed of a dried-up lake.

At the foot of the glacier spreads a river, and we elect to take the lateral moraine on our left. Mountain cock dart to and fro on the heights like so many gambolling rabbits. Setting foot to the ground, we take leave of Matkerim and the horses.

We note the tracks of earlier travellers on the stones, and like sinister landmarks, quantities of bones. It is impossible to walk fifty yards without seeing ribs, hoofs, or the vertebrae of domestic animals.

Across the valley a gigantic peak, reminiscent of ' l'Aiguille Verte,' dominates the scene with all its northern face plastered with a jagged glacier.

The moraine we are on seems made up of immense stony waves. Between each we find a tiny plateau some ten yards square, white with scattered bones.

Each of these troughs must have served to shelter the flying nomads and their exhausted herds. Sometimes it may have been in winter, with the animals falling into the deep drifts piled by the snow against each rock. Dying of hunger, they perished where they fell. Skulls of horses lie among them, all but buried in sand.

After the national uprising of 1916, when the Cossacks were exterminating the Kirghiz, all who were able fled into Sin Kiang. But the Chinese inhabitants saw no reason for offering protection to these Kirghiz-Mussulmans of Turki-Mongol origin, and by degrees their herds were stolen from them. Stripped of everything, they decided to return whence they had come. It was winter and they perished in thousands on the way.

131

Those who regained their villages found that Russians had taken possession of their lands; and there was obviously little to be expected from that quarter.

Once more the now starving Kirghiz rose up in revolt and avenged their wrongs as best they might. It was the end of the great year 1917. Little by little the demobilized Russians filtered back from the Front, all Reds now after the Revolution. On every hand signs of destruction met their eyes. They too began to make reprisals, and in their turn started shooting their captives.

People who were living in Kara Kol at the time have told me: "It was atrocious. One can hardly talk about it: words don't exist for the sort of thing that took place."

But at the beginning of the revolt, was the only cause their reluctance to serve in the army?

It's not very easy to say. We don't really know yet. At the Duma held in St. Petersburg in 1916, three separate demands for an investigation were made, one by a faction of Socialists, another by the Cadets, and a third by the Mussulmans. But nothing was done, and by February the Revolution had broken out.

According to the official version 'agents-provocateurs' were at the back of it all: the Tsarism of that time wanted some pretext for vigorously repressing them.

However it may be, the unfortunate wretches made their way over the very trails on which we now happened to be. Yet this pass is little used owing to its height—some sixteen thousand feet—and because of a crevasse in the glacier near the summit.

The moraine comes to an end and we are standing on an immense snowy plain encircled by mountains. We ascend slowly towards the crevasse, which we negotiate roped one to another, on our stomachs, and casting fearful glances into the depths of the dark fault.

Still a quarter of a mile of deep snow to battle with: then we are at the pass, a rock-strewn ridge, where we sit down.

At our feet, virgin of snow, a black gravel valley sweeps

steeply away from us. From this point only a very few miles would lead us to Turfan, the nearest Chinese town.

But there, straight in front of us, when we raise our eyes over the nearer mountain-spurs, what is that yellow vibration in the air, stationary and like a sea of dust, rising to assail the skies? Guessed more than seen, the line of the horizon lies where the yellow merges with the blue of the sky: it can only be the Gobi, the trackless ocean of sand, Takla Makan, the terrible. . . .

Here at my feet is one of the objectives I had set myself in coming so far: the Chinese mountains inhabited by Kirghiz, and Sin Kiang in the turmoil of opposing currents. And still remoter, still calling me, were Kucha, Basaklik with its temple-grottoes containing the hundred thousand Buddhas, and Tokharian frescoes which bring to life again a whole Indo-European aristocracy whose amazing civilization flourished in the seventh century. . . .

I had everything with me I really needed, all but my sleeping-bag. There was nothing to stop me setting off alone for Turfan: and the few miles on foot were in no wise frightening. The only thing was my lack of a *visa*. In Berlin and Moscow I had been told it would take five or six months to get an answer from Urumchi, the capital.

What would I not have given to have gone on into the unknown? . . . "Adventure is not as some people think it, a romance. It cannot be acquired from a book. Adventure is always something lived through, and to make it part of oneself, the most important is to have proved worthy to live it, to live it without fear," Blaise Cendrars has written.

What joy it would be to go down there and burn my boats behind me, and go on always, intoxicated by the Unknown's thousand faces! . . .

No! I'm not foolhardy enough. This once I let myself be influenced by what people had prophesied: 'immediate imprisonment as a suspicious character.'

Immediately north of India we are here on the 80th meridian of longitude, almost on the line of Delhi.

Sadly I turn my back on the country of my longing and begin the protracted descent under a tormented sky.

Tension

Back at the camp we find the rice has been overcooked. Mila and Capa are out of temper at not seeing us return. The atmosphere is tense: it has not yet been decided by what route we are returning.

" The route to Kara Kol by the north-east, passing at the foot of Khan Tengri is impracticable, it appears, owing to the bad condition of the trails," says Auguste. " But before leaving, I very much want to go down to the end of this valley."

" Then," says Volodya, " we must separate, for Mila and I have to be back by the time the Institute opens. The detour you suggest represents at least another four or five days of travel, and we have not one extra day to spare, owing to all the accumulated delays due to one thing and another."

We fall asleep without having come to any decision.

But as we are breaking camp Auguste at last makes the propitiatory gesture.

" Let's return by the Jengart pass," he says.

We begin toiling up the crumbling path leading over the gravel mountain, and once more icy shudders shoot through me. Decidedly I am not made for the kind of expedition that I dream of. When, however, the steepness of the path forces us to set foot to ground, it helps enormously to hang on to the tail of one's horse and let it drag one after it.

The return is exhausting; in one stage we cover the distance to the O.G.P.U. outpost where the Comrade-Chief has temporarily assumed the rôle of mason and is helping his men to build an enclosure. Two young Russians have arrived from Frunze for some shooting. One, very pale under his too new Kirghiz hat, asks have we seen any game?

" Yes, lots; but why? "

"We personally haven't seen an argali, steinbock, or marmot yet!"

Later, we find that the whole native encampment has moved to a valley some three miles off. It takes our done-up horses a good extra hour to get there, and a biting wind turns into a snowstorm before we arrive.

As usual, I have forgotten to put some biscuit in my pocket to stay my hunger. And so I offer thanksgiving to the feldcher's wife, who quickly hands me two pirojkis sopping in fat, as an instalment on my supper.

The indefatigable Mila begins playing cards with passion.

We prepare to depart. To get a look at the shoes of Capa's horse, now healed at last, we hobble and cast it, and then hold it down while Matkerim does what is necessary.

Near us, camels are cropping at yellow tufts which push through the red earth every other yard or so.

CHAPTER XIV

THREE NEW PASSES

JUST BEFORE WE leave the trail by which we have come, we pass a number of ancient tombs, simple heaps of stone. Then, struggling against the wind and snow, we begin climbing up towards the Ichigart pass.

The load roped to one side of my saddle turns out to be too heavy, owing to a sack of flour that has fallen to my lot. It crushes my foot, drags my saddle askew, and violently irritates me. Volodya gets down from his horse and risks taking his gloves off to give me a hand.

When we get to the pass, at no great altitude, I find a couple of planks lost by some caravan, and take possession of them for our evening fire. The cold is so intense that we have to proceed on foot to keep warm. A momentary break in the clouds permits us to see subsidiary mountain ranges all round us.

Descending a slope facing north, every step of our horses' hoofs turns the snow into yellow mud. On the lower levels, however, the thick snow lies as it falls, and cakes, crunching under foot.

Half-way down the last spur, before we get to the River Irtach, and while I am still on foot, my saddle and its ' barda ' swivel round once more. Intensely exasperated, I hurl everything to the ground before preparing to buckle it on again. Jocubai, very displeased, comes up to me; then, after a furious argument in which I let myself go in French, he loads his own horse with the sack that bothers me so.

A lonely camel, unsaddled, watches us pass. How on earth has it got here?

Our camp, which we set up near the grey river whose steep shores rise at our backs, for the first time in its history sees flying sparks and flames rise into the air, for we have found some small, dry bushes. All round us dash scurrying hares.

In the morning our fire burns brightly in the serene air. Floating above the mists, the mountain summits are white with new fallen snow. A passing Kirghiz couple dismount, and, squatting in front of our fire, warm their hands and share our tea.

Again we climb out of the verdureless, deserted valley; our stirrups clanking at times against some rock bordering the trail. Then we are deafened by the tumult of a torrent quickly forded as we plunge through sudden cold gusts of air.

To our right, a steep track rises towards the Kouiliou pass which would have got us speedily to Kara Kol, save that the route is impracticable for horses. We are forced therefore to follow the course of the Irtach, whose leaping waters have soon to be crossed, to my great terror. Auguste's mount slips on a sharp stone and cuts a deep gash in its foot.

Suddenly in front of us a herd of camels, grazing at liberty, appears. They have thick coats and two humps, but one of them is white, unreal looking, as though covered with hoar frost.

In company with them we climb towards the near-by aul: they go in front of us, their immense shadows lengthening over the earth stripped bare save for the pale splashes made by clumps of artemisia.

The vision of this evening sinks deep into me: the strange animals cross the river, hesitant, up to their bellies in the water white with foam.

A Visit to Jocubaï's Sister

The clear outlines of the mountain ridges glow in the soft light. From the mushroom-shaped yurts, calm blue smoke escapes into the sky.

Climbing the banks of the river, Mila's horse stumbles and falls, but in a moment is on its feet again, unhurt.

Conceitedly, I begin to reload my camera, as Auguste does,

while still remaining in the saddle; but a dog barks, my horse steps forward a pace or two as the reins are loose, and the camera falls to the ground. When I have picked it up it is impossible to load it again.

I leave the setting up of the tent and the search for stones to the others while I try all ways to fit in the new spool. Volodya, divining my distress, comes to my aid.

"Volodya, be careful or you'll smash it altogether! You don't even know how the thing works," Mila says.

"Come away now," Auguste cries; "it's too dark to see anything. I'll fix that up for you to-morrow. Get the canteens, the sugar, and the flour."

Tea is ready in the yurt of Jocubai's sister. Company is present and the carpets have been spread. A kid, white as snow, is brought close to the fire by a man in leather breeches. The flames can be seen leaping in its yellow horizontal-pupilled eyes. They prod it with their fingers, and a few moments later it appears again in dismembered pieces that are plunged into the cauldron.

The scene in the gathering darkness pierced by the gleaming firelight is unforgettable. My neighbour whittles a stick to a sharp point, which then, like a deliberate impalement, he slowly buries with a sharp cracking sound in the skull of the small creature.

Then the head with its horns is held over the flames, whereupon the hairs splutter, curl up, carbonize, after which, with the point of a knife, veiled by smoke that smells of burnt leather, the man scrapes the spongy, dried black mass, peels the ears, and drops it into the cauldron also. The feet are set in the embers, and later, thoroughly gnawed, will delight those to whose lot they fall, and who will suck away at them like true connoisseurs.

In order to see how the cooking is getting on the woman takes a brand which she holds over the smoking cauldron.

The blood, which has been caught in a bowl, is lapped up by the dogs.

The wait is a long one, but, when all is ready, how eagerly

we fall upon the delicious flesh! The dry grasses of these high plateaux are, it seems, richer in vitamins than even the green shoots of English pasturages. No doubt this explains the succulent richness of the meat only to be found in these regions.

I smile when I think of the vegetarian credo. The Kirghiz feed exclusively on meat and milk. Yet they live long, and, like the Esquimaux, are able to put up an astonishing resistance to cold, privation, and the fatigue of the long treks.

To eat as much as possible when one has the chance, so that the unexpected may find one with every reserve stored full, that is the principle on which the camel works. In unconscious obedience to this rule I stuff myself daily and put on flesh visibly. I am the terror of Mila, who is in charge of our victuals. Either her eyes or her voice remind me daily:

" It's frightful. Ella eats more than the men! "

Jocubai's sister, her laughing face shadowed by the white kerchief, passes the night making ' toukatch ' with our flour.

When the first beams of the rising sun glitter on the glaciers that frown down on us, I begin to investigate what has happened to my camera. But it is Auguste, as he promised, who discovers a scrap of film stuck in the catch.

In my delight I photograph everything in sight: a pile of kisiak in front of the smoking yurt, a girl with twelve plaits and a fur toque on her head, and a father, with a curly lambskin hat on his head, smiling delightedly at the sight of his little devil of an offspring disappearing under a peaked proletarian cap much too big for him. The fathers know that some day they will depend on their sons, and therefore, fearing reprisals, they spoil them, and treat them always with indulgent kindness.

From the heights of Sari Chat on which sheep are grazing we see our handsome Sari Tor from behind. Then we come out into the upper valley of the Narin through which we had passed before reaching the Meteorological Station. Thus, tying a bow in our journey, we proceed among the edelweiss towards a new pass, leaving our old Chuguchak to the right.

All through the day we trot over a soil riddled with argali tracks. A herd comes into sight, and our two Kirghiz gallop away to cut off their retreat with the object of beating them back to us, and in their panic getting them within rifle shot. . . .

But these mouflons are faster on their feet than any of us.

Kashkassu

The net result was that our party was scattered. Slipping, and leading our horses, we were going down a schist gorge when suddenly we realized we had lost Auguste. Consternation! Capa hands her beast to me and goes back up the trail to call to him.

At last we come upon the trail to Kashkassu again in the hollow of the valley and begin to make rapid progress. But night falls as we are skirting two small, dark circular lakes. Matkerim says:

" It's useless to go farther, we can't get over the pass to-day. We must camp where we can."

No grass, no kisiak. A lunar landscape. The cold stings.

Once again on waking the roof of our tent sparkles with hoar-frost, and Mila plays at throwing the discus with the round of ice she finds in the saucepan. Our sleeping-bags, however, soaked through by condensation, must be dried first. Capa makes a scene:

" Ella, you've lost my fine flask for me. It must have happened when you were leading my horse yesterday. It was strapped over the pommel."

The lakes follow each other, strung together like a chaplet, with great glaciers stretching down to their very waters, like a Greenland landscape. But in front of us the huddled mountains write a sharp V on the sky.

Among them, two glaciers face each other and almost join, their steep black moraines overhanging a lake of unimaginable turquoise-green, in which the shimmering outlines of the glacier are mirrored. The unequalled beauty of its colouring dazzles and ravishes the eyes; satisfying them so wholly that they cannot tear themselves away from it.

The perilous track disappears when the lake overflows, turning into the dwelling of a giant enraged, who holds in captivity an immortal creature whose snowy body undulates amid tresses of billowing, wayward turquoises.

But a rugged descent begins on the flank of a glacier at the foot of high cliffs of rock. Then the horses fearfully descend the blocks of stones projecting in steep stairs.

Our difficulties are at an end: a valley of green pasture grounds is at our feet. It seems miraculous! Trees emerge by degrees, more and more clearly, a forest of firs, the first to be seen again after so long an absence.

The Caravan

Galloping at times, we catch up with a strange procession.

Under their double load of enormous bales of wool, it is hardly possible to see the feet of the thirty moving beasts. But their bells can be heard, and by their abundant tails I recognize them to be horses.

Their loads, however, are never more than round about two hundred pounds, while a burden of nearly five hundredweight hardly incommodes a camel.

In front of them walks a man on foot: another, skinny and with a black beard, grinning with all his teeth, sits on an ass, a handkerchief folded in a triangle knotting a white robe round his loins. The third, sitting on a white horse, fat and bearded, looks discontented. Stuffing his saddle and heaped under him is first a sack of flattened flour, then a mattress covered with geometric designs, and finally a pile of quilts. He it is who owns the caravan. He is wearing two padded gowns, and, like his men, a black sheepskin toque. In the stirrups his feet are on a level with his horse's shoulders.

" Where do you come from? " I say in Russian.

" From Kashgar in twenty-six days! "

" What is your race? "

" Uzbek."

" And the man laughing behind you? "

" He's only a ' Sart.' Heh! What are you doing? " he says in terror as I sight my camera at him, after making my horse's pace fit in with his.

' Sart ' is what the natives of Turkestan, who have become settlers, are called in derision. The word comes from Sari-it, or yellow dog, I was told. Sarts are Iranians who have been crossed with all the Turkish races that have occupied their land. In the fourteenth century the Uzbeks, descended from the Turki-Mongols, seized the country, adopted its customs, and became its aristocracy. They go back to Jenghiz Khan through Uzbek Khan, Cheibani, and Djoudi. Nowadays every inhabitant of the new Soviet Republic of Uzbekistan is an Uzbek.

A stop enables our beasts to graze, while we eagerly start a wood fire with which to cook our dried peas. When the tin of melted butter is passed to our Kirghiz, each takes a piece and adds it to his tea.

Matkerim, unlike Jocubai, has no penknife, and so he waits until we have finished to use one of ours. Mila scolds me because I pass him a blade we have used for cutting sausage.

" Not that one, do be careful; you'll outrage his feelings: take the butter knife. . . ."

Our descent continues beneath narrow, slim firs, the smell of which wraps us as closely round as though we were taking a pine bath. When we come to the torrent Jocubai washes his hands and face in it.

In the half darkness of the forest we meet a camel so monumental it takes my breath away. On its back is a folded yurt, topped with a cradle and various cauldrons.

The landscape broadens, flattens out, and leads down to the valley that descends from the Jukka.

Despite nightfall and our fatigue we continue to press on. To cheer us on our way I sing Swiss songs at the top of my voice. They are the only ones I know, and it is the way in which, at times, I give expression to my delight.

Not before the following morning do we reach the Gostorg depot. A number of encampments of caravanners have been set up, simple tents on the very ground, or surmounting bales of wool doing duty as walls. A cauldron is simmering on the ground, and men of all ages squat round, waiting. An Uzbek juggles with a skein of ' lapcha,' then drops it into the boiling water. I am invited to join, but my companions are far ahead, and I must follow them.

Chinese Colony

Since we are anxious to reach Kara Kol the same evening, we keep on at a quick trot with a short rest to give our horses time to graze. The sudden return to the heat tries us sorely, and, grown accustomed to glacier-water, the temperature of the neighbouring arik astonishes us by its warmth.

I have a marvellous yellow ointment against sunburn, and every time I use it Matkerim comes up and asks for some, just as he does when I use my pocket mirror ; but as he takes far too much, and bursts the tube by squeezing too hard, I refuse to give him any. Whereupon, like a spoilt child, he comes and sticks his finger out with a supplicating air.

A yurt has been set up near the road. In the doorway a woman stands with noisy laughter, pressed by a couple of Kirghiz who seem drunk. ' Booza ' is written on a sign. It is a sparkling liquid, the colour of _café-au-lait_, and Matkerim pays a rouble for a bowl. I put it to my lips. It tastes like medicine, insipid and astringent. They make it with the fermented grain of millet.

We shall not see the rest of the southern shores of the lake. An alphabet of Syrian origin, dating from the period when the Manichaean religion extended to the shores of the Chou, has recently been found there. (Manichaeism was founded in the third century by Manes of Ecbatana. Its principle is the conflict between light and darkness, like

Zoroastrianism. For many centuries disciples were to be found in Turkestan.)

A stone has also been found which bears the Buddhistic invocation in Thibetan characters ' *Om mani padme hom* ', ' The Jewel is in the Lotus.' But the inscriptions found at Djargalan have not yet been deciphered.

We were now on our way to Marinovka, a Doungan colony of Chinese Mussulmans, who in 1883, with the consent of the authorities, were permitted to settle in the country.

In the fields of blown poppies we see small yellow men swiftly scraping the slit seed pods. Rain had begun to fall as we passed through the streets of the almost deserted village. There were ruins everywhere! It does not take the houses long to return to the earth from which they are made.

Those which still remain standing are constructed in a special manner: under the projecting earthen roof are four rows of beams and untrimmed logs superimposed horizontally, and then a long frieze of highly decorative pierced wood.

From the shorn heads of the children a single plait always sticks out stiffly.

In the time of the revolt, houses and an agricultural school in this village were burnt, and women were stolen away.

Jog-trot, jog-trot, jog-trot, all day long. We shall have covered nearly forty miles: fatiguing in the extreme. One puts out every effort not to be outdistanced by a yard by the Kirghiz at our head. From time to time we have to use the whip on the pack-horse who drags more and more. At moments a hasty glance at the sky over the lake fills me with anxiety: from the Kungei range a black wall with a sulphurous border advances upon us, predicting an imminent waterspout.

Hardly are we in before the storm bursts like a cataract, and joyfully we eat our boiled potatoes served with salt.

I go to the Post Office, but my money has not come. On several occasions I make inquiries about it from various members of the staff, but all in vain. (There had been no hitch at all; the warrant was waiting for me: four months later in Moscow I was to see the counterfoil proving it had been sent, and the form returning it as unclaimed.) I send off a telegram for the same sum to be sent me at Alma Ata.

What will my friends think of me?

We are unable to pay our two Kirghiz off until we have sold our horses; thus they will be forced to go on with us, though much against their wills. To hearten them I give them each a ten-franc timepiece bought at Woolworth's. Jocubai can hardly believe his eyes, yet, nevertheless, refuses to accompany us. He has a really beastly abscess in the thigh. I feel no little pride at the thought that my skin has held out, when that of an old ' dziguite' cries surrender. I had been wearing ski-ing trousers, and had used my sleeping-bag to pad the high cantle of my wooden saddle.

Matkerim, however, is willing to accompany us, and in order to tempt him we promise to buy him stuff for an overcoat at Alma Ata, where there is a cloth factory. . . . On the way we shall find a guide to take us over the high Kungei passes.

CHAPTER XV

LAST DAYS IN KIRGHIZIA

WITH CHINA ALWAYS at our back, we cross the grey waters of the Djargalan River on a great wooden bridge of modern construction, pass through the immense village of Tioup (Preobrajenskoe), and come out again on the northern shore of Lake Issik.

As I ride I think of Sultan Gasyeva, the tiny woman editor of the *Tuoussu Kolkhoz*, whom I had just left, and of her Komsomol comrades.

A round head wrapped in a white kerchief knotted on the nape: a full, round face with practically no salient feature save for the flattened tip of the nose projecting a little. The broad cheeks spread from the corners of the firm mouth to the top of the smoothed-out cheek-bones were surmounted by a bulging forehead with barely visible eyebrows. Now I begin to understand the amused interest on her face as she looked at me, with one eye gleaming intensely black out of her saffron-tinted visage while the other was half hidden, so that I only caught a glimpse of it, veiled by the strange Asiatic eyelid so typical of her people, protuberant and over-hanging and taut to the very corner of the eye.

She was evidently thinking what could I understand of their life, this woman who says she has come so far and from a town that contains millions of inhabitants? What could I know of the life that has made her what she is, or of the toil that wore out her mother and sister?

I understand now. Somewhere in her she felt the world was not wholly made up of desolate plains like those which once surrounded her. Therefore, when she heard three years ago that there were schools available for all, she abandoned the high plateaux and yurts to settle in Kara Kol.

And now she knows something about the world: she can read and write, and even express in articles—though written with difficulty, for I saw her in the act—what made her develop as she has. Her husband said to me:

"Sultann is my second wife. She cost me nothing and earns a hundred roubles a month: she is much better than the first. I had to pay twenty horses for that one in 1920, and hadn't even seen her first."

No longer has she the open sky over her head, but her salary is a splendid sign of freedom, like the long khaki blouse that hangs over the very short black skirt which reveals her bow legs. She went among her people, and with the enthusiasm of the neophyte converted them to collectivism, thereby adding greatly to her prestige. Now she is as important as Comrade Yildenbaivar Kulsoun, who wears a mantle of green velvet at New Star Kolkhoz, where she drives a tractor, or Takta Khunuva, who has been studying at the Educational Technicum for the past three years.

In the past, I imagine, the Senegalese rifleman on returning to his village must have enjoyed a prestige similar to hers. It marks the rise to power of the technified barbarian, the man-who-drives. Yet the far-flung motor will finally destroy the European.

But as applied to you, Kirghiz women, you are the pillars of the new regime—that is, so long as the promises that have been made you are respected.

This day our stage was a short one: we must not force our mounts too hard in view of their approaching sale.

At the village of Kurmenkte we find the leader of the Volunteer Force, to whom we have an introduction. In the yard are stalls for the horses, and in the gallery in front of the house quilts and pillows have been laid out ready for the night.

Coloured koshmous are spread over the floor of our room. Behind us is an iron bedstead—one must be modern at all costs—which is never used, then a dresser for the pialas, and finally a brass-banded coffer studded with nails containing articles of clothing.

When the samovar is brought in we unpack our provisions. I open the last tin of fish in tomato sauce, and make a pretence of helping myself.

" Offer it first to our hostess," Mila hisses.

" But she would never dare touch it, and anyhow there's not enough to go round."

Nevertheless, I obey, meekly accepting the merited rebuke. The young woman tastes the fish discreetly and passes it on. She is wearing laced bootees and a mantle of black velvet; her regular features are framed in a pink silk kerchief from under which long plaits hang with coins tied to their tails. The man is stalwart, tanned, with a ferocious-looking moustache, and wears his white hat all the time.

We Lose a Horse

When we start off again my horse develops a limp which continues to get worse. At our side carts roll on their way to the fields in the vicinity.

' Mazars,' the tombs of saints, rise by the roadside, dignified and impressive in spite of the ignoble earth with which they are constructed. Generally their shape is a crenellated cube flanked by severe geometrical porch.

We proceed, chewing sunflower seeds bought from the women who dry them in the sun on vast sheets.

Impossible to set out to attack the Kungei on a horse with only three good legs. Happening to be near the bypath that leads off to Bolshoi Ouroukte, where there is a stud-farm, we suddenly decide to go there.

The veterinary surgeon, whom we find among the vast stables containing hundreds of thoroughbreds, keeps his counsel. Next day the inflammation has spread to the whole limb: in less than a week there is no possibility of saving the beast. The marks of the metal crampons can be seen on its rump. The horses must have been fighting together, as a result of being tethered too close.

LAST DAYS IN KIRGHIZIA

Since I knew my comrades were in a hurry to get home, I began to wonder whether I should have to stay on by myself. But then Matkerim turns up, saying:

"The 'viouk' (pack-horse) is ill. His withers have swollen so, it looks like a belly on his back."

Thus the others are forced to stay, too. Matkerim is right, though we had somewhat scoffed at him owing to his habitual exaggeration. Every night in the same pitiable tones he used to say:

'Koursak savciem propal.' And then, "my stomach is right down in my boots."

The farm is delightfully situated at the mouth of a defile from which the eye commands the whole shore and lake. A vacant room adjoining the office is put at our disposal. We take our meals in the communal kitchen, used by all the employees and situated close to the torrent. There we meet two hirsute geologists, tremendously enthused by their discoveries.

The cows come in for milking to the dairy sheds only a few paces from us, and we buy our milk by the bucket. It goes wonderfully well with the delicious, very dark bread of the region. It appears that this colour is due to an unhealthy condition of the grain. As always, however, I eat enough for four.

The stud-farm is grief-stricken, their prize English stallion having died the day before as a result of eating wet lucerne.

Matkerim, having gone off to look for some koumiss, discovers a Kirghiz with whom he hopes to make the following bargain.

"The Kirghiz has a strong little horse that he would quite like to exchange for Ella's and the pack-horse. The latter, with its sore withers, is hardly resaleable, and in any case has never been worth much. The Kirghiz himself is in no hurry and is quite able to wait until the animals recover."

"An excellent arrangement! Let us start at once!"

So here I am on a little roan beast with a belly as round as a barrel, whose natural pace is a canter. How nice that is!

That evening we set up our last camp in the plains. We

guard the horses turn and turn about, for fear they may be stolen, or in spite of their hobbles stray too far into the fields. To keep awake I spend my night watch counting my paces and warm my hands in alternation on the bowl of my pipe.

The sky seems altogether too small to hold the stars that press so thickly on each other, collide, and topple over the edge at every instant.

At moments I realize I am a horse short. I count and recount them, and then go running off to find the stray looming out of the scattered bushes.

Only towards noon does Matkerim return with a guide, and we begin our climb out of the valley of Ak Su, the White Waters. The mountain slopes that face the south are all worn bare; but when they swing round to the north they are covered with pines.

My wretched mount, or rather my lack of equestrian training, has changed the pleasurable canter of yesterday into a disagreeable jog-trot which pitilessly bumps my poor carcase about.

By evening we are up in the heights. After the heat of the plain the cold pierces, stings, bites, and lashes; the muscles of one's jaws set fast. But I have not the courage to get down and climb the flanks of the oversteep grazing-grounds on foot.

At last we see an aul of thirteen yurts perched on a grassy promontory. It is the last we shall see, and also the last lamb we shall have offered us.

It is night, and so the lamb's throat is cut in the yurt. The head is held stretched back while the thick blood pours into an enamelled bowl. Skilfully the white, smooth body is peeled out of the veined hide that spreads wider as the operation proceeds. We all fall fast asleep while the meat is being cooked. That night I do believe I managed to eat as much as a Kirghiz: it is impossible to say more!

All night I have frightful pains in the hollow of my clavicles, with neuralgia and extreme exhaustion, as a result of the new jog-trot plus the intense cold. If there had been no one in the tent I know I should have groaned for all I was worth; but as it is, my only possible diversion is to balance myself on one hip and a shoulder-blade. At daybreak one of Volodya's citric powders relieves me in ten minutes.

I notice that children are chewing gum, and am about to assume the recent visit of some American to these regions when Volodya says:

" No, it's the Chandrilla plant which grows round here. It was discovered by accident, but now it is going to be developed on a large scale as a source of artificial rubber: it contains 20 per cent of an elastic substance."

Farewells

The entire aul is present to see us depart. The white-bearded elder sits astride a bull, which he drives by means of a ring through its nose. He is going to bear us company as far as the main trail.

With a last glance I bid farewell to the incomparable beauty of the scene in front of me, bathed in the new-born iridescent light. The round yurts, solidly roped down, with plumes of white smoke; and, like a watch-dog at the door, an immobile eagle standing under its hood, with drawn-in neck and shoulders hunched; the plump, tiny horses, curly as spaniels, bearing the high, padded saddle; women with heads bundled up in white turbaned head-dresses, and men distended by quilted ' chapans,' or disappearing under many sheepskins.

Solitude. Now there are no more trees: stones only!

" Halt! What's happened? "

Matkerim is cursing for all he is worth.

" Cheitan. I've cast a shoe. And we haven't a nail left."

It is hopeless now to expect to cross the glaciers and moraines that await us. None of the horses that belong to the aul are shod. And it means two days lost if we wait for Markerim to return from Semenovka. There is nothing for it but to separate.

" Say. You won't forget to send the stuff for my overcoat! "

"Good-bye! Khoch! Vsio horosho!"

The climb becomes steep and precipitous. The guide, by signs, gives us to understand that the Ak Su pass is long and dangerous.

From our escarpment we are in a position to admire two glaciers at our feet and the summits of the Kungei. Dismounting and spacing ourselves out, we cross a steep, sloping *névé*, which luckily supports our weight. At the top of the pass our altitude is nearly fifteen thousand feet: then we descend rapidly in a northerly direction towards a narrow glacier valley that is already in shadow.

I begin to understand why our new Kirghiz betrays anxiety. Progressing quickly and surely, he quits the moraine and advances over the trackless glacier, avoiding the long crevasses with consummate skill. At every moment the thought we may disappear assails me.

I, who am so tormented by the need to prove to myself that I could, if necessary, follow in the tracks of my heroes of the Himalayas or North Pole, tremble with fear when the least difficulty arises, and begin asking myself, "Why on earth have I got myself here?"

All ends well, but I have had neither the necessary calmness of spirit nor the leisure, like Auguste, to take some photographs. Mila asks:

"Have you read Pilnyak's book on Tajikistan, and his descriptions of the passes he came through? I wonder how he would have rendered this crossing of ours over the Ak Su. Two years ago we were at Darvaz and 'Peter the Great,' only a week after he himself had been there, but I swear to you I would never have recognized them from his descriptions. Maybe he had never seen a mountain before?"

"Well, you've discovered a secret there. To talk about anything in a striking way, it's best to know nothing about it, then one is tremendously affected by what one sees, and can indulge in lavish superlatives with all sincerity. I tried myself once to imagine I had never seen a glacier, but I couldn't take myself in."

We sank exhausted into the first patch of grass we met. The region was a dangerous one on the frontier of Kazakstan, in the deserted Kebin valley. No herds are led to pasture there for fear of reprisals, since the two republics have not yet succeeded in delimiting their frontiers.

Our guide has a fine spare head, blue eyes, and fair beard. He gets us up early, as he is not accompanying us over the Zailiski pass. His idea is to leave us at the foot of the easy pass into Alma Ata, in order to give himself time to get back to his aul the same evening.

This long valley makes me think of a deserted lunar landscape: the river has hollowed out holes in the cliffs and worn them into ravines like craters.

" But our guide's crazy," says Auguste. " We must have passed our tracks some time ago."

And certainly he is behaving strangely. He loads his rifle and gazes intently at the opposite bank. . . .

" Over there! Three men! He must have seen them long before us. Can they be Bassmatchi? At last, after all that has been said about them! "

Our Kirghiz wants to make sure what sort of people will be following on his heels, for in a few minutes he will be returning alone, on his horse of great price.

Urged by the same curiosity, the three armed men have already crossed the river and catch up with us. We all burst out laughing. They are botanists armed with spades.

Farewell, taciturn and pale-eyed Kirghiz! In a moment he is no longer to be seen.

The pass, bravely taken, leads to a long and final descent which will land us in the plains of Kazakstan at an altitude of two thousand three hundred feet. The horses advance over the stones as though they were dancing, lifting high their bent knees.

On the borders of an Alpine lake, situated at the foot of a mountain covered with dark firs, the bright and intense green colour of the water makes me exclaim:

"Preposterous! It's the exact colour of bathroom tiles. There's something very unhealthy about such a colour."

It turns out as I said. No fish have elected to take up residence in these strange waters.

The first habitation we encounter is a chalet of modern construction for the use of lumbermen. At an immense distance in front of us can be seen the vast plains of the steppes stretching to the endless Siberian boglands, where only flatness reigns.

As we issue from the valley, large fruit trees bow before us in the passing wind. A strange white cow lies on its back under an apple-tree, its hide, stripped off, flattened out like a large, supple carpet under it. The carcase is still whole, bulging, smooth, well-knit; and pale and shiny with fat.

Capa is incapable of proceeding at a regular pace: sometimes she urges her mount into a trot and overtakes me on the trail that is often only just wide enough for one, then suddenly she drops into a walking pace under my horse's very nose. At last I can contain myself no longer.

"You're maddening. If you get in front, then set the pace as head of the file. This is the tenth time you have overtaken me and made me break my rhythm by having to slow down."

Alma Ata: the Capital

That must be the town, that verdurous sea upon which float the bright onion bulbs of the church towers. Towering masts for wireless rise into the air, an astonishing plantation to see arising out of this yellow earth.

On the outskirts a kind of zone of half-yurts; huts made of packing-cases, miserable tents. There are even inhabited holes in a cliff.

Founded in 1854, Alma Ata, the capital of Kazakstan and its six million inhabitants, was originally christened Vierny. In 1929 it numbered fifty thousand souls, but by 1933 the number had risen to one hundred and fifty thousand.

Finding the tourist base is like looking for a needle in a

haystack. The Government building to which we go for information is a fine new structure which Le Corbusier would delight in. Our difficulty comes from the fact that all the streets have been rechristened. We are glad to be on horseback, for the surface of the wide avenues has disappeared under a thick layer of liquid mud. At last we are back in the fold!

Horse-dealers

We have accomplished the remarkable feat of using the same mounts for months in the upper mountain regions, and then selling them at a profit. There are numbers of dealers, it appears, whose main occupation is bringing horses from Kara Kol to Alma Ata, where they fetch better prices.

But the saddles which we found such difficulty in procuring are unsaleable, and in any case it is not our best animals that fetch the highest prices. Draft horses are what is wanted. Auguste, who has to spend whole mornings on his feet in the horse market, must keep on answering the same question:

" Well, and tell me, does it buck in the shafts? "

The profit we make is all the more important to me, because there is still nothing for me at the Post Office. (The money was dispatched, as I heard later, but disappeared completely on the way.) It appears that in autumn it is always impossible to come by liquid money in sums of any importance even at the banks, where it has all been requisitioned to pay the peasants. The horse market is only able to settle up for part of the money due to us: the rest it promises to send to Moscow later.

Mila finds a shop in which cloth is being sold without any restrictions, and spends the greater part of her available money in it. Materkim is not forgotten. At the Post Office, however, the regulations controlling the fashion in which the cloth wrapping must be sewn are truly Chinese in their complexity.

In one of the Co-operatives I discover some honey at

twelve roubles a pound, as well as some dried ' ouriouks '—
tiny apricots with a delicious flavour.

But the great bazaar is simply pitiful. Five or six roubles
for a musk melon, and two roubles for a kilogram of
potatoes. This spring, all the blossom of the famous apple-
trees of the region was frost-bitten; and at Alma Ata, which
signifies ' Father of Apples,' a kilogram cost two to three
roubles.

I go to the bazaar with Mila, who wants to get rid of her
worn-through mountain boots. We wander about among the
crowds of people, all with something to sell, the boots dangling from our finger-tips. Finally, we relinquish them for
fifteen roubles.

Kazaks from the Steppes, burnt black by the sun, are
selling all their possessions: embroidered koshmous, braided
velvets that decorate the yurts of the rich, saddle-bags,
carpets, multicoloured traces, damascened knives and saddles.

I go about looking for some small souvenir which I should
like to present to myself, when my eyes fall on the legs of
a sitting Kazak woman wearing bright-striped stockings of
crocheted camel-hair. She takes them off and lets me have
them for six roubles. Under the stockings white bands are
wrapped round her legs in the Russian manner.

The man in charge of the base has supplied us with bread
cards and a permit to eat in the printers' restaurant. Groats
with herring, or herring with cabbage, soon begins to get on
our nerves, and we go back to cooking on our own stoves at
the base.

In vain I try to discover Mr. Ba Tou Tchin, the consul
for Sin Kiang. The dye is cast. I give up definitely the idea
of going into China. I shall leave for Tashkent and the
legendary cities of Turkestan: Samarkand, Bokhara, and
Khiva.

PART II

A VAGABOND IN TURKESTAN

CHAPTER I

ALONE

Now I SHALL have to manage as best I can. My friends
have gone, bound for Moscow. I laugh when I think
what an odd person our Capa was. No longer will she be
able to call each evening:

" Ella, come for a stroll with me ! "

She thought I could see in the dark, and would keep close
to me when we withdrew to find some discreet corner. . . . It
was she, too, who every morning, with loud cries, looked for
our Balzac, whose many pages we found of the utmost service.
It was funny to hear the desolate mountains re-echo daily to
the names of Balzac and Giraudoux. Some day I shall take
up my most eloquent pen in order that the particular master,
who still is in a position to savour the originality of the
compliment, may realize how unexpectedly popular he was
with us.

Another Exile

Before leaving Alma Ata there is another political exile I
mean to visit. On my way to him I look over the Ethno-
graphical Museum, the lay-out of which was then undergoing
rearrangement. The principal church, now disestablished,
has been given over to it, though the glittering crosses still
gleam over the cupolas.

Exiled over a year before to this newly established capital,
the man I was looking for had found work immediately in
the local university, where he now occupies the chair of
history. In pursuit of him I wandered through empty
lecture rooms, for it is late afternoon. A wing of the building is under repair, ' remont,' as they say in Russian. I am

unable to find a porter, but in the end three students, with slits of eyes, direct me to the professor's lodgings at no great distance.

In the presence of his wife and a young student, and in a room littered with disordered piles of books, the professor explains what happened to him.

" I was exiled after being accused of belonging to a newly established religious sect, an accusation that was utterly false. Then I was hardly in this city before I was offered a post at the university and the job of Chief Archivist. But in any case I have reason for believing there is a likelihood of my sentence coming up for revision soon, and that then I shall be recalled to Leningrad. In one sense I shall be sorry, for I have become very attached to my work here."

" What do you think of your native students? "

" They are quite as intelligent as the Russians, and certainly at times more industrious. The Kazak is not quick-witted, but what he takes in he remembers. The Kirghiz in contrast is quick, intuitive, more inventive, but very honest."

" Are they devout? "

" Their parents were only very superficially Mohammedan, so that the present absence of any official religion does not really seem strange to them."

" Do you think it will be long before they are mature enough to govern themselves? "

" Certainly not, there is nothing to prevent them becoming so, and it seems to me that within the next few years they should even be able to dispense with all Russians."

" And do you think that then they will see eye to eye politically with their Soviet administrators? "

" Certainly."

I notice numbers of French periodicals on the table, including the latest publications from the ' Left Bank.' In a copy of the *Temps*, dated barely three weeks earlier, I read the sudden death of Virginie Hériot! Opening a copy of Luc Durtain's *D'homme à homme* at hazard, I stumble on the following phrase, which seems to crystallize all I have been thinking. " Briefly, the world first: then in the world, man: and in man, other men. The threefold desire the writer conjures from his white paper and the public from the ink-blackened sheets."

Coming as I have from the very confines of the earth, my sudden plunge into the contemporary finds me unprepared and completely at a loss.

I take my leave of a bald, smooth-shaven, and remarkable man, whose elegant and meticulous phrases are interlarded at every instant with remarks such as " On the 28th April 1912, as we were dining at the Petit Vatel, John Somebody said to me in these very words . . . "

I hurry through the park at top speed. Ouf! I'd rather be here than in the Petit Vatel, in spite of all my desire for a really good meal!

Immediately the three main avenues have been crossed the streets become terrifyingly black. It is by no means a simple matter to get home without being lost. Startled, I listen to the booming sounds struck from an echoing piece of wood. It is the night watchman on his rounds, and this is the curfew knell.

How to Leave!

All I have to do now is leave! A difficult operation I know, but I saw the way my companions went about it. It is the Society for Proletarian Tourists that is responsible for me on my travels. Therefore I go to the director in charge of the ' base,' who fills up a form for a given date, approving my application to be supplied with a railway ticket, which entitles me to enter the category of ' bronniy ' or ' armoured ' tickets.

Armed with the form, you turn up at the station two or three hours before the ticket office opens on the eve of the day you propose to travel. There you find a queue already waiting. The very first comer has noted down the successive arrivals, so that everyone knows the order in which he appeared; then, according to the kind of form you produce, you are put into one or other category.

Those who remain in front of the window, tired and pale, are the first to be supplied with tickets : they are 'kurortniys' going to sanatoria. Three have already arrived before me. Then come the Communists, who need only produce a corner of the red card that proves them members of the Party. No vouchers are demanded from them; it is certain they are travelling on urgent business.

The 'bronniy,' among whom I find myself, form the third category, and to them is conceded the right to travel with the least possible delay. Then come the 'kommandirovka,' those dispatched on various missions by the Departments employing them, and finally at the tail come those who are travelling on their own account, without the backing of an organization. Possibly, when their turn comes no tickets will be left, in which case they will patiently return the following day.

I calculate that with my place in the queue I have a good two hours in which I can look round. In the station buffet rolls and matches are being snatched up fast. A rouble buys a bottle of lemonade. When I get back, thanks to my number, there is no difficulty at all about taking up my place again. Some passengers try to cheat by sneaking into the ticket office through the back, but are noisily thrust out, much to the joy of the unoffending. Others turn up, saying 'Krasniy,'[1] and take their place behind the last Communist arrival. When, however, they are asked to produce their documents, all they have is a scrap of red cardboard.

"But I've come for my brother, who is a Party Member."

"Here, what's the game? Go and take your turn. You think we've been here for the last three hours, seeing which of us has the flattest feet, to have you sneak in front ! "

Nevertheless, when some worn-looking female arrives with an infant in her arms, the person whose turn it is to pass in

[1] Red.

front of the window will get her ticket for her without the least demur.

At Alma Ata, from which numbers of coaches leave, it is an easy matter to book a seat. I pay thirty-four roubles fare to Tashkent, but my seat is reserved only as far as Aris, on the main line, where I have to change.

And that is how, next day, I climb into a ' hard-class ' coach and find my numbered place, while a fresh queue crawls slowly towards the booking office window, and those travellers who have not yet joined the elect wait on the platform huddled against their bundles. The view is magnificent. Over the verdurous city majestic mountains rise sixteen thousand feet, blue at the foot and half-way up, white with snow to the summit.

This same Turk-Sib line is scheduled to convey annually nine hundred and sixty thousand tons of grain from Siberia, as food for Turkestan, where cotton has almost completely supplanted every other form of crop.

At the ' base ' the chief permits me to lay in victuals, and I sell my ice-axe, rope, and crampons at the price I paid for them. In my sail-cloth sack I have my clothes, climbing-boots, four kilograms of bread, two kilograms of sugar, two kilograms of rice, some underclothes, and a dictionary, in addition to my lined sleeping-bag.

In my rucksack, its usual fifteen kilograms more than amply made up, I am carrying the rest. Cooking stove, spirit flask, films and camera, waterproof, medicine box, socks, linen, butter, tea, honey, a kilogram of oatmeal, two kilograms of apples, my inseparable frying-pan, and my pipe for lonely vigils.

Aris, or the Migration Continues

At Aris my difficulties begin. Now my problem is how to procure a place on the trans-continental Moscow express.

I set my belongings down against the station wall and establish acquaintanceship with my neighbour, a typical shrewd peasant with long, fair moustaches, who has spoken Kazak-Kirghiz since babyhood. He, too, wishes to travel to Tashkent.

" I leave it to you to get ' platzkarte ' for us. I'll look after your bags. Take my ticket with you."

In the big railway hall I hardly know were to put my feet down, so closely are the groups of human beings packed against each other. This is where they camp out, waiting for hours and days on their way to new jobs, or better living conditions, or toward some completer devotion to building Socialism, wherever it may be.

At two in the afternoon the ticket office for Tashkent shuts down. All the places in the train arriving in an hour have been sold. I have therefore to return at ten, before the night train leaves. The most courageous are already in the line, drawing up a list of the order of arrival of those present.

Suppose I try and imitate the cunning ones, and sneak into the booking office by the back? The door is bolted, but just as an employee comes out I go in, looking as if on urgent business. I find myself in an ante-room in front of another window.

" Please, Miss, what does one do to get to Tashkent? I am a journalist, and in a very great hurry."

" Oh yes! So am I. Come back again to-night, and apply at the main-line window.

Clearly, it is not thus one has to go about it.

But I shall not go to the O.G.P.U. office where, to oblige a foreigner, they may possibly find me a seat that will be taken from someone else.

At the station buffet I get some good cabbage soup, but the chopped meat is uneatable.

I walk round the station to get in the shade. Opposite the building is a garden protected by wooden railings. The ground is littered with melon seeds, husks of sunflower seeds, backbones of herrings, cigarette ends . . . and still more encampments.

To my right are a number of filthy gipsy families with

voluble gestures; the older men with long black locks, thick beards, and the deep eyes of fakirs. The young men—slim, brown-skinned, and coffee-coloured—flash lightning glances from under their bristling eyebrows, and seem like tied stallions ready to leap forth. One old woman with beringed fingers, most venerable of them all, lays down the law, flies into rages with her daughters-in-law, and indefatigably gesticulates with glittering eyes: then, because a scarlet petticoat with hundreds of pleats in it, hawked by a passing peasant woman, tempts her beyond all reason, she begins cajoling a brigand with ferocious moustaches, who evidently holds the purse strings.

I can't help wondering at one of the women. She is pale, with an auburn glint in her fair hair, and dressed all in pastel shades, from her brick-red skirt to the mauve bodice and the pink kerchief knotted under her chin. The face is a lovely oval, the nose coarse and aquiline, with green eyes that disappear between inflamed and puffy eyelids. She lays her head on the knees of her neighbour, who pours some drops into her eyes. They will make her eyes water for hours as she wipes the tears away with a scrap of cotton-wool. Her little girl, whose eyes are as inflamed as her mother's, stands just as much in need of attention. Then with dignity the brigand hands a few roubles to a half-naked youngster, who returns with a water-melon which is soon cut into pieces with a dagger, and then handed round to them all.

There is a queue at the cold-water tap for washing and a queue at the hot-water tap for the tea kettles.

No success with the night train! While having my place kept at the ticket window, I had gone off to try my luck with the stationmaster.

A native woman lying by the track has a bad cough; I hear her through the night whenever I wake. On my right, against the wall, a young Russian woman is lying under her blankets. Pretty, and with a yellow skin and violet lips, she smokes incessantly. Her cigarettes have cardboard mouthpieces that match exactly the colour of her skin.

" Have you any quinine? " she asks.

I give her some, after which she answers my questions.

" I'm returning from Tajikistan. Infernal . . . cotton . . . malaria. The wildest things are being done . . . it's crazy . . . the scale's so vast. Are you a foreigner? "

" Yes; but tell me, can't one buy quinine there? "

" The little there is the girls mix with iodine to procure abortions. . . . As for all their terrific engineering jobs, well, the workers don't get paid, and so they have to stay. But where's the point of killing off thousands by starvation in order to construct a hydro-electric station among uninhabited mountains? Who cares if the Indians sit up or not? " [1]

Her lovely baby sits impassive, its legs crossed, a Buddha incarnate, with a star of flies sucking at the corners of its half-shut eyes.

Beneath a tree in front of me two Kazak couples are sitting on a carpet. The women wear green velvet jackets and splendid turbaned head-dresses of the finest wool, a fold of which passes under the chin and closely frames the face. They rinse their hands with tea before eating a lipiotchka: all their movements have dignity, even when holding out the baby which has diarrhoea. The fair gipsy—how vulgar she suddenly seems to me—openly expresses her disgust.

As for the afternoon train, I am firmly determined that this time it shall not start without me. At last it appears. But at every coach there are conductors blocking the gangways. An inspiration! The restaurant car! It is empty. I make inquiries.

" Can I get in here? Yes? I'm only going to Tashkent."

I rush off to get my bags, and return immediately, but the train has already started. All I can do is watch it dwindle in the distance.

A painful spectacle somewhat distracts me from my mortification. Two youngsters, decently clad but horribly common, with large mouths, prominent ears, and insolent expressions,

[1] These, again, are individual reflections, which though repeated the author holds no brief for.

have got hold of two Kazaks in waistcoats, and all four are picnicking lavishly on a chicken. A walking skeleton passes in front of them: a young, fair boy with scabs on his face, begging. He is given an already half-eaten musk-melon. He scratches away at it with his nails, trembling in his haste to drink off the juice, and at the same time takes three or four mouthfuls of lipiotchka in quick succession. In guise of thanks, he begins to sing in a bleating voice while smiling pitifully, the half melon worn upside down on his head. . . .

In front of the ticket window I hear someone say:
" Can't be helped! I'll take the Maxim then! "
" Is a ' Maxim ' leaving for Tashkent? " says someone else.
" Yes, there's a ' Maxim ' in now."

Can they be speaking of an armoured train carrying maxim guns on which passengers have the right to perch themselves? No! they are fourth-class trains, Maxim Gorki trains, ' tavarpassagirov,' trains that are put on sometimes to help clear the railway stations.

Maxim Train

With some difficulty I find the train in question, a mass of passive humanity jammed in two layers on planks laid like shelves across cattle trucks. Not a vacant corner to be found anywhere.

Three Kazak women climb up and squat on the metal plate which links two of the coaches. I settle myself in a somewhat more sheltered position, on the tiny platform at the top of the stairs, already occupied by a couple of ancients. One of the Kazak women seems to me quite the most absorbing person I have seen till now. What first strikes me is her immense white cashmere turban, tucked in at the back of her head, and permitting a woolly fringe to escape like a mane cascading down her back. Her forehead is framed in three bands of dark red embroidery, and her head is swathed in hundreds of parallel folds. She is also wearing a band under her chin which, continuing as a long veil, practically covers the whole of her body: this band is also trimmed with red, and completes the sumptuous nun's head-dress that she wears. The narrow oval of the face delineated thus, seems to overflow with contemptuous nobility. Can she be a descendant of the most noble tribe of the Adai of the Golden Horde? [1]

The youthful Abdul Khair, the indefatigable archer who slew the Kalmuck Goliath, was a descendant of this tribe. The Adai, with their one thousand two hundred families or ' Kibitka,' constitute the Kazak-Kirghiz aristocracy. The Turki-Mongols claim descent from Grey-Wolf and Doe of Brightness. This was the sort of face that baffles description: the proportions of the lines, the relation of the masses, were a poem in themselves. The raised corners of the perspicuous eyes gleamed with intelligence, the straight nose followed after the singular accent mark of the sparse and straggling eyebrows, and the voluptuous yet secret lips pouted indulgently as though to say: " What if I do travel on the footboard of a cattle truck; how does that affect my rank? "

On one of her fingers, in place of a ring the woman wore a large circle of chased metal, and on her wrist numerous bracelets of wrought silver. She was carrying a baby in a cotton quilt, whose ' tiubiteka,' or cap, was adorned with trivial coins. She handed the baby to her mother, the dark skin of whose wrinkled, expressive face made the baby seem still paler in comparison. The third woman looked rather coarser: her face was rounder, and beads of sweat which she rubbed away with a finger perpetually broke out on her shining temples.

Twilight! Every ten miles or so we come to a halt on a siding to allow the regular trains to pass, for this is a single track.

My loins hurt me as a result of trying to keep my balance sitting. If only I could stretch my legs. I creep into the waterproof cover of my sleeping-bag, and then, needing no longer to fear the filth on the floor, rest my back against my

[1] From Ordu = encampment—settlement.

packs, insinuate my feet behind the baskets of the two Russians . . . and fall asleep.

Nevertheless, I am awakened several times by people kicking me in the ribs, and passers-by muttering to themselves:

"Some people have a nerve to stretch out in the corridor when others can't even find room to sit down."

How superior these Kazaks, with their native dignity, which bears certain testimony to a culture whose traces still persist, seem to all these Russians. And to think I once thought them a primitive people.

We drag slowly into Tashkent, the moon a glittering sickle, the sky turning pale over the fields and gardens bounded by mud walls.

CHAPTER II

TASHKENT

A MOTLEY CROWD at the station! I manage to hoist my sacks, one on my back, the other on my shoulder, my opposite arm passing over my head to prevent the weight from slipping. I take the tram as far as Voskrochensky Square, then proceed to the Ikanskaya, only to find the offices of the 'base' still shut. However, I go in through the yard and make myself some tea. Then an employee arrives and breakfasts on some bread and an apple.

When the secretary appears I show him my papers, and he sends me off to the real 'base.'

I get on the tram again at Lenin Street, which soon leaves the Russian city by an avenue lined with poplars, ariks, and low houses. At the entrance to the native city I get down at the Chai Khan Taour.

Some steps, then a gateway topped by a cupola, a stone-paved alley lined with the booths of barbers, an avenue of poplars in which rows of Uzbeks are selling apples, grapes, lipiotchka, sliced carrots, and confectioner's delicacies. A dis-established mosque, a polytechnic in a low building through the windows of which I see the pupils at their desks, the large platform of a chai-kana in the open air with the portraits of the most important figures in the Soviet Union nailed to the uprights, an alley. . . . I find I have to stop a moment to rest. But at last I come out into the second Djarkantcha; and at No. 58 find a yard full of trees and a gallery giving on to two rooms, one of which, reserved for women, has a dozen bunks in it. A young woman welcomes me and allots me the last available bed. This base in the past was the 'Itchkari,' the part of the dwelling reserved for the women of some wealthy 'bek.'

I shall have to get my meals in the city, but every night I shall meet my room mates—journalists, economists, students, some of whom have husbands living in the adjoining room. We exchange impressions and share our discoveries with each other.

Roamings

Pilnyak found Tashkent a most unusually boring city; but no doubt he was referring to the Russian half of this immense capital of half a million souls—if among souls, as Kisch says, can be numbered the souls of Communists who deny its existence and of Mussulman women to whom the Koran refuses any.

But for the first time I find myself in a vast concourse of Orientals, and hasten to take stock of what remains of the ancient life before modernity overtakes it.

It all astonishes me: the narrow, stone-paved streets, labyrinthine, the numbers of veiled women, in the stiff, unbroken lines of their 'paranjas,' looking like silhouetted upright coffins, with some package or basket balanced on every head. It is nonsense to call them veils: trellis-work is far more to the point, so dark and rigid is the horsehair which scarifies the tips of their noses, and which they pinch in their lips when they bend down to see what quality of rice is being offered them, for their sight is only able to filter through when the 'chedra' is hanging straight down in front of them. Where the mouth has wet it a damp circle remains when the woman stands again, quickly powdered by the floating clouds of dust. When old the 'chedras' look rusty and full of holes, as though moth-eaten. . . . Most of the women wear factory-made short frocks, shoes, and stockings.

And here come three approaching, grey and mauve heaps squatting on the floor of a cart, possibly a harem moving house. Wearing a waistcoat, with an embroidered skull cap on his head, and squatting on his horse's back with his feet on the shafts, the man in front may very well be the husband!

The ' arba ' or native cart, with its immense spokes, is a source of great pleasure to me. It has only two wheels, each over six feet high, admirably adapted for travelling through mud or deep sand: they do not have iron tyres, but instead enormous nails with round heads are driven into the rim, and these glitter in the sun and leave a curious-looking, rack-like, zigzag tread in the damp clay. So high are the shafts that I am always in terror they may swing up into the air, taking the horse too.

I hear the trickling of tiny subterranean ariks, the waters of which flow into the opaque waters of a pond situated at a cross-roads. There is a lovely harmony in the colours: the sombre green of the water in shadow, and its bright green in the sun; the silvery green of a round, leafy willow, then the yellow of the banks; the yellow of the dusty mud walls, and the whitey-yellow of four ' arbas ' abandoned at the foot of a wall with shafts pointing down.

The street is blocked by an immense rectangular load of hay, wider than it is high, borne on the back of a camel with a ruffle and black muffs, whose driver sits perched on top.

I try to get to Urda, the native city, by a roundabout way, and keep on finding I am lost.

Here is an open door in the middle of a wall, with a tiny minaret-keep over the gateway. I go in. To the right a garden with an aspen trembling in the breeze, fig-trees, cactuses, and a pond. To the left a huge veranda raised on two rows of grooved wooden pillars shut in waist-high by a parapet of pierced wood. The ground is covered with mats in front of the ' mirhab,' the alcove which faces towards Mecca, in front of which people pray, for this is a mosque. The walls are simple panels of plaster. Peace, sunshine, solitude . . . absorbed by my reflections I gaze up at the coffering of the ceiling carved and gilt with arabesque designs. It seems to me that this is how the ceilings of Chinese temples must look.

TASHKENT

What there is in the Native Market!

Now I am in all the bustle of the crowd: the vendors of
sherbert, of mineral water, and the barbers operating at each
house corner: like some new convict, the patient bends his
head forward and his hair falls into the towel tied round his
neck which he holds in front of him.

Outside the bakery an impressive queue waits for the door
to open, while loaves of black bread are being piled into an
' arba ' with an arched roof that stands by the kerb. The
men are wearing ' khalats '—wide, quilted robes with vertical
stripes of green, mauve, black, and white, which make their
sleeves look like enormous caterpillars. The large piece of
cloth that serves as a belt forms a triangle over the loins.

A bridge spans green water: from the banks an alley
ascends, steeply skirting a mosque with a veranda. The other
cliff-bank reveals the stark nudity of yellow sand between
posts and piles that support wretched hovels about to be
pulled down. The housing shortage is due in part to all these
demolitions in the old city, the process of reconstruction not
having proceeded as fast as calculated.

Seven barbers wrapped in waiters' aprons operate side by
side; one of them, oldish, has a white pointed goatee, and
iron spectacles on his nose. Across his forehead, sticking out
of his skull cap, is a sprig of fennel. His client wrinkles his
brows pitifully: half of his skull is covered with thick black
fleece, the other half glitters perfectly white.

A weeping willow bends over the rapid waters of a main
arik, in which a water carrier is filling his two buckets suspended from a thick staff: then the water disappears under
the platform of a cool chai-kana, where skewers of mutton
splutter over a brazier.

The street climbs up towards the immense dome of a
mosque, and passes under a portico decorated with scarlet
bannerets. So dense is the throng that walking is difficult.
Here is a row of tobacconists; their yellow leaves heaped
upon newspapers on the ground, and at their sides their

pipes, calabashes surmounted by a bowl, with a long bamboo stem sticking out at the side.

A fight! Two men going at it hammer and tongs. A fearful market woman removes herself and her saucers of butter. I follow her, and for fifteen roubles buy a little of the flabby yellow paste. She assures me it is pure cow butter.

A busily chewing circle squatting on the ground have not thought it worth while to move for so little. An Uzbek woman, with a white headcloth and a black waistcoat over her wide, white robe, is selling pilav. The rich rice containing cut-up carrots fills an enamelled wash-basin and is set on a pail half-full of glowing embers. One goes up and pays a rouble, she takes a bowl and hands it to you, with a wooden spoon and hardly anything else. The young and Russians use the spoon, but my hairy neighbour converts the tips of his fingers into a highly useful receptable. My other neighbour eats his portion with a great sack of grain balanced on his head.

In front of me, with a basket on his arm, accompanied by a beautiful fair woman, I think I recognize the incredibly tight waist and grey cloth boots of one of our neighbours at Chulpan ata. I follow him, but a savage brawl in front of a soap booth makes me lose light of him. However, I run into him again, and we are both exceedingly surprised to see each other.

" Yes, our journey into the Syrt was magnificent, unforgetable. But how are you? Did you have a good holiday? "

" Imagine my luck! I've only just got out of hospital after a bad bout of dysentery. I can't imagine what I can have eaten. . . ."

" And did they look after you well? "

" Oh, yes! I can't complain."

" And what were you doing here? "

" I was looking for a bit of meat for the soup."

We are under the roof of the butchers' market. To get near a stall we have to push through a five-deep row of other seekers.

" It's all camel! " he tells me.

And indeed, I recognize the huge, barely curving ribs, like those which heap the tracks of the Tien Shan.

" What does it taste like? "

" Oh, it isn't bad, but I feel it's beef I want, although it will cost more, fourteen or fifteen roubles the kilogram, I should say."

I abandon him to his exhausting quest, and go off to the saddlers' quarter. On the pavement shoemakers are selling the very supple boots the women wear inside their goloshes. Vera, in Paris, had asked me to bring her back a pair.

" Fifteen roubles! " I say.

" No, twenty, leather . . . very fine! "

" Fifteen roubles, not a penny more . . . at Co-operative only twelve roubles! "

" Co-operative . . . skins bad . . ."

All this passes in surroundings impregnated with the odour of dust, of chopped straw, of camel excrement, and of horse and man, the latter recognizable by its nauseating sweetness.

I abandon these unrelenting salesmen to seek repose in a neighbouring chai-kana: there one feels the slightest breeze that passes. A Russian and an Uzbek talk together at my side. The Russian departing, I offer a lump of sugar to the man, whose appearance I like, and whom I would like to make talk to me.

" Yes," I say, " the life here is extraordinarily interesting: I come from a long way off to visit you and see how things are working out! But hang it, your pilav is pretty dear! "

" Ah, you come from far away. In your country, in Frankistan, do you grow rice? Do you know what they've done here? The order was given out to plant cotton all over. So the plough went everywhere, blotting out the tiny irrigation channels of the rice fields that were made so long ago and kept up with such care. And after that, when they saw the corn wasn't coming so easily from Siberia, they said to us, ' Replant a third with rice.' But now it can't be done, all the irrigation channels are dead. . . . And another thing, you

know: keys! In the past such things didn't exist: everything
was open, houses and shops. Now we ruin ourselves in pad-
locks, and you can't keep anything safe from thieves."

Wanting to visit the Women's Club, I return by a parallel
street, stopping at every moment to look at new and absorbing types of humanity. Pale Iranians with black moustaches,
tanned Tziganes with large, bony foreheads, Tajiks who
remind me of faces I have seen along the Mediterranean, ten
women sitting on the pavement, all ten behind their black
trellises, with piles of 'tiubitekas' on their knees for sale.
Joints of horse-flesh hang at the corner of one of the houses.

An Uzbek is busy near two splendid, kneeling dromedaries:
the proud outlines of their aquiline muzzles has not been
ruined by a hole; a chain only serves as a muzzle strap.

A blind couple approaches with outstretched stick and
playing an accordion.

Reading Lesson

In one corner of the square is a large printing works. In a
square in front of an ancient 'Madrasa' (Mussulman
university) is a statue of Lenin, the arm eternally uplifted. A
few more steps, and here is the club, a building that looks
like a school.

I ask a caretaker, who appears to know no Russian, where
I can find Comrade Achmetof. In a class-room on the first
floor a reading lesson is being given, with the aid of a booklet
which outlines the story of the proletariat. Fifteen girls and
young women listen absorbedly, their 'paranjas' and the
lattice-work of their 'chedras' piled up on the window-sills.
Their bushy eyebrows are linked together by an artificial black
line, for it appears that eyebrows that join bear witness to a
passionate temperament. Their faces are typical of the Otto-
man Turks, round and pale and with large eyes.

Not to embarrass them I sit down on a bench and try to
obliterate myself as much as possible. My neighbour is suck-
ling a little boy lying all but naked, save for a tiny blouse with

a sailor collar, in its blanket: first she follows the text with her right hand, and then she uses it to keep her baby's feet from kicking.

I wait till the lesson is over; and they put the 'paranjas' back on their heads. When I go up to them, desirous of examining a 'chedra,' they hold one out to me, at the same time making signs to me to wear it, which I do, to their delight. The teacher, in a waistcoat, after explaining to them that I have come from a very great distance, shows me over a crêche, the clinic, the library. On the ground floor is a large concert hall.

" This evening there is going to be a lecture. You should come to it."

" No, thank you! I have another engagement."

I dare not tell him that these eternal lectures bore me. They are all exactly the same, whether at Nalchik, Kara Kol, or Moscow. They make me think of Tibetan praying wheels: " importance of developing culture among the natives of educating the masses, of constructing Socialism by levelling the classes, Socialism whose triumph alone will save the world from capitalist bankruptcy! "

Even if all our salvations depended on it, surely it could be orchestrated with a little more variety.

After countless detours through the old city we arrive at the schoolmaster's house, for I want to see the manner of life his wife leads. Blocking the end of a dark passage is a wall pierced by a door: then a tiny courtyard bounded to the left by a reed screen, and on the right by a colonnade. In front of us is the spick-and-span living-room, in which the only article of furniture is a little bed, which turns out to be so hard that I feel sure it is only a plank.

A pile of school-books is on the ground. The walls, white-washed and divided into symmetrical panels, have little hollow niches to take tools, teapots, and plates. On the ground is a carpet, a chest, and some quilts. A cloth has been laid on the carpet. The cooking is done outside. The woman, her feet bare, for her slippers have been left at the door, brings in a brass tray on which is a tureen containing 'lapcha.' We eat with wooden spoons.

I like the young woman. She is slim under her billowing robe, and has large, quick eyes, freckles, and long, curling chestnut hair. Her face is expressive, and I guess her to be intelligent. But she knows no Russian. Her husband says:

" You really find her pretty? I don't. She's studying at the Educational Technicum. Of course, she doesn't wear the veil."

The young woman waits till her husband has finished before eating and drinking herself. Sprawling on the ground, her baby plays with a shoe.

We go out again, without the husband troubling to say good-bye.

Everywhere the water supply depends solely upon the ariks: pipes and water-towers are only beginning to be installed in the districts where the houses have been solidly constructed. It is a colossal undertaking, for the city covers a tremendous area, the houses being only one story high as a precaution against earthquakes.

I end my evening at the Uzbek Theatre. A native company is performing a clever adaptation of Lope da Vega's *Fountain of Sheep*, a play I had seen excellently acted by the players of the White Russian Jewish Theatre, two years earlier, at the time of the first theatrical Olympiad in Moscow.

CHAPTER III

Pravda Vostoka

No one has yet asked to see my *visa!* I shall act as though I obviously have one, and go forward with my head held high. I decide to pay a visit to the offices of the *Pravda Vostoka, Truth of the Orient*, the newspaper of the Communist Party, which is published in Russian. It is a large office, bustling with activity.

Tall and likeable, with blue eyes, and young in spite of his bald head, the editor, Tselinski, astride his table, listens to me with interest. I show him my book, whereupon he wants me to inscribe it to him. I tell him where I have been, that I want to see a cotton plantation, and that the restaurant at which I have the right to eat is too dear for my modest resources.

" I'll see to all that! " he says. " Here is a permit which gives you the right to eat free of charge at our trade union restaurant in the town: you'll find it in a basement the other side of Voskrochenski. Then I shall send you with someone in our cotton section to see a kolkhoz."

Summoned, young Naskof begins to make objections. . . .

" Oh! the car is under repair, is it? That's a pity. I should have liked you to go and see Pakhta Aral, the plantation which has been awarded the Order of Lenin. Well, then, Naskof will hire a ' lineiki,' and you shall go and see Baumann. But why don't you come with us to Boz Su the day after to-morrow? We are spending the free day together."

Every moment we are interrupted by telephone calls and callers: there is only one subject, and that is cotton and again cotton. I am shown the photograph of a lorry equipped with a vacuum hose which mechanically picks the cotton. Graphs all over the walls depict the percentages delivered by each region every six days. Far from feeling I am in the editorial offices of a newspaper, I feel I have strayed into the G.H.Q. of the Cotton Offensive. The figures laid down by the Five-Year Plan must be fulfilled before the end of December, cost what it may. The fate of Turkestan depends on it, for the peasants will be supplied with grain only in proportion to the cotton output.

"Yesterday," says the editor, showing it to me, "I published the translation of an article from the *Frankfürter Zeitung*, which said that the eyes of the whole world were turned upon our Central Asia. We are ruining American and Egyptian commerce by producing our own cotton. The example of our Republics, liberated from the Imperialistic yoke, will inspire the Asiatic colonies, now dominated by France and England, to revolt. . . ."

A Cotton Village

A few days later, in company with Naskof, I alight from the tram at the Lunacharski terminus: and here be it said in passing that the crowds that fill the Moscow trams are less brutal than those of Tashkent. He hires one of the conveyances stationed there, and we set out for a village eight miles off.

I had already been in the vicinity, having come out one day to take tea with a Jewish family which happened to be celebrating a birthday, the table as a result being covered with a wonderful assortment of cakes. The son of the house, an irrigation engineer, had gone on improvising on the grand piano while talking to me about Tajikistan. He was just back on leave to get treatment for his malaria.

"There's a country you ought to see. It's astonishing the way things develop month by month. Out there, young people not afraid of work have every possibility in their grasp. There the future belongs to anyone smart enough to seize it."

"And the Bassmatchi?" I objected.

"Since the capture of Ibrahim Bek in 1921, we hardly hear of them," he replied.

The wheels of our 'lineiki' sink to a depth of twelve to fifteen inches into the thick dust, which like a yielding liquid flows back and levels all: at every step the horses' hoofs sink with a dull thud.

Walls, gardens, fields! Then a tiny dreary village, where we stop in front of a house, beside a chai-kana. In a dark room we find the office of the Dourmen Baumann Kolkhoz.

The five-hundred-odd acres are all under the same administration. The year before they delivered two hundred and nineteen tons of cotton (of which the best quality, picked before the rains, was worth thirty-two kopeks the kilogram); a quantity, translated into the proportional allocation of grain, equal to twenty-five tons of bread.

We walk through uneven fields separated by irrigation dykes, the ariks, but for which nothing at all would grow. Some of them date from before the Christian era. Their waters were released on certain fixed dates, which were regulated by ancient custom. Officials called 'arik-aksakals' controlled them through 'mirabs' under their orders.[1] The taxes payable to the Emir of Bokhara were calculated on the quantity of water the taxpayer had the right to demand. The 'aksakals' or 'white-beards' were paid in kind once the harvest was gathered in. But the rich beks who owned the water and distributed it as seemed good to them, compelled the peasants to pay whatever they demanded. Nowadays all this is scientifically regulated and the Co-operatives provide for the needs of the workers.

In the book written by Prince Massalski, a functionary of the Board of Agriculture, and published in 1913, I read that the author estimated the canals watering the country at stretching for twenty-five thousand miles. He was struck dumb with astonishment by what had been achieved by the primitive science of this people. It made me think at once of the 'fogaras,' the canals that, twelve feet under the earth,

[1] Mir=Chief. Ab=water.

carry water for hundreds of miles into the heart of the Sahara, and as to the origins of which nothing whatever is known.

The pink and yellow flowers I see, and which last but a day, belong to the Navrotski variety of cotton which grows only in the northern part of the United States. According to the Research Institute of Tashkent this plant suits the region best. A cotton of very inferior quality has been grown in these parts from prehistoric times.

It is a bush whose hard, pointed, separated leaves make me think of ivy. Sowing takes place in the middle of April, and picking begins in July when the first pods burst, and lasts until the end of November, or even into December, when, under the influence of the frost, the pods burst for the last time.

Here are women at work, picking. Young and old, all gaze at me, laughing because I photograph them. Their faded gowns are held up above the knees, full to bursting with great balls of snow, and the long, tight muslin pantaloons descend down to the ankle. They move forward, plucking the plants with a single precise gesture.

The white boll is composed of four or five pads of longish cotton-wool closely bound together, each of which contains a round, hard seed, difficult to separate from the stuff in which it is enveloped. The crushed seeds render oil, and the residual husks are converted into flat combustible cakes.

Khàlissa, a woman with a laughing expression, and gold rings in her ears, picks on an average over fifty-three pounds a day. The amount collected by each is noted down, for payment is calculated on results. The average income for the preceding season worked out at one hundred and fifty roubles per worker. In all, two hundred and seventeen families are dependent on the kolkhoz, which includes three hundred and fifty woman workers.

In a corner of the field each worker has her enormous coarse sacking bag which little by little she fills.

I cross a number of deserted fields to reach the crèche

where Khalissa keeps her baby. Fringing the bank of an arik, an immense plant ten feet high with long alternate leaves like those of the maize plant and seeds hanging in membraneous clusters like the inside of an unripened melon, brings me to a halt.

" Jugara used for live-stock," explains Naskof, " though not so good as maize."

It is ' Sorghum,' the ' Great Millet,' the Doura of the Africans which the Kazaks with whom I am to stay live on, to the exclusion of practically all else.

A woman squats under a tree, from a branch of which hangs a wooden frame with a solid piece of cloth nailed to the sides: this makes a large cradle in which three or four babies lie kicking. When she glances in the direction of Naskof and our guide, the woman drops her white headcloth over her face.

In the shade of large fig-trees stand samovars, and there is a shelter for the workers who come to drink their tea here in the middle of the day.

I ask to be allowed to visit some of the houses in the village, both rich and poor. From the main street a passage runs off at an angle, and leads into a yard formed by the façades of various houses. To the left I hear someone groaning. It is an old woman, ill. What is wrong with her? Is the doctor coming? Questions that remained unanswered.

We go towards the house in the middle, and find a three-sided room open to the air with a mud brick floor which a carpet covers. Against the farthest wall is a pile of quilted coverlets. This is where the family lives in summer. It is all absolutely clean, though the task is no difficult one considering the absence of furniture.

My hostess, an old woman, bears herself with much dignity. She has been away down the yard, and now leaves her over-shoes on the step and walks about barefooted. She spreads a tablecloth and cuts up an enormous water-melon for us on a brass dish, at the same time offering us pieces of stale bread. Naskof has remained at the office, as he would not be allowed to penetrate into the 'Itchkari,' and the boy who serves me as guide knows practically no Russian, so that my visit is confined chiefly to using my eyes.

" In your country things are better, I don't doubt! " says the boy.

I like this sober interior reduced to its most simple expression. And how do they keep warm in winter? The room, built entirely of dried mud, has a rectangle some four feet six inches square hollowed in the floor, the 'saundall.' During cold weather the bottom is strewn with glowing embers, and a low table round which everyone squats then covers the hole, with a quilted coverlet placed over it to keep in the heat. There are carpets, chests, quantities of teapots, a heap of apples, and in a niche in the wall the photograph of a group, for the son is a student in Tashkent. In one of the corners of the floor a small cavity has a pierced slab shut down over it, through which the water used for the general ablutions runs away: that is, when the hole is not stopped up.

Under the roof is an open loft in which maize hangs drying.

The poor house I visit is arranged after the same fashion, but there are fewer objects and far less ceremony. Two girls are at work in it: one with unkempt locks is drying melon seeds, the other gathers together rice straw. The latter is dark-skinned, with finely bred features and delicate eyebrows laid parallel over the horizontal yellow eyes. Her solid breasts make the threadbare stuff of her gown jut out.

" It's terrible how dark she is," the boy says; "don't you think so too? "

They do not understand any Russian.

With Naskof we go walking down the road, intending to leap aboard the first passing lorry, but none of them slows down for us. The dust is one of the ten plagues, and the women's 'chedras' must certainly have been invented to protect their faces.

A string of unloaded camels approaches with supercilious

expressions as though the strides they took were far too long for them. To photograph them silhouetted against the sky, I hurry across the sunken track and suddenly sink into a deep pocket of dust. The jolt jerks open my mouth in which I am holding the yellow filter that I do not need. I take my photograph, then begin to look for the filter which has fallen somewhere at my feet. Purposely, I have remained standing in exactly the same spot, but no trace of it is visible in the dust. Methodically I begin to search, plunging both arms deep in; they disappear up to my biceps, then touch the underlying gravel.

Naskof waits for me. Passing natives help me in my search. In spite of all my obstinacy, for I feel the filter must be somewhere there, I give up after half an hour. Near us a lorry has broken down and is trying to start up . . . during the hour we wait for it, I see two men go on searching in the dust. They had asked me what I lost:

" A yellow round of glass," was my reply.

Convinced, no doubt, that only a gold piece at least could have made me kneel there in the dust, they refuse to be discouraged. Possibly they may be there still.

Boz Su: 'Pale Yellow Waters'

For the day's outing two trams have been specially hired to convey the staff of the newspaper out of the town. Boz Su is a public park with a lake in the centre, on which we go boating. As in Moscow, everyone enthusiastically employs his free day in qualifying for the 'Ready for Labour and Defence' badge.[1]

There are bathing cabins, a diving-board, and a minimum of clothing as at Juan-les-Pins. Surprised exclamations burst forth, " Oh, how cold it is! "

Accordions, guitars, balalaikas! The orchestra plays wild

[1] The tests cover running, jumping, swimming in clothes and without, rowing, shooting, putting the shot more than forty yards, raising and carrying a weight, and ski-ing three kilometres at the rate of about a mile in eleven minutes.

dances and couples whirl in the roadway. The spectators munch muscat grapes.

A woman takes charge of the youngsters, who amuse themselves dancing rounds, while the parents take their ease.

The men practise putting the shot.

Inside an enclosure is a vast open-air theatre, in which speeches are being made in honour of the fortieth year of literary activity of the hero, Maxim Gorki.

A young girl passes with a rifle on her shoulder. . . . Suppose I shoot, too! There are plenty in front of me, however, and I have to wait my turn. We lie flat on our stomachs, the targets being set against a wall. Three trial shots are allowed and then ten more which count. Pretty well pleased with my score, I press the trigger for the seventh time. A flash, then darkness, and a burning pain in my eyes! I am led away. A handkerchief is lent me, for I am weeping copiously. I keep on repeating to myself : " Blind, and alone in Tashkent! "

Soon, however, my eyelids relax a little, then open, and I can see. It was only some gunpowder in the eyes. Returning to the canteen, my stomach hungrily gnawing as a result of the emotional disturbance, I find I am too late. The queue is breaking up; the pilav is all sold out.

CHAPTER IV

A Visit to an Anarchist Exile

E VERY EVENING I pay him a visit.

Had I but known how soon he was to die, how many questions I should have asked him and how much more important the words he uttered would have seemed to me! How different our relations with those we esteem would be, could we but always think we were speaking with them for the last time!

But then I listened as he talked thirteen to the dozen, conjuring up the past and his life in Geneva, where he had taken refuge during the war. I remember how he said:

" Do you know that little restaurant in the Plaine de Plainpalais? I used to go there often to eat ' fondues.' [1] "

Fifty-two years old, and tall and strong, he had a mighty forehead, fair moustache, and eyes somewhat too wide open, which revealed the excitable temperament.

" Nicholas, don't get so excited," his young, over-pale wife would caution him. She held herself with dignity, sure of herself, though she broke into frequent laughter and then seemed almost like a little fair girl.

She alone of the two has work. She works in an office; and her pay has to support the household. In the evening, when she gets back, the supper has to be prepared. To reach their room we have to pass through that of the landlord, separated from it solely by a curtain doing duty as a door. On account of their neighbour, we have to be careful what we say in Russian, for he is only seeking an excuse to turn Nicholas out and let the room to one of his friends.

And because they do not want the conversation which we carry on in French to excite his curiosity too much, Anna

[1] A Swiss dish of boiled melted cheese.

tells him we are old friends who have known each other in exile.

Though Nicholas has no idea why, he is met with hostility at every turn. The posts he would like are refused him: and yet in the past he had given ample proof of intellectual capacity in a field far removed from anarchist politics. For years at Tiflis he worked in the Scientific Institute of the Caucasus, which was founded by himself. In those days he roamed the mountains on this work. " Now he is weary of seeing every opening prove abortive," Anna confided to me.

So it is with enthusiasm that he greets my suggestion for a possible means of getting out of the blind alley. Born in Russia, he had assumed a Russian name at the beginning of his career as a militant anarchist, but through his father he is Czech by nationality. If Masaryk, whom he had known well in the past, could be got to intervene, he might perhaps get himself repatriated.

" And Anna? " I said.

" She would rejoin me sooner or later. It would not be the first time she has smuggled herself across the border to come to me. Even in the Kerensky days she managed to smuggle herself into Russia to nurse the wounded, for she had a presentiment the October Revolution was coming. An officer was going to disclose her identity, but she had the courage to shoot him in cold blood."

" Let him go," she said, " if he can manage it. He ought to have medical attention. When they arrested him in Tiflis, though no charge was ever formulated, he was sentenced to three years' imprisonment. But as he was still suffering from the after-effects of an attack of pleurisy, they granted him permission to settle in Tashkent."

" Yes, I caught that in 1923, when I was doing propaganda work in Kabul. I had only just got over a bad attack of malaria which compelled me to leave Angora, where I was working for our Political Information Department."

" Nicholas, eat your grapes. . . . And you haven't drunk your tea yet."

A VISIT TO AN ANARCHIST EXILE

" Ah—grapes . . . to think of all the grapes I wolfed in the vineyards of Valais. . . . You know, I've been over all your mountains on foot. What wonderful memories I have of them! My father was an agronomist, but he loved zoology too, and it's from him I inherit my one religion—Nature. Life was pretty difficult for me in those Geneva days. The Social Democratic International had surrendered its position and turned chauvinist. There was also a breach in the International Anarchist Front: Kropotkin was calling for help to defend the French Revolution against German Imperialism. My faith was in Bakunin's idea as expressed in his masterly work, *The German Empire of the Whip, and the Social Revolution.*

" We decided to pool the resources of such anarchist Internationalists as still remained faithful to the cause. We put down our last money to publish the *Tocsin* (Nabat), which could only be smuggled into Russia. Shockingly badly paid, I was then working on a farm as a gardener, but managed to attend lectures in law and social sciences at your university.

" It was only after the October Revolution that I could hope at all to get back to Russia. I was one of the last group of *émigrés* to arrive at Fort Dunabourg in January 1917. We crossed the frontier in a special extra-territorial train, with the Swiss comrade Platten driving it.

" And the Pyrenees and Andorra and the South of France, I've been through them all on foot. For a long time I was working in Catalonia with the Spanish workmen, and I took part in the general strike of 1911."

" But how, or rather why, did you turn anarchist? "

" Well, you see, my father had democratic tendencies. And then we had lived in the Donbas region of the Ukraine, where they all are miners and peasants. I got interested in the local traditions. Our ideal was to unite once more with the Zaporogue Cossacks, and we detested the Russian Imperialism that was crushing the life out of the Ukraine. My mother was Russian.

" Then there was a coal strike. The Government had

worked up the peasants' feelings against the miners, so there were masses of murders, and many workers were sent into exile to work in the mines.

"At school, leadership was almost forced upon me. I used to give the boys talks about the revolutionary movements. We had a schoolmaster named Strumuline who provided us with lots to read, so that we were fairly well grounded in elementary Marxism. I began to attend evening classes, but for years I interested myself in the lives of the workers, and laboured in the Social Revolutionary cause. To complete my education in that respect, I decided to go abroad. Ah, the *Alexander I*: that was the name of the freighter I engaged in; then, of course, I had a dispute with the captain, and he gave me my passport—which was a false one—to an agency whose business it was to repatriate me. But I managed to escape in a port of the Dobrudja."

"You'd interest Ella a lot more," broke in Anna, "if you told her something of your life in Bokhara. Ella, you know, you absolutely ought to try and get an interview with Faisulla Khodjaief, and try to photograph him in his turban. He's so handsome that all the women are in love with him."

"Faisulla, the President of the Board of Commissioners for Uzbekistan?"

"Yes, and one of the seven members of the Central Executive Committee of the U.S.S.R. The strangest rumours are current concerning him. They say he is exceedingly rich, an out-and-out nationalist; that he beards Moscow with the utmost effrontery; and that no one could toe the Party line closer; that he must have been in league with the British. . . .

"I knew him well about the time they were 'liquidating the Emir of Bokhara.' I was working by orders of Frunze and Kuibyshev at the Revolutionary Military Bureau. As secretary, I was responsible for establishing the Committee of the Young-Bokhariots, Faisulla then being their leader. They were working on the lines of the Young-Turk movement, and would have liked to have got a constitution for themselves based on the 'shari'ah.' Little by little, however, the Young-

Bokhariots came over to the Communist Party, and after the ultimatum which Kolesso sent to the Emir Said-Mir-Alim in '18, when we had to beat a retreat before the opposition of the peasants, the Emir, who was executing everyone he felt he could not absolutely rely on, set a price on Faisulla's head.

"In 1920 our troops finally proving victorious, I went as head of the delegation to Bokhara, which had become a People's National Republic, with Faisulla as president. It was not till '24 that the regions of Khiva, Bokhara, Samarkand, Tashkent, and Ferghana were welded into the Soviet Republic of Uzbekistan."

"But what is there in all that to make him suspect?"

"I forgot to mention that in '18 he was expelled by the Soviet Government of Turkestan. He took refuge in Orenburg, but there the Ataman Doutof, who was one of the White leaders, arrested him. However, he was liberated again after giving Doutof a lot of valuable information about Tashkent. At the end of July Faisulla left for Moscow in order to defend his caracul skins, worth half a million roubles. When he came back he was a fully pledged Bolshevik."

"And how did he win the Party's confidence?"

"I can't say for sure whether he has that confidence. He has been threatened with expulsion three times. In '25 he was against agrarian reform, then he was opposed to the liberation of the women—he even has two wives himself, one at Tashkent, the other at Bokhara—and the third time he was against the drive for collectivization. On each occasion he got out of his difficulty by writing a letter exculpating himself. But the Bolsheviks need him as a go-between for themselves and the natives. Now he is the last remaining representative of the one-time Young-Bokhariots Revolutionary Committee."

"Do you think the Uzbeks would be capable of governing themselves?"

"Indubitably: some day or other. They are all madly ambitious. Before they even know how to write they want to be heads of departments, and scorn subordinate positions.

Where in Europe one person would be needed, here you need four at least: the output is very poor, but what is astonishing is that it's done at all, don't forget that. They are very proud of working in an office, but if they are put in responsible positions, then they are timorous and don't know what to do. I saw a letter once, at the bottom of which some head of a department had written, ' Agreed, but feel I cannot sign it.' In '23 the President of the Executive, Akhun Babaef, was still illiterate. Ikramov, the Party Secretary, states that according to the official figures of the Department for Central Asia, illiterates number 48 per cent of the Party members."

" And what do the ' Nationals ' say about the high cost of living ? "

" They get shown the electricity, the water mains, the schools. And then they are told how the Second Five-Year Plan will provide for the tenfold increased demand in articles of consumption. . . ."

" At the post office the other day, as I was sending a telegram to France, the assistant asked me if I was a foreigner. Then, in a flat, monotonous voice which was in great contrast with the conviction that sounded in what she was saying, added: ' I can't stick this. I'm about through. We hardly know how to get enough to eat. By working overtime I make ninety roubles a month, enough to pay for nine days' decent meals.' " [1]

" Yes, thinking of how to get enough to eat is the eternal problem here ! You, however, can go to the ' Torgsin ' shop."

" I have only been there once, and that was to buy soap."

" And did you not meet our negroes there ? "

" No ! What negroes ? "

" They had six brought over from America to act as advisers in regard to cotton. Every day they're in the ' Torgsin ' shop, stocking up with whisky, biscuits, and tinned stuff. . . ."

[1] Once more it is worth noting the danger of a too hasty introduction of one general form of culture, which, before necessary adaptations have been made, brings many difficulties in its train, similar to those being experienced in so many European and Asiatic countries to-day.

CHAPTER V

THE ANSWERS OF AN ORIENTAL PRESIDENT

AT THE *Pravda Vostoka* building the editor picks up his telephone, connected by a private wire to that of Faisulla Khodjaief, tells him there is a young foreign woman who would like to ask him some questions, and gets me an interview.

" Take an interpreter with you so as not to waste time in unnecessary explanations. He allows you half an hour. At ' Glavkhlopkom ' (Central Cotton Committee) there is a man thoroughly conversant with French and English."

In a large grey building with orange canvas sun-blinds, I find the man in question surrounded by piles of reviews.

" I keep a check on every publication throughout the world that deals with cotton," he explains.

We make an oppointment for going to the Sovnarkom. As I am preparing to leave, a negro enters, radiating intelligence. He has splendid eyes, a silk shirt, and well-cut clothes, and looks almost a Cambridge dandy. He is one of the North American specialists of the Cotton Institute: an engineer.

I stand there gaping! Because unconsciously, I now realize, the first impressions of childhood are so strong in us that the story told me by Anna had crystallized itself into six woolly-pated negroes, plantation beasts of burden. The black cotton-pickers of Hallelujah, the inspired people of the ' Spirituals ' illustrated by Covarrubias were taking their due revenge. Their sons have crossed the waters and are now masters who teach in their turn.

" I have just spent a number of months in Kirghizia, during which I had time to see something of the varied problems that face the Soviet State in Central Asia. I thought you would be the person best qualified to correct my impressions, if need be. I am grateful to you for receiving me. Will the ' Nationals,' do you think, be capable of governing themselves some day without the aid of Russia? "

A vast chamber. . . . An immense T-shaped table! Faisulla is sitting at the middle of the cross, with myself facing him. He had come towards me when I entered, smallish, in a dark suit, with magnificent black eyes, an oval head and face, and golden-brown complexion. Meeting him in a drawing-room, I should have taken him for a Spaniard.

" It is difficult to answer you. We should have to make much progress first. Everything depends on the sort of organization we can build. Up till '26 the official language was Russian for all matters of government. Now the villages and the Central Organizations correspond in Uzbek. All teaching is now carried on in the native language. In '24 only 10 per cent of the population was literate, but in '32 the proportion had risen to 60 per cent. Where education offers the least difficulties perhaps is among the settled Tajiks."

" Is that the reason why Tajikstan is developing so much more actively and energetically than Kirghizstan? "

" No, that is because it is the Central Asiatic region most exposed to pressure from without. At this very moment we have ten thousand Uzbek students ready to step into the ranks of our various organizations. In addition, we have some twenty thousand Russian students."[1]

" How do the Uzbeks feel towards the Russians who colonized them in the first place? "

" They see now, of course, the difference between the two regimes and all that has been done recently to help in their development. You must remember that in the past only the Russo-Native schools were open to the Uzbeks, and that only in Tashkent did the Government permit non-sectarian schools to exist. All the national schools were confessionals, in fact. At Tashkent there was a seminary where schoolmasters were

[1] In Uzbekistan the Russians form roughly one-tenth of the population.

trained, the Turkestanskaia Utchitelskaia Seminary, with the Russian missionary, Ostroumof, at its head. The Turkestan schoolmasters who still retain their Moslem faith had the same political credo as the purely Russian officials, so far-reaching was the colonizing influence.

" The merchants had not even the right to build factories this side the Volga. All they could be was middlemen between the banks and manufacturers.

" The Russian peasants were sent where there was no cotton, for they did not know how to cultivate it, and meanwhile the Uzbeks remained working the land which practically belonged entirely to the banks. The Government would not help them, and so they would mortgage their harvests to the banks two and three years in advance, and then as soon as a bad harvest made it impossible for the natives to meet their obligations, the banks foreclosed and took possession. Now the land belongs to the people who live in it; they retain their nationality, their tongue, their litera-ture, and their theatre."

To myself I was thinking, however: You know yourself, that in order to stabilize this agrarian revolution, the Bolsheviks, who say all religion is foreign to them, have had to win over the Moslem priesthood in order to get them to make clear to the natives that the new division of the land is not in opposition to either the ' shari'ah ' or the Koran.

" What is the reaction of an Asiatic peasant to the Soviet and the Communist regime? "

" What strikes him most is the enormous tasks to be accom-plished in all directions. But there is no great such diver-gence as you imagine: the Uzbek peasant has never been an individualist."

" What do you think has made the apathetic Orient pre-pared to accept the Communist ideal? "

" That has come about as a result of the introduction of piece-work, which marked a special phase in the progress towards collectivization. We were digging ourselves in: it was an inevitable stage in the progress from Individualism to Communism."

" And you personally, why are you a Communist? "

" My father, who was very rich, died when I was thirteen. A year later I was leading the Young-Bokhariot Nationalists. In '17 our one object was to wipe out the 'Mir,' the big estates. But we were not strong enough alone, we had to link up with someone, and so we turned to the Russians. That was the first time the Emir passed sentence on me; the second time was after the uprising of '18. During the Civil War I was in Russia. At the time of the split in the Young-Bokhariot group in '17, the Emir had the British behind him. . . ."

" Rumour says you were working for the Intelligence Service."

" No, that was Ubaidulla Khodjaief who, in Kokand during '18 was Minister for Foreign Affairs of the Enemy National Government."

" Would you say the Nationalist movement, so contrary to the Communist ideal, is dangerous here? "

" The Nationalists have made attempts to gain control of the Bassmatchi movement, which originally depended mainly on 'Kulak' support. Enver Pasha was connected with them. But as the people began to realize more clearly what our objects were, their power steadily dwindled."

" But by nationalizing your language, schools, theatres, and literature, aren't you bound to develop a distinct and non-Soviet view-point? "

" No, controlling the Nationalist movement are our Soviets, so that it would not be possible for the movement to develop in isolation. We stand at the head of the movement, armed with our special powers, our one ideal the betterment of the peasant and worker. In Stalin's phrase, ' Nationalist in form, but proletariat in content '; or, put differently, Nationalist in appearance, but striving towards one Socialist Culture."

" Another thing! In old Tashkent practically all the women still go veiled. Do you think women are happier as a result of the great reforms that have been introduced on their behalf? I'm told that prostitution has increased since their emancipation."

"The fact that the ' chedra ' has been cast aside has no particular significance; it must be taken as a symbol of liberation merely. All the emphasis has been laid on the fact —hence the family complications. What is of real significance is psychological maturity, and that we are achieving through our schools, our propaganda, and wage-earning, which makes the woman independant of her husband. Admittedly, the new-found liberty has swept some off their feet, but they must be educated. As for prostitution, there will always be found idlers to practise that occupation."

"Another thing interests me particularly. Do you think it possible for a nomad Kirghiz to turn himself into a town-dwelling proletariat working eight hours a day? "

"Certainly, when he realizes all the advantages it means to him. He no longer freezes in winter; he gets bread, sugar, boots, a stable wage, a regular existence, amusements. These advantages were the main factor in deciding our peasants to carry out the ' Plan ' for cotton cultivation. In 1916 Central Asia produced sixteen million poods[1] of cotton, in addition to which a further eleven million poods were imported. Now we produce thirty millions. Even by '27 we had exceeded the area sown before the war. And now that the Turk-Sib can bring us the grain which was pushed out by the cotton, we are moving ahead at an extraordinary rate. We have made ourselves completely independent of the capitalist Cotton Mart. And all this we have achieved thanks to Socialist competition."

I should have liked to make an objection, which Faisulla must certainly have been as clearly aware of as myself: namely, that the inhabitants of Turkestan were bitterly complaining that, while the process of adaptation was going on, living conditions had become practically impossible. The Russians I had visited—doctors, school teachers, architects—

---

[1] A pood = 36 lb.

were unanimous on that point, and it was true also for the natives, who were returning to their nomadic conditions of life, seeking better conditions, and abandoning the kolkhozes, where the promised abundance was not always to be found, for the quantity of wheat imported was far from being sufficient. . . .

And if there was so much cotton, how did it come about that there was such a scarcity of cotton-seed oil? Late one evening, having missed the last tram, I had seen a dozen women sitting on the pavement in front of the shut doors of a Co-operative store. At about ten the next morning, on the same spot, there must have been a hundred, most of them hidden behind ' paranjas,' and all with bottles in their hands. " Za khlopkovoie masla! "[1] they explained.

But Faisulla has looked at the clock. I must take my leave.

" If you're in difficulty as to where to eat," he adds, " ask my secretary to make you out a permit for the Sovnarkom restaurant."

" Thank you for your kindness. I should also like to ask whether you could help me to obtain a ticket in the Samarkand aeroplane, for the seats are always booked up in advance."

" You can arrange that with my secretary."

The interview was over, and not once had the man revealed himself or abandoned his official tones; not once had I succeeded in establishing any real contact between us, though we had often spoken without the help of the interpreter. In the anteroom some twenty people patiently wait their turn for an audience, and look ferociously at me as I pass. I had been in the audience chamber an hour and a half.

With the help of my interpreter, everything arranges itself nicely. I receive a permit, and a motor-car takes us to the aerodrome. My fare will cost me seventy roubles.

On the return journey the car breaks down in front of a large church, the club of the metal workers. Above the porch

[1] " For cotton-seed oil."

is an immense portrait of Lenin framed in red electric light bulbs. The chauffeur begins his attentions to the car by filling the radiator with water taken from the near-by arik, but it proves impossible to start the machine up again. Unlike the average Asiatic chauffeur, he curses for all he is worth.

" This brute will make me miss my English lesson," he says in explanation.

CHAPTER VI

UP IN THE CLOUDS

AT EXACTLY EIGHT the tiny three-seater Junker takes off, bumping along the ground. . . . Then it smooths out: we are up. The earth sinks away. . . . " Hi! your left wing's falling! " No, it's veering, and the other wing sweeps the earth as we turn. The sun is now to our left, behind us. " Hi! I say, can't you climb a bit, don't you see those huge trees in front of us? "

The massive towers of the concrete silos that we saw as enormous grey cylinders designed by some futurist architect have dwindled to mere rows of piled pennies. The church has become a white chessman moving over a grey plain. The sinuous irrigation canals ramify in the dusty green of the gardens. The cotton-fields are yellowish, dark stippled. Then the yellow band of a cliff bordering the Chirchik, a tributary of the Syr Daria, appears.

We have left the oasis of Tashkent behind us.

Tawny lights and velvety gradations flit restlessly over barren sands.

There is the Syr Daria and its huge meandering curves. I know it of old . . . and remember well how I saw it first, all small in its icy, swaddling bands. It was called the Narin then, as it cautiously slipped from stone to stone. No one sought its good graces then, or put stout bands around it to test its strength. Then it was free, and little knew that some day it would be forced to kiss the feet of every tree in Sogdiana. No matter: however supple its spine may be, it will avail it little against the wretched doom that waits for it at last when, joined in marriage with the hemmed-in brackish waters of the Sea of Aral, the Amu Daria forces itself into their nuptial bed.

But at the moment nothing could be more ingratiating: to the south it is one mass of glittering liquid gold, and to the north a lovely turquoise blue, but which, when we pass over it, turns to dirty grey.

In spite of the strict prohibition against doing so, I photograph its huge blue S, surrounded by red earth, through the mica window. Farewell! Yet I may see it again if, before reaching the Caspian Sea, I get sick of travelling by the intolerable train. No one has heard the shutter click. My neighbour goes on reading with a frown, and the pilot fortunately has no side mirror.

The railway line pushes south towards Ferghana, clearly outlined amidst the zigzagging trails.

Now we are over the 'Golodnaya': the Hungry Desert, immense steppes, bald and yellow and glittering, frosty with white salt.

> We are the pilgrims, Master; we shall go
>   Always a little further: it may be
> Beyond that last blue mountain barred with snow,
>   Across that angry or that glimmering sea:
> White on a throne or guarded in a cave
>   There lives a prophet who can understand
> Why men were born: but surely we are brave
>   Who make the Golden Journey to Samarkand.[1]

These pilgrims desired to discover to what end we are born, and their womenfolk could do nothing to withhold them. Their caravan would take three weeks to reach the famous city, a journey that takes twelve hours by train, and two by air.

Overwhelming contrast of dreary plain and fertile oases! In the distance are the highest mountains on the globe and their icy slopes. And again stifling deserts, salt-covered and perpetually in motion. Then nomads under their eternal tents of felt, and the workmen's barracks in Tashkent. Then veiled women of the Moslem, and their fastory sisters, now shock brigaders: then Tamerlane's ruins, and in their shadow

[1] Flecker, J. E., *The Golden Journey to Samarkand.*

an Asiatic proletariat coming into being to establish Socialism in the land.

From my journeying speck of corrugated aluminium high in the sky, all these lie below me at my feet.

And the negroes? I had not questioned them. Nor had I interviewed the wife of the Grand Duke Nicolas Constantino-vitch, once banished from the Court. A worthless fellow, who at Orenburg had stolen away and married the daughter of some governor or other. . . . She had her head tied in a lace veil, her hair was waved, and the loose skin of her face was plastered with powder. A bitter expression was on her lips as with inquisitorial eye, inspecting the merchandise, she went from stall to stall. She wore a grey, braided jacket of excellent quality, a white dress with frills, used her umbrella like a cane, and carried a portfolio under her arm. A ruin of the past . . . . I could not take my eyes off her, but she did not notice it, so busy was she buying nothing, getting angrier as she went, because the grapes, the most abundant product of Tashkent, were nowhere cheaper than two roubles a pound. . . .

No, I am weary of this ceaseless search for information, the asking questions, the effort to imprint the answers on my mind. I yield myself up to the joy of existing in silence!

Out in the hungry steppes the caravans dare not stop, for ' karakurts '—black, venomous spiders—attack the camels.

The sky, like mother-of-pearl, is of incomparable loveliness.

The brown patches that covered the ground have given place to a yellow carpet streaked with spurts of mauve. Then we are over green squares that should be clover fields; Djizak appears below us, built near Tamerlane's pass. Our plane mounts steeply to leap the mountain that now bars our way. "Hi, there! Hold on, look here now!"—it is to the plane I am talking—"Don't swing about so." Of course, I know the pilot knows his business better than I do, but that's just it, for when they get so sure of themselves they may respond too mechanically through force of habit. . . .

The valleys of this mountain in the desert are divided into small regular squares. Why? No, no more questions! Gliding into the valley of the Zeravshan, the Gold-giver, we arrive. Below, the Samarkand oasis stands out clearly marked, the verdure interrupted here and there by tiny beehives that are the courtyards of houses. And the ruins? Already they are behind us, and we are again flying over the desert, which then comes up to meet us, so that we can land on its flat back.

Getting out at the same time as our frowning passenger, the pilot opens his mouth for the first time:

"Nine forty-eight. Two minutes ahead of time on the hundred and seventy-eight miles."

I haul out my two bags, and look enviously at the S.S.S.R. L.85 leaving in ten minutes for Tajikistan. It is still early. The shadow it casts on the sand is a long one. It will take it four hours to cover a distance that takes three days by train. Solitude! In the distance I see a new mountain, and near me a house. That is all.

The pilot has breakfasted. The plane roars and sets off.

"A fortnight earlier you would have met an Englishman straight from England," says the youthful and handsome head of the aerodrome. "After spending two days here he went back to London. He was stand-offish and said nothing. Are they all like that over there?"

"Yes . . . that's their way towards strangers."

We travel the seven-odd miles separating us from Samarkand in a lorry, then pass through the Russian town. I am dropped at a street crossing.

"All you have to do is go up that avenue as far as the Registan: the tourist 'base' should be somewhere round there."

CHAPTER VII

SAMARKAND THE INCOMPARABLE

WHEN, AS A time-pressed traveller, I visit some place that moves me deeply, I long to be able to spend days there in order to soak in its atmosphere at leisure . . . to see the sun weave slow shadows through the cloisters of Monreale, or wake at morning above the ruins at Delphi and feel the air vibrate to the first beams of the sun, or live in the square courtyard of a Samarkand madrasah . . . and behold . . . the dream has turned into reality.

What more lovely present could a traveller have in return for having come so far? There are practically no tourists and I have a room entirely to myself, an ancient cell, whitewashed and with a stone floor and very high ceiling, a tiny window over the door, a bunk, an enamelled wash-basin, and a table on which to spread out my cooking things That is all. And yet it is a whole universe.

It takes me two days really to know my way about the Tilah Kari Madrasah, which in Persian means the Golden Mosque. In each of the four walls that make the courtyard are ten large alcoves with ogival arches. The central alcove in each wall is enormous, set in a frame of glittering polychrome mosaic. This is the ' Iwan,' or classic portal.

The Iwan, to the left as one enters, is surmounted by an immense cupola that covers the praying floor, and this part of the mosque is enclosed.

From my cell I see two Europeans, in suits and grey felt hats, enter the courtyard with red guide-books in their hands. I have just emptied my wash-basin with an ample gesture outside my door as they begin to walk towards me, having been sent on by the office to which they had gone for information. It is for me they are looking, and they have brought me kind messages from a German friend in Moscow.

SAMARKAND THE INCOMPARABLE

The hem of my only dress is torn ragged: I am quite unpresentable, as my mother would say. So much the worse: it doesn't bother me (though I must say that every morning I do attempt to mend the unmendable). I hope that perhaps they will invite me to dine with them at their hotel, where there should be real meat to eat. But no, of course; I look too much of a scarecrow! They go away. Heavens! they look simply stifled in their tailored suits in contrast with the lithe and supple Uzbeks.

An Uzbek goes past, his flowered chapan belted with a triangular handkerchief, and carrying a teapot in his hand.

Four women are squatting in the middle of the court, like dark, shapeless mounds under their ' paranjas.' I go over to them. We smile at one another. They are not wearing the ' chedra,' and two of them look ravishingly beautiful, with a fold of the paranja pinched between their lips. What's happened? Suddenly serious, they veil their faces, get up, and trot all four towards their lord and master who calls them from the gate.

In one corner of the madrasah an Uzbek, standing in a cellar, piles wood into an immense circular oven. It is the potter preparing to fire his kiln, and later I come here often to keep him company. The glowing furnace turns the place into some vent hole out of hell and my head fills with fiery visions. Then the man stuffs up the cracks with bricks and muddy earth. He tells me that the formula for preparing the blue enamel of the mosiacs has been lost.

On my way to the latrines in one of the backyards I discover a heap of mud bricks, thanks to which I can climb on to the madrasah roof, a long wind-swept terrace dotted with quivering, sapless plants. Every native, before shutting himself in the little house at the rear, crumbles a piece of brick and takes some fragments with him. Of course, not everyone carries newspaper about, and a whole brick might be somewhat cumbersome, you must admit. . . . In the desert, or in the ditches, I notice that wherever I see someone squatting, they always make the same gesture of sweeping up a handful of sand. . . . Later I learnt that thus they replace the ritual ablutions imposed by the Koran.

From my solitary terrace, where I spend many hours, my gaze soars over a sea of flat roofs surrounding the tiny interior courtyards of houses. Spreading trees give shade to the cisterns in which the water is stored. On top of the mosque where I have got myself, the roof bulges at regular intervals into perfect hemispheres casting oval shadows; lovely convexities that the hand yearns to caress, and that, like the terrestrial globes, glitter in the light of the sun. Still higher I reach the narrow gallery running round the drum on which the dome is supported.

From this point I get a good view of the common brick which like a backcloth forms the rear of the Tillah Kari whose true façade is in the Registan Square. I see also the tops of gigantic minarets that look like smokeless factory chimneys.

Worthy of note! I am about to visit a city of which I know nothing save the magic of its name. As in the case of Baghdad, it is a name weighed down with associations, but however deep I seek in myself I can find no preconceived image of it. In no event, therefore, can the city fall below my expectations: all that lies in front of me is pure discovery.

I set forth!

The Registan

In the shadow of a doorway the public letter-writer, his head on his folded chapan, sleeps away the time while waiting for a client. In front of him, by the side of his satchel and ink-case and held down by a teapot, is a specimen of his writing.

On the opposite side of the street the while-you-wait photographer also has the results of his efforts on exhibition. He is operating on a client approaching her term, who for an instant draws aside her chedra, revealing a face that is too round, though with splendid eyes, and eyebrows artificially bridged with khol. Her friend, on the contrary, is very up to date. She wears a short skirt, blouse, and embroidered skull cap, and pays the photographer.

The Registan Square is strikingly impressive, shut in on three sides by the lofty façades of the madrasahs lovingly restored by the architect Viatkin. The work begun at the birth of the century still goes on. Wherever the wretched brick that was used in the structure has disintegrated owing to wind and sun, rain and frost, concrete is now replacing it. The enamelled facing tiles are beginning to peel off.

Ulug Beg madrasah is lovely in its stark simplicity. The immense Iwan is a sombre opening, the whole arch being set in the square frame of walls whose façade is covered with geometric designs in enamel.

At each angle a solitary minaret rises, the bricks arranged in such a manner as to make patterns in lozenges of dark blue. The cupolas that linked them have long fallen into decay. The minaret on the right is under repair. It was beginning to lean, but a very slow pull exerted over a period of eighteen months, by cables which encircled it half-way up, has now restored it to perpendicular again. This process had the merit of preventing the decorative bricks from springing or falling away.

Viatkin's death was the occasion for a most solemn ceremony in the Registan Square.

This madrasah, the most important and most ancient in Central Asia, was built in 1417 by Ulug Beg, scholarly grandson and successor to Tamerlane. He was a great mathematician and astronomer, but his enemies hated him because he wished to take the universities out of the hands of the priests. Then his generals, under the leadership of his son, plotted together and killed him. His favourite pupil managed to save all his valuable scientific apparatus, and sought refuge in Constantinople in 1450.

Opposite it, either to satisfy some desire for symmetry or through lack of inventiveness, the Shir Dar rises, a replica of the Ulug Beg, though constructed two centuries later. The architect Jalank Toush was an important personage at the

Emir's court. The ribbed egg-shaped cupolas still stand, over-shadowed by the immense façade. It is mostly in Turkestan that the domes are raised on lofty cylindrical drums. Also, something that is not found anywhere else, the angles of the walls as well as the minarets curve outwards near the top.

Contrary to custom, an animal is figured on the mosaics of the façade, a sort of lion, and on all sides phrases in Arabic characters are woven into the decoration. One says: " The architect has built the arch of this portal with such perfection that the entire heavens gnaws its fingers in astonishment, thinking it sees the rising of some new moon."

In another place occurs the phrase, " Only the eagle of thought could presume to attain the peak of this madrasah "; and again, and this still enchants me, " Never in all the centuries will an artist, thought's acrobat, even with the bow of phantasy, scale the forbidden peaks of this minaret." And again: " Thou art the great warrior, Jalank Toush Bahadur, and were the numbers of thy name summed up, the date of the foundation would be given " (1028 of the Hegira).

I found it impossible to go over the Shir Dar, for at the time of my visit the Bassmatchi, whose trial had been in preparation for some months, were then imprisoned in it.

The façade of the Tillah Kari, built in 1630, presents some differences however, for a double range of arches flanks the central Iwan.

In the middle of the Registan stands a thick crowd, which I penetrate into with some difficulty: it is drawn up in a circle, and gapes with astonishment at the feats of an acrobat.

Behind the Shir Dar I find a round open space, occupied by a small market, under a cupola filled with a swarming mass of humanity. Every imaginable article is being sold: embroidered skull caps, soap, tobacco, laces, stuffs, silk hand-kerchiefs, stockings, ribbons, greasy pancakes in frying-pans, scraps of mutton on a great tray protected by a muslin dome-shaped cover, and snowy sherberts glittering with icy crystals.

Some riders appear, pushing aside the crowd with their hands. Look out! A coachman is trying to get through. . . .

I see my Germans again, and my best drawing-room smile greets their uplifted hats. . . .

Alleyways of different trades, where in the half-light of the roof-pents the minute and identical booths face each other; squatting artisans, cobblers, carpenters; and at a short distance blacksmiths disappearing into the earth up to their knees to be on a level with their anvils which rest on the ground, Whenever the bellows are put into motion the coal blazes up, and a sudden vision of a rain-sodden England rises before me, so clearly does the smell of the anthracite recall the odour that impregnates everything in that country. . . .

In the resounding alley of the tinkers a booth gleaming with antique copper objects makes an admirable foil for the head of a young Uzbek who has brought some knives to be sharpened: the whites and blacks of his flashing eyes shimmer in the shadow of the enormous silky-haired, russet head-dress he is wearing.

" Fox, no doubt ! " I say to him.

" No; cat ! "

Ah, I forgot: Bokhara cat!

Bibi Khanum

Bibi Khanum, the ruins of former grandeur !

Two immense mounds at the entrance, massive piles of bricks strewn in places with squares of faience; a vast court-yard over three hundred feet long, once paved, but now planted with trees. In the centre, raised on two steps and borne by eight cubic pillars, is a splendid lectern of carved stone, set there with the intention of supporting the Koran of Osman. Originally it stood in the sanctuary, and one of its inscriptions is to the effect that Ulug Beg caused it to be removed from Djitti in Mongolia. It is the Kursen, the stone beneath which sterile women crawl at morning, fasting.

To the left is a tiny mosque with a gallery, from the top of whose tower the *muezzin* wails and cries aloud.

And here at last, facing me, I perceive an enormous eighty-foot arch, the portal of the immense mosque, dominated by a segment of the crackled cupola, a glittering turquoise dome that makes the sky seem pale by comparison. It is the same blue as the dazzling little lake of Kashkassu, the classic Mongolian blue that ravishes one with delight. The porch is flanked by huge octagonal minarets in which the turquoise and sea-blue bricks are built into the walls in raised designs; while slabs of faience make a facing for the walls that surround the portico.

To get a better view of what remains of the dome, which rises nearly one hundred and eighty feet, I climb over the outer wall. From that position I see an acrobat moving about in the heights. He is collecting wood for himself, which he drags away from the beams supporting the brickwork of the vault. The wood is smooth, hard, and raspberry-coloured. The man goes off with his booty, leaving the ground strewn with glazed bricks. The intensity of the dark blue is indescribable against that of the joyous turquoise blue.

It took five too rapid years to construct this cathedral-mosque,[1] 1398–1404. Aged seventy, just before he died in 1405, Timur had himself borne in a litter to the site to superintend the work. The passage of time, earthquakes, and the cannon-balls of the Russian conquest of 1868 have made of it a ruin that nothing can save now: the dome fell in 1882.

But what has become of the numerous stone columns that stood around the mosque? The contemporary writer Sherif-Ed-Din writes that in all there were four hundred and eighty of them, each nineteen feet high. Ninety-five elephants were brought from India to help in their transportation, and innumerable workmen and technical experts were dispatched from all the surrounding countries to execute the work.

The story goes that Bibi Khanum, a Mongolian princess

---

[1] There are three kinds of mosques: the ordinary mosque for the prayers of every day; cathedral mosques for the Friday (Sabbath) gatherings of the populace, and a special cathedral mosque found only in the great cities: these are not generally used, but services are held in them twice a year.

and Timur's favourite wife, decided to have a magnificent throne-room constructed for her lord, and that Timur, who was warring afar, scattering destruction in his train, dispatched all the most skilful workers among his prisoners to help her to this end.

Day after day the princess visited the site, but her Arabian architect, madly in love with her, invented innumerable delays for holding up the work, so that she might not cease her visits. Impatient to see its completion, she asked:

" What must be done to hasten the work? "

" Grant me permission to kiss your cheek."

She refused. But news was brought that the returning Timur had reached Merv. Then she consented, at the last second, however, interposing her hand. Yet so ardent was the kiss that it burnt through to her cheek, leaving a dark spot that nothing would take out. Whereupon, she commanded all her women to veil their faces. Timur, returning, wondered what the cause might be.

" It was done that our modesty might be preserved," she explained.

Timur learnt the truth, and commanded that Bibi Khanum be buried alive in the mausoleum already built for her, which stands opposite the mosque. As the Arab architect was being pursued to the summit of the minaret in which he had taken refuge, wings appeared upon his shoulders, and he took flight towards Meshed.[1]

As early as 1369 Timur was using Samarkand as his capital and had largely restored the city laid in ruins by his ancestor Jenghiz Khan in 1218. At that date the population numbered one hundred and fifty thousand.

[1] Some attribute the appearance of the spot to the fact that Bibi Khanum betrayed her husband, even though merely in words. Others, on the contrary, claim that the spot appeared because Bibi Khanum had not kept the promise given to the love-sick architect. The spot did not remain very long on her cheek, but a custom grew up by which those who forswear their promises, or fail in their duty, are called ' black faces.'

Tamerlane's Mausoleum

The Gur Emir, or Mausoleum of Timur, completed in 1402, stands in another part of the city, shaded by diaphanous acacia-trees. He himself had wished to be buried at Kerk, his own city. This superb edifice had been raised by him for his grandson on the site of an ancient tomb in proximity to the tombs of two holy men. But his successors decided otherwise.

Seen suddenly at the end of some tortuous alleyway, in the shade of which some 'cloistered' woman passes, it is exceedingly impressive, with its dome glittering over the low, windowless earthen walls of the city, looking like an enormous melon raised on a cylindrical drum of the same diameter. Approaching closer, one sees shining in the sun on the walls of the twenty-foot drum, enormous Kufi characters decoratively inlaid with white bricks set in dark blue borders.

Approaching closer, one perceives the lofty, octagonal-shaped structure which supports the whole edifice. In the court of entry an isolated arch stands, surrounded by trees. It is covered with arabesques and geometric motifs executed with the utmost delicacy in blue and dark green. In close proximity to the mausoleum, when one raises one's head towards the cupola, appear huge melon slices in relief, that seem to belong to some strange spheroid balloon caught in the foliage.

One enters through a vaulted winding corridor. The chamber of the tombs is dark, and white spots of sunlight enter in through a small, fretted window. Behind an alabaster balustrade Timur's sarcophagus appears, a simple rectangular block of dark green nephrite, a rare jade brought from India. About him sleep some of his ministers and children, Ulug Beg among them. Standing by the gravestone of the Sheikh Said Bereke rises a rough 'buntchuk,' the mast which always indicates the tomb of a saint. Above a wainscot of marble and alabaster encrusted with jasper, traces of gilt and painting may still be seen on the walls.

In a crypt beneath this chamber lie Timur's remains, with his teacher at his side.

Though the ruin sowed by Tamerlane, the 'Iron Limper,' stretched from India as far as Egypt, yet in Samarkand he created monuments that still astonish the beholder. . . .

At the exit from the mausoleum a holy man stands mute, waiting to sell his copies of the inscription carved in the nephrite of Timur's sarcophagus. "This is the the tomb of the mighty Sultan, the benevolent, the Khan Amir Timur. . . . Gurkhan (Khan's son-in-law) Jenghiz Khan is of the lineage of the ancestors of this worthy Sultan buried in this holy and magnificent crypt. The mother of the Emir Buzandshara was named Alankuwa and was unique among women for her honesty and irreproachable uprightness. She was impregnated by a beam of light which entered her open door, and which, assuming the form of a man, announced that he was the descendant of the believer Elijah, the Son of Talib, 'whose true descendants would reign for ever on the earth.' "

The Street of the Tombs

Outside the town, however, what made the deepest impression on me in Samarkand was Shakh Zinda, the Living King and its street of tombs. Begun in 1326, it is the most ancient of the monuments erected after the Mongol conquest to the memory of Koussame, son of Abbas, Mahomet's cousin.

From the verdurous alleys of a park can be seen the yellow, waste, abandoned, and dried-up monticules of Afro Siab, a vast dead surface covered with tombs. And among them, scattered far and wide over the solitary slopes, the pointed projectile shapes of the domes of a dozen mausolea, on the walls of which still glitter vestiges of enamel.

Below, by the roadside, bearded Uzbeks sit at the foot of the varnished panels of the main door of entry.

Inside appears a wide staircase, above which to the left rises the turquoise-domed mosque of Timur's wet nurse. But when one reaches the white arch at the head of the stairs, one stops in astonishment, for five façades of mosque in miniature stand in line along each side of a paved alleyway.

The riot of colours, arabesques, carvings, and inlay; the exquisite workmanship of the mosaics, the exquisite taste of the contrasting motifs is indescribable. (Personally, I am little inclined to rhapsodize over the products of Persian art, except where carpets are concerned, for their traditional elaborations, warm and velvety, enchant me always.)

To the left the façades of the mosques of the Emir Zade, of Timur's son, and of his first wife, Turkan, stand in line touching each other. And then suddenly I realize what a Persian carpet really is. It reproduces the miraculous façade of the mosque, the ogival-framed portal, the Iwan-arch as immutable as our cross itself, which is an exact replica of the ' mirhab,' that oval alcove shaped like a beehive that serves as the sanctuary, and before which the mullah always kneels, " never weary, it would seem, of his holy gymnastics."

The interior of the Turkan Aka is very fine, and contains many tombstones. The inside of the dome is covered with glowing geometric designs in mosaic. Facing it lie buried the Emir Hussein, one of Tamerlane's sisters, and also a daughter.

The alleyway makes a turn: the walls have lost their facing of enamel. Then come three mausolea, after which follows a second porch near two ancient trees, cuttings from which afford a sovereign cure for all diseases. Then one enters a tiny courtyard, incomparably beautiful. Ultramarine blends with turquoise, sea-green with emerald, cobalt with burnt siena, lapis-lazuli with ochre; the colours seem reflected in each other, and, enhanced by the warm glow of the earthen bricks, leap like a chant of glory towards the blue sky.

The mosques of Kutluk and Nuri, Timur's wife and daughter, face each other. Last of all, blocking the street, is that of Saint Achmed. The dazzling pillars of the Kutluk mosque are pure turquoise in colour, and carved in high relief, an art found nowhere but in Turkestan.

The mullah standing under the dome of the portico throws open the incredibly fine fretted door of wood, which by devious dark chambers leads to the mosque of Shakh Zinda, Saint Kassim, also known as Hussan. He converted the whole of Sogdiana to Islam in the seventh century, but then the Nestorian Christians attacked him. His army annihilated, he fled away, and an angel revealed a grotto where he took refuge and is said still to live. As his horse was dying, he flung away his 'kamtcha' (whip), which took root and became the two trees near the porch. It is said of him also that, decapitated by the pagans, he withdrew into a well, carrying his head in his hands, till the moment should come to purge the earth of every infidel.

In the antechamber to the tomb 'buntchuks' stand erect. Horses' tails hang from the poles round which bits of stuff are wrapped, each testifying to some offered sacrifice. The tail is an emblem of might, for the horse made good its escape, leaving its tail in the hands of the man of invincible might. Darkness shrouds the tomb, railed off and unapproachable.

Afro Siab

The vast abandoned expanse known as Afro Siab stretches beyond Shakh Zinda, unenlivened by even a blade of grass. It is composed of dusty hills, at times of superimposed tombs, simple vaults of brick, and narrow tunnels crumbling into dust.

Afro Siab is the name by which the ninth king of the Pechdad Persian dynasty, a Turk by birth, was known. He was the most celebrated of the kings of the ancient dynasty, and his name represents whatever is most ancient and traditional in the annals of the country. He is said to have lived eleven centuries before Christ.

This immense and shapeless mass, over which each century has heaped fresh layers of dust, and which at every step is strewn with shards of pots, what story does it tell? Clearly defined, one sees the circles of four hills. Excavations reveal that in the centre lived the reigning dynasty, round them lived the merchants, and on the outer ring came military forts, and finally the circle of market gardens.

The Uzbeks have not yet lost their love of reading of the high deeds of Iskander D'hulkarnein [1] (Alexander of Macedonia), who, as legend says, founded Marakanda. The great conqueror reached this spot in 334 B.C. There he slew his friend Clitus, then wedded Roxana, daughter of the Iranian chief of the region, and married his warriors to the women of the country. His intention was to unite Europe with Asia by the ties of legitimate marriage, and in one common descent.

Alexander did not meet with any Turks in Turkestan, then known as Sogdiana or Transoxiana. He encountered Parthians, and Bactrians, whose country was the original home of the camel. The principal religion, Mazdaism, followed the precepts of Zoroaster, and was founded on the conflict between light and darkness. Later Mithraism would continue to make adepts even into the Roman era, while Nestorian Christianity spread in the contrary direction from Roman Syria as far as China. To the north, beyond the land of the unknown Scythians, innumerable hordes of the unsuspected Huns dwelt.

Alexander's great international ideal crashed down with his death; he died in Babylon at the age of thirty-three, as the result of a fever caught after a too copious banquet. The terrible Roxana assassinated her rival, the daughter of Darius and second wife of Alexander, and gave birth to a son, who was to be assassinated later with her.

After which the general, Seleucus, took over the direction of affairs, and founded the Seleucidan dynasty in Persia which endured for nearly three centuries.

Then the Sassanids dominated Iran for four centuries, finding little to disturb them in the inroads of the first nomads, the hephthalite Huns, who in 475 conquered and took Gandhara in Afghanistan.

But with the coming of Islam in the seventh century the

---

[1] " The two horned, the prophet."

kingdom of the Sassanids fell into the hands of the lizard-eating Arabs. In 643 a conqueror named Samar begins to make himself heard of, and it is possibly thanks to him that the city was named later Samarkanda.

From 873 to 1004 the Iranian dynasty of the Samanids was established at Bokhara, and defended Iran against the Turan and the Turki-Mongol hordes who were beginning to raise their heads. In 980 was born at Bokhara Ibusina—Ibn-Sina, or otherwise pronounced Avicenna—the prince of healers, celebrated throughout the Arabian universities.

In the eleventh century the Seljuk Turks, issuing from the Kirghiz steppes, invaded the country, establishing petty states, becoming dwellers of houses and Sunnite Moslem. Soon they were powerful enough to go to the aid of the Abbasid caliphs of Baghdad.

But the terrible thirteenth century approaches. In the distance the son of Jesugi Bahadur, the Inflexible Emperor, conquers China with the aid of his four sons. What magnificent crowded hours these five men must have lived together! Then he sets about recreating the empire T'ou Kiou as it existed in the sixth century. In the eyes of Jenghiz Khan, the Shah of Kharezm and Bokhara, Mohammed the Seljuk is a mere Turkish baron converted to Islam. But the Shah gets into a panic, refuses to offer submission, no longer protects the caravan routes, and in 1220 Jenghiz Khan ravages Samarkanda and Bokhara. The country is laid under the yoke of the Mongol terror—the yassak—outlawry. The generals of the Khan come up with the expiring Mohammed on the shores of the Caspian Sea and conquer every Turkish stronghold between them and the Black Sea.

Six centuries of Islam have been wiped out. Hulagu the Mongol, who reigned over Persia, slew the last Abbasid caliph in 1258.

In the fourteenth century Timur welded Turkestan together once more. In place of the Persian tongue he substituted Jagatai Turkish (which comes from the name of Timur's second son). Massacres took place on such a scale that pyramids were built with the victims' skulls, and only the poets, scientists, and dervishes were spared, to do him service in his court. From very birth his hair was white, and it was said he had never shed a tear. He limped, and yet could have struck down the hero Rustum, so great was his strength. Beyond all things he loved truth, and whoever lied to him was killed. . . .

The Tajik Timurids were driven out by the Uzbeks in the sixteenth century, and the latter, starting a reign of terror, put themselves at the head of the Khanate of Kharezm (Khiva). They were descended from Jenghiz' eldest son Juchi, who had reigned over the Kipchak, and from Uzbek Khan, the eighth and celebrated Khan of the Golden Horde.

In 1717 the expedition sent by Peter the Great to discover a route into India was massacred at Khiva. The Emirs of Bokhara from 1784 to the date of their extinction belonged to the dynasty of Mangites who issued originally from the mountains of Tajikistan.

The Russians under the leadership of General Perovsk began to penetrate into Turkestan in 1839. Tashkent was conquered in 1865. General Tchernaief defeated forty thousand Bokhariots with three thousand six hundred men. Samarkand was taken, and the Emir bought his peace for a sum of £75,000.

In 1920 it was the Republic of Faisulla Khodjaief. Later, in 1924, with the aid of the Reds, it was transformed into the Soviet Socialist Republic of Uzbekistan. This was a new marriage of Asia with the West, Russian, however, this time, and Macedonian no longer. What will its issue be?

CHAPTER VIII

THE PRESENT

I HAVE MADE some friends, and every day when they finish work I go to meet them at the big chai-kana facing the Registan, where we chat together while munching pistachios and the kernels of 'ouriouks' (tiny apricots).

Maroussia is lovely, no one would think of questioning it. In Leningrad, where she was once a dancer, her heart had been set on becoming a film actress, but her narrow face and sombre periwinkle blue eyes proved somewhat too subtle for the screen, I imagine. Tall, over-tall perhaps, her broad shoulders are habitually bowed as though discouraged.

All she lives for is her motor-lorry. Her hands are long and delicate, yet she can sit at the steering-wheel eight and ten hours on end when working overtime. Even when her male colleagues have been laid out by fatigue, she still manages to keep a smile on her face. And take it from me, lorry-driving in Turkestan is far from being a sport for girls.

Departing from the grain-store, we deliver sacks of corn in the surrounding 'kishlaks.' What goes by the name of a road is full of such deep ruts that Maroussia, without ever relinquishing her delighted smile, is always miraculously balanced on the edge of the embankment. Every minute I think we are going to roll over. . . . At intervals the road is cut by irrigation ariks, deep runnels which turn the loose soil into sticky pools of mud.

The chic thing to do in the narrow alleyways of the old town appears to be to take the corners at full speed without knocking pieces off the walls. To give us passage, the wayfarers leap into the first door-way. But it is a dangerous game, for the 'paranja' deadens sound, and often the women do not hear the warning.

If she breaks down, Maroussia is expected to repair her own machine, but the men on her job do all they can for her. I verily believe that even if she began hacking them to bits they would still say " thanks."

" Hi, you great goose ! " our black-moustached Persian with the handsome head, bald under his embroidered cap, shouts to a woman in the road.

" Here, Ella, I've something for you." And he hands me some nuts and a biscuit.

Maroussia has always got something nice in her pockets for them. She earns a hundred and fifty roubles a month, and is studying to qualify as a mechanic, which will entitle her to still more.

In the grain-store canteen, where we get cabbage-soup and potatoes cooked with pimentos, she introduces me to a young Armenian driver named Reuben. He is set upon our visiting his wife and young son, and is small, with magnificent golden eyes, overshadowed by black lashes that seem to curl up to his very brows.

So we set off in a band together, arm-in-arm as we go down the wide, descending pavement of the boulevard.

" It's like this," Maroussia explains. " When I'm with my workmates I can laugh frankly, and I don't feel sorry for myself : we understand one another. And then I like them ; they're alive, it does me good to be with them. They don't merely fall back on words when there's trouble ; they lend each other a hand. Yesterday Vanya took a bag of potatoes to the Persian, and said, ' I hear your babies haven't played ball with potatoes for a long time.' And Yann just now saying, ' with meat at ten roubles a pound, it will soon be worth while turning one's own rump into steak.' They're square and open, not like women with their eternal grousing."

Going past an open booth selling beer, I take the liberty to express some scepticism as to its quality, whereupon I am told it is incomparable stuff.

" A round for five ! " the Persian orders.

The liquid is refreshing but watery, and the glasses enormous for a rouble. Reuben then insists on offering another round. There is nothing to do but sit down on the pavement to collect oneself a little.

At the house of the Armenian, when they hear I may possibly be going to Merv, a letter of introduction is written for me to take to the father and grandfather who live there, in order that I may visit them and bring them news of their children. . . . The room is minute, very poor, and in the European fashion, with white curtains.

The Jewess of Khoudjoum

Every day Maroussia has stuff to deliver at the Khoudjoum factory, so I go with her to see how silk is made. The moment the door into the main hall is opened one begins to stifle in the hot steam of what practically amounts to a vapour bath.

Women stand in front of high tables, their hands blanched and softened by the boiling water, and watch the yellow cocoons that look like floating beans simmering in the pans. These must be seized at the right end or they will not unwind. They are lifted out with a skimmer. Then the next worker takes up the filaments, seven by seven, and these form the thread which is gathered up into stiff and glittering skeins.

Some of the women have transparent gauze over their heads, others a handkerchief rolled turban-shape, others again wear the traditional skull cap. All have small black plaits hanging down their backs and straggling over the shoulder-straps of their coarse aprons.

The plates on the machines show they are of Italian manufacture. Built in 1927, the factory then employed one hundred and forty-four workers, but at present the number of emancipated women employed is eight hundred and fifty. On the first floor one wanders about between long rows of glittering skeins, white or yellowish-gold, the natural silk, that is subjected to meticulous scrutiny. The employees are paid at piecework rates. From the skeins turned out by each worker, four hundred turns are taken as samples and the result noted down in a register. Eleven implies that it is too coarse; thirteen to fifteen, satisfactory.

Descending again into the filature, I look round for a young and sympathetic worker whom I can accompany, to see something of her home life. Nearly all are old and ugly and I lead the supervisor to the only pretty girl I see. She is tall and wears a brown velvet blouse. Her thick black hair grows low on her forehead. She has long eyes with still longer eyebrows and a straight nose, and smiles at me as she juggles with her invisible threads.

"She is a Jewess: an excellent worker in one of our shock brigades. You know our factory has fulfilled its plan 112 per cent. . . ."

I notice that the Jewess is the only one who plucks the ends of the silken threads with her lips: her hands are thus free and she works with great rapidity.

We wait for the young woman after her work, but she seems disturbed as we walk by her side. She knows no Russian, only Tajik, that is to say Parsee, the ancient Persian; and we have to wait to be able to converse until we reach her home, when a neighbour acts as interpreter.

Surrounding a large yard dotted with green growing bushes stand new houses, all of the same earth, all on the ground floor, with recent washing and quilts hanging in front of them. It is in one of these that our Jewess has her room. On the floor is a kelim, on a plank trestle coverlets hidden under a 'souzaneh,' a cloth with large round red-embroidered motifs, and in the corridor a Primus. That is all. Apprehensive, she makes no reply to my questions, and continues to remain alarmed. "Has my work been bad?" she asks. "They must be dissatisfied with me if they send you inquiring like this to my home."

I find it impossible to set her fears at rest or straighten out the furrow that joins her eyebrows.

The Armenian with the 'Chilim'

"How depressing! Heaven preserve me from ever working

in a factory," says Maroussia, as we leave the knit-goods factory.

"All the same, do come with me to the embroideress's 'artel,' and don't laugh when I ask for the hundredth time 'unveiled, married, illiterate?'"

Maroussia is disengaged: her lorry has broken down: I saw it in the garage pit. Can the break-down have been calculated, and is Maroussia in the pay of the O.G.P.U., with the task of keeping a watch on me? I cannot tell, but I shall do and say as I wish.

In the sun in a yard, and on tiers, women squat upon mats, embroidering. By their sides stand slippers and a tea-pot. All bear themselves with great dignity; even the spectacled old women under their large dark kerchiefs.

The directress is an energetic, very thin woman dressed in a belted grey waterproof, her head wrapped in a piece of mauve-coloured gauze on account of a sore throat. The white knot of a handkerchief shows on her forehead, and I presume it goes round her head. She is precise and intelligent.

"When we began, in 1929, there were seven of us. We went from house to house and talked with the women, all of whom knew how to embroider. Now, when we have enough materials, we employ two hundred and fifty women in the town and one hundred and fifty in the 'kishlaks.' A good worker earns one hundred and twenty roubles a month, but a woman who comes to us merely to have the right to a bread-card earns only twelve. It takes four days to make a shirt. Those who come here work seven hours a day: those who work at home cannot, of course, be supervised."

"But you yourself, are you Uzbek?"

"My father was a Persian."

"And did you wear a veil?"

Maroussia does not smile.

"Yes, till '27, in spite of definite orders to the contrary from my husband, who was a schoolmaster. But I had to obey him when I saw he was beginning to get really cross with me."

"And the family dramas that they say take place in connection with unveiling: do they still happen?"

"Yes: we must go carefully. The liberation of women has created discontent in the home. The old women who gain by it jeer at it, and as for the young, it's always the same story: 'I won't have you go out like that,' says the man. We've established a small court for dealing with these family differences. It's the husbands who have to be made to see reason: for all they can see is pitfalls everywhere. But education will open their eyes in time."

After looking at tablecloths, blouses, shirts, and embroidered napkins, reproducing the classical motifs of the 'souzaneh,' we visit the 'tiubiteka' corner. One could almost think oneself at the booth of the melon vendor, for the skull caps are stuck one within another and lie along shelves among piles of brocade, cut into sections, waiting to be sewn.

"I am having brought from Moscow," says the Armenian woman, "two wagon-loads of priests' chasubles and surplices that I have got to pay cash for. But this is the difficulty. According to the old way of making deliveries to the Trust, I have to give long credit, and as a result I am always short of money. Some workers here have not been paid for two months now, but we make a point of paying the Russians, for they have neither a cow nor a kitchen garden and are unable to wait."

The directress lapses into silence to puff at her gurgling 'chilim,' the water-pipe that passes from hand to hand. A simple tube of bent tin does duty as mouthpiece.

As we are laughing at the sight of tiny fair angels' heads painted on cardboard and held in place on the crowns of the skull caps by bits of embroidery, the woman says to us:

"Yes, in the past the Russians crossed themselves before such images: nowadays it is just these skull caps that are most in demand in the mountains of the Pamir."

The women chatter as they work. They seem to be here because they like it. How different the atmosphere is from that of the two preceding factories.

THE PRESENT

" The old ones talk less, and they drink less tea too, and work much harder," the Armenian says, smiling, as we take our leave.

I Am Still Not Satisfied

As we sit eating plov in the gallery of a native café, I tell Maroussia that I am still far from satisfied.

" I want to enter into more direct contact with the native women, both in town and country. I should like to find a village where I could live and work in the fields with the women."

" Serge will help us. I find him a little irritating, but it can't be helped: he is a painter, and has spent some months in the country."

His job at the moment is reorganizing the museum housed in the Ulug Beg. We find Benkof, the well-known artist, in the courtyard of the madrasah working at a striking canvas, the subject of which is *The 8th of March in the Registan Square*, a date which celebrates the emancipation of the women, when the chedras were burnt in great heaps.

Serge makes us climb to the top of the minaret to admire the view. 'Samarkand, most beautiful of worldly cities,' lies at our feet.

To the east the upper third of the mountain ranges is white with snow. At our feet the paving stones of the Registan Square are being removed so that the surface may be restored to its ancient level. A crowd stands in a queue waiting for the bus that serves the Russian town and the station. Little asses bray in the caravanserais, and the noise they make is as inseparable from the landscape as is the crystalline light found only in Turkestan.

In the distance, on the stark mound of Afro Siab, beyond the great mosque Khazrat Khaisar, with its lovely wooden pillars, a smaller mosque with a simple peristyle suddenly brings to my mind the sober temple of the Wingless Victory on the Acropolis.

225

Serge is so affected by the presence of Maroussia that it makes him stammer. It must be wonderful to have such a capacity for emotion in oneself. I slip away and pay a visit to the directress of the Women's Bureau.

"Yes, Soviet law does not permit marriage under sixteen, demands a health certificate, and prohibits second wives. You must realize that in the past the birth of a girl was considered of less importance than that of a dog, whereas the coming of a son was greeted with feasting: it alone was baptized.

"In the towns a girl had practically nothing to do: she sewed, watched her mother work, and wore the chedra for a year or two before her marriage. She was not taught to write, for fear she might start a correspondence with some man. According to the 'shari'ah,' the exegesis of the laws, if a wife did not give due heed to the words of her spouse, he was entitled to beat her. In the country they work in the fields unveiled and lead much freer lives. The 'kalim' which bought a wife could not be less than ten 'dergamofs,' equal to five gold roubles, and the wedding feast cost the whole of it.

"A widow could remarry whom she pleased. Among the Kirghiz she married her brother-in-law in order to keep her possessions in the family.

"They did not go into the mosques, but prayed on tombs and gave money to the Sheikh, the chief mullah. They knew nothing of the simplest medical attentions, and at need consulted only the 'falban' or female shaman, who practised exorcism. Thus the victims of venereal diseases were almost countless. You can imagine, therefore, how much there was to be done everywhere. In the past there was only one midwife on the staff of the Samarkand hospital. To-day we have ten thousand beds in our hospitals, as against only nine hundred in 1916."

What a labyrinth the countryside round Samarkand is! Serge leads us from field to field, from alleyway to alley. We ask, "Is it far to the ruins, to the right of the road?" and the wayfarer replies, "as far as the voice carries."

THE PRESENT

We knock at the wooden door of the house of a 'tchorny rabotnik,' a journeyman-worker, and hear voices of questioning women.

" It's I, Serge, Mustapha's friend! Is he at home? "

No reply.

Tired of waiting, we are going off, when the door opens. A tiny yard, at the end of which is a gallery, divided into two by hanging lengths of cotton. We go into the division reserved for the men and find Mustapha lying down.

" Yes, I've had this fever for two months now : but I'm feeling better. Serge, this is the first time you've come to see me, in spite of your promise. The women did not realize who you were, and that's why they did not ask you to come in."

" I've brought a foreign woman to see you, who would like to see how the women live and the way things are done in your house."

A little girl brings in the tea, two bowls for four people, and some 'kishmish,' the delicious dried grapes that are quite pink and seedless. The shivering Mustapha with difficulty sits up to do the honours. " Yes, I understand. Let your friend go through and join the women."

In the adjoining division children are playing on the quilts, a squatting woman spins, teapots stand in niches in the walls ; there is a cradle, a coffer, and that is all. In the yard is the oven

" Mustapha ill! I'm sorry. Where does it hurt? " and I point to my head, my stomach, and my back in turn.

" Two months already . . . "

" Tabib (doctor) been? "

" Yes, yes."

" What did he say? "

" Tiffy."

It's typhus that he has. What a delightful piece of news! And I have drunk out of the bowl with him.

" No," I say to Mustapha later. " Thank you for your invitation. I cannot pass the night here. I have seen all I want to see."

CHAPTER IX

Yann Tells a Story

Yann and Maroussia are arguing about magnetos: his job is inspecting omnibus engines, and he is trying to catch her out. He is fair, with a roving blue eye, and burnt by the sun. Maroussia tells me that anyhow she can stay good friends with Yann because he has only just got married, and so there is little likelihood he will suddenly begin pestering her with his love.

"Yann, you should introduce Ella to your Uzbek friends, so that she can get inside the women's quarters. But to-night tell us a story about the Bassmatchi, to make us forget the fright we got over the typhus."

Yann knew Uzbek before he learnt Russian, and his youth had been wild and unruly. The expression in his eyes changes, he turns dreamy, and suddenly looks like a Scandinavian.

"Would you like a story about a horse?"

Like a nibbling mouse, his story proceeds in short, brief sentences, colourless, and with intervals of silence.

"Well. A peasant house with fields. A son and a daughter with their mother and stepfather. The woman lacks character, she cannot do anything that needs initiative: she is afraid of her self-centered husband. The white-handed daughter, Anna Gul, dislikes work, quarrels with the domineering father who interferes in everything that goes on inside the house. She has large, grey, dreamy eyes, and long curling eyelashes.

"No one bothers about the son, Gul Murad. His nature is sullen: and when someone slights him he shows no resentment, though he never forgets. His work is laborious, for he guards the herds. The mountains and the tracks of the wild are familiar to him; he can snare birds. He is a good rider and he does as he likes, for the mother loves only her daughter.

" With the money got for the birds he has snared he buys a lamb which he fattens. And so that his parents shall not take it away, leaves it in the care of a neighbour. At last, he is in a position to buy a foal. He is young, he wants his steed of Arab blood. To begin with no one notices his horse, Hindu Kush, but then his stepfather commands that no more barley be fed to it. The son gives up his own bread.

" In the part of the yard that faces the section reserved for the women, a barn stands which belongs to an usurious kulak, as well as the sheltered winter yard for the animals. When one passes the door one can see the house is a well-to-do one. There is a great room with a carpet, ' souzaneh,' cushions, ' sandouks ' (coffers). The stranger, coming from afar, can find rest there both for himself and his beast. The son attends to everything. Dirty workmen dare not presume as far as the carpet, but sit down near the door and eat the scraps left over.

" In the daytime there is sunlight round the ' karagatch ' (the Asiatic elm) ; in the women's quarter there are flowers, fruits, grapes ; round the fountain there is music, tea-drinking, and idle gossip. The stepfather comes in. All fall silent. You can hear the flies buzz. He looks angrily at his daughter, and she goes out. The woman takes off his khalat, washes his hands, gives him food, and brings in his ' chilim.'

" Opposite them lives the fox of a usurer, with his son Kakim, who envies Gul Murad.

" The time for the ' kurban ' comes round, the riders dispute with each other the capture of a goat, the trophy. Both sons take part in the hurly-burly, and Kakim gets the goat. But his horse is a weakling and Gul Murad snatches the goat and wins. The defeat rankles in Kakim's breast, and he begs his father to buy Hindu Kush for him, and the father promises.

" Gul Murad has taken the bridle off his horse and they run together in the yard. The son cries, ' Hindu, Hindu ! '

But he has forgotten to shut the gates. The father rides up on a mare, and Hindu wants to play with it. The father's white turban rolls into the mud. When he picks himself up, his sleeve, too, is covered with mud. The son manages to catch his horse again. The father takes his whip and begins to beat the son, as he ties up Hindu and the other horse, and shuts the gates, and picks up the turban. Then he starts kicking him about and completely loses control of himself. The women scream, the mother weeps.

" The son clenches his teeth. He is badly hurt. The fox of a usurer, who has seen everything, comes up and says to the father :

" ' Your son neglects the flocks and gives all the barley to his horse. Sell it to me, I'll pay a good price for it.'

" The father orders the horse to be brought. The labourers are fond of Gul Murad ; he winks at the groom who is holding Hindu's bridle, seizes his father's whip and cries, ' The horse is mine, you will only get it over my dead body.' Taking them all by surprise, he leaps into the saddle, strikes his father and the usurer with the whip and seeks refuge in the mountains.

" He turns into an ' abrek ' (vagabond) and joins up with a group of rebels. People love him. He organizes a raid on his own village, and beats Kakim within an inch of his life, saying :

" ' That horse is not for you, not even a hoof-paring.'

" At times he helps the poor and oppressed.

" The mother is exceedingly unhappy, and begs her husband to send for Gul Murad. He refuses. The husband has invited his friend Bala Bek, who wants to marry the daughter, to a pheasant shoot. Bala Bek pretends he wants to go shooting and so he gets a chance of seeing Anna Gul. She detests him, however, and begs her mother to prevents the marriage.

" It's the beginning of the Revolution, during the civil war. In the village they are very afraid of a near-by band of Bassmatchi whose flocks have been stolen by Gul Murad's comrades. To revenge themselves, the Bassmatchi fall on Gul

Murad's village and take the young man's best friend with them as prisoner. Gul Murad, however, succeeds in setting his friend free, but an unseen knife makes a deep wound just under the ankle bone.

" Weakened by loss of blood, Gul Murad can hardly remain in the saddle; but he brings the flocks back to his village, to the great joy of the villagers. The mother begs her son to remain. He goes on refusing, but at last his stepfather says: 'Forgive me, I was in the wrong.'

" Then, greatly weakened, he lies down. His comrades depart.

" Kakim has seen everything: he urges the representatives of the powers-that-be to make a search. Whereupon Gul Murad escapes, without arms, without a horse even, and worn out takes refuge in the earth of a jackal. Kakim mounts on Hindu's back and cries out before the people: ' I've got Gul Murad's horse; I have achieved my object.' Suddenly frightened by a dog, the horse throws Kakim to the ground and gallops away.

" It is night. The jackal, which has retreated deep into its earth, wants to get out. It has smelt the fresh blood of the wound. Gul Murad sees the shining green eyes, he fights and almost kills it with his knife. Utterly exhausted, he crawls out of the hole with the jackal and drags himself to the top of the mountain. His horse is browsing there, ready saddled with the best saddle of all. The young man calls to Hindu, and, making it kneel, manages to get on his back.

" Returning to the village, he has to pass near the house of a female shaman. She hurries out to meet him; the horse shudders, the jackal falls. Although mortally wounded it utters a long, lugubrious howl. Gul Murad wants to pick it up again. 'Don't take it, it's unlucky, I see it.' But he refuses to listen to her, pulls the beast back, and finally dispatches and cuts it up. It is past midnight. The moon shines over the snow. He hears the cry of a distant jackal. Then a baying and the bellowing of a cow. Gul Murad fastens up his beloved Hindu, unsaddles it, and covers it with blankets against the great cold. He is home again.

" Below sleep the brother and sister : upstairs the parents. Outside the shut gates is heard the noise of a horse. Kakim knows his way round the house, leaps over the hedge, and opens the gates to the Bassmatchi led by Bala Bek. The servants are speedily tied up. Kakim promises Bala Bek to deliver the sister over to him and to keep Hindu Kush for himself. The Bassmatchi fire through the door, the children seek refuge upstairs with the parents.

" Gul Murad breaks a hole through the wall in the attic, behind a coffer. The mother says to Anna Gul, ' You must go through, whatever happens ! ' She falls in the snow in her night clothes. ' Go, too ! " says Murad to his mother, holding her up by the hand as long as he possibly can. When it comes to the father's turn he says, ' You go to my friend ! ' Kakim gets in through the window and sets fire to the hangings to see better. The others dare not do anything. They are afraid that Gul Murad may be armed, but he has hidden himself and waits till the coast is quite clear. In the morning he returns. Everything has been destroyed, scattered ; the forage set on fire, the servants bound. Little by little the animals return, first an ox, then an ass, then the cow and its calf : they were too well fed, and so were not able to stray very far. But the saddles have gone, and Hindu. . . . The broken hobble still lies on the ground, and there are traces of blood in the field where the horse has tried to tear itself free.

" Gul Murad, in the midst of his sufferings, hears the sound of hoofs. Hindu Kush staggers up to him, sinks down, and dies.

" Gul Murad cries for a long time : he refuses to allow it to be cut up and orders it to be buried. He sells whatever remains, and carries to his family the clothes he has saved and their jewels. Anna Gul is in love with a young man and follows him. Gul Murad conveys his mother to a place of safety and rejoins his bandit troop.

" The power is in the hands of the Soviets : the bandits join the Red Partisans and help to ' liquidate ' the Whites. Bala Bek is caught and handed over to the authorities ; but

YANN TELLS A STORY

Gul Murad is not allowed to cut off his nose and ears. Bala Bek sues for pardon, and, deprived of his opium, loses his reason. Kakim is caught at last after a sharp exchange of shots; he implores pity. Gul Murad does not permit him to escape, but orders his feet to be cut off, saying, ' Now ride Hindu Kush!' Soon Kakim dies of hæmorrhage, and so his story ends."

" What became of Gul Murad? "

" He had no education. He becomes a komsomol. Works day and night. Then he helps the others through their apprenticeship. . . ."

A long silence.

Yann wakes to reality again and looks at Maroussia.

" Did you like my story? "

" Oh, yes. . . . Not bad, but too long! "

Hurt by this reply, he says:

" Right. . . . I'll tell you nothing more then. Good night."

" What's got him now? How touchy men are," says Maroussia.

" He seemed to me wrought up. I think he was telling the story of his life in a roundabout manner."

But Yann means nothing to her: she pursues her own thoughts.

" Ah, I've got it," she says. " Riza will help us. He knows all Samarkand. He sells me my butter."

Riza

What an extraordinary man! He knows everything that's going on, gets the better of everyone, talks his head off, and even half drunk will allow no one to squeeze the least kopek out of him. On several occasions he has arranged to take us to see his daughters, then at the last moment there is always something to prevent it.

We go to see him.

" Well, Riza? You must be making fun of us! We've emptied four teapots waiting for you."

" Just a moment while I finish my butter."

His sleeves are rolled up and he is stirring the thick cream in a pail with his fist. At moments he places it on a stove. Then he makes some ' blinnys,' delicious pancakes made with whey, which we eat standing at the table. All he has is the minute room, dark but clean.

He asks fourteen roubles a pound for his watery butter.

" But you must be very rich with all this butter. What do you do with the money? "

" With any wits at all one can become a millionaire in no time. Before the Revolution I was one of the richest men here. Sometimes I would buy a thousand sheep without the wherewithal to pay for them, and sell them the same day at a profit. When I worked for the Co-operative, all the peasants kept their ' kishmish ' for me, because I knew how to talk to them and trusted their word for the weights of their sacks. When the careful buyers who never bought anything without weighing it turned up, there was nothing left for them.

" Riza, it's getting towards night, too late to visit your daughters. And you said you were going to take us to a ' kishlak.' "

He begins to shave himself, smoothing out his skin, that is one mass of wrinkles, with his finger. Then a young woman enters who appears to be Russian. She seems quite at home here. I did not know the wily Riza had remarried. Small, and wearing her hair in a flat coil on her neck, she turns out to be Georgian, apprenticed to a photographer. Speaking through her nose, she says:

"I'm in a hurry to get to the cinema for the seven o'clock show. Riza, give me two roubles! They are showing the *Sniper*."

I had seen this film, the story of a spy during the Great War.

" Nothing doing, my girl: no more to-day than yesterday! "

The girl departing, we tease Riza and congratulate him on how lucky he is.

" But it's they who run after me. For two years I've been trying to get rid of that one: I kick her out, I don't give her a penny, and yet she won't clear off. She means nothing to me. But you, Ella, you're just the person I want: have you thought over my proposition? "

We burst out laughing. Riza had wanted to marry me the day before, too, and I had thought he was joking.

" But why not? Ella wants to get to know the country: she needn't have to work, I'll see to her food. She wants to go to Bokhara, which I know well. I'll be her guide. . . ."

" I must have time to think about it," I say, determined not to put him off before he has done what I want of him.

" Riza, you must take us to the Armenian café so that Ella can hear the native music."

We had already been there on our own, but we wanted at all costs to get Riza to put his hand in his pocket.

" And if you were really gallant I think you would present that scrap of butter to Ella."

" Not at all! That half-pound is worth seven roubles."

In the big crowded tavern there are at most five or six women, not one of them Uzbek. There is American cloth on the tables, and beer or vodka is being drunk. Before the door scraps of mutton are grilling, spitted on metal skewers. Noise, smoke! The orchestra is a stringed one and the sounds sharp, grating, and very monotonous, with a constantly changing rhythm which alone reveals the feeling proceeding to a climax. In comparison our own use of richly melodious phrases seems quite orgiastic. The songs are Persian, the dances Uzbek.

Four of the patrons have each a rose at their temples, stuck between the skull cap and the shaven head. A staggering man, supported under the arms, is led out on to the pavement by two ' comrade-waiters.' Another falls down in his own vomit.

Nothing, however, can distract me from the pleasure of listening to the ' barraban,' a large tambourine whose rich muted resonances form, as it were, the skeleton of the music.

The performer is a tall, bearded man, who accompanies all his movements with expressive mimicry.

Before beginning to play, he rolls up his sleeve, uncovering the stringy wrist and the long brown fingers. Then he moistens his thumb which rests against the rim of the tambourine. His dry fingers flatten themselves rapidly against the taut skin. They follow their own cadence, repeated in a slower rhythm by the arm and still more slowly by the bust; a threefold articulation of the body, a threefold accentuation of the time. During a crescendo the knee introduces a fourth beat, and with an ample gesture the man sweeps up the 'barraban' with its small metal jingles and rocks it passionately. It is when she dances that Tamara Khanoum stands rigid, with transfixed shoulders, and rhythmical movements of the seemingly disarticulated head from which a hundred tresses float, while beating time with a metronomic chin. I had already seen her in Moscow with her company.

Riza begins telling me about a village near Khiva inhabited only by women, all the men having been executed. He will take me there if only I say yes. He is very unhappy because we have insisted on having expensive shashliks, and vodka to go with it.

On our way to visit Tula, Riza's youngest daughter, we pass a swarm of Uzbeks, with men hurrying forward in turns to put their shoulders to some shafts. Thus the saddler abandons his work to walk ten yards before returning. Over the shafts a long oblong of dark blue material is spread. It is a funeral, and by helping to carry the defunct some few yards of the journey to his last home, every Mussulman is doing a good deed. . . .

Tula, from her expression, seems to have inherited the obstinate will of her father, and looks by no means easy to get on with. The determined brow under the disordered hair is held down by a black bandeau, the nose is broad but clean-cut, and a black coat pulled over her wide, white, gaping shirt covers worn boots.

The oval mud oven in the yard, protected by an awning,

smokes gently: and inside its blackened maw I see lipiotchkas browning. An Uzbek saying asserts that, ' blessed is the
visitor who arrives during baking.'

Tula, as she spreads a koshmou for us in the yard, hardly
deigns to reply to her father. She offers us some apples.

" No, she has not abandoned the use of the ' chedra.' "

" No, she has no desire to learn to read ; no, the cinema
does not tempt her." She does not care to talk about her
husband either, and so we do not discover what his work is.

But her wrinkles smooth out when she sees me playing
with her baby. I go into the dark room where the ground is
covered with carpets. The child is smiling as it lies strapped
to its bed. The cradle is of carved wood, and two heavy-
quilted coverlets, parted like curtains, lie on the thick wooden
bar over it. The child is playing with a necklace of many-
coloured beads hung over its nose.

To suckle her baby, which remains lying on its back, Tula
leans her arm on the crossbar and squats motionless. Then
she strips the bedding from the cradle. Where the child's
bottom comes, the mattress and the wooden base have a
round hole pierced in them, under which an earthen pot
stands, containing ashes. Now I realize the function of the
small wooden utensils made in hundreds by the carpenters:
pipe-shaped for boys and flute-shaped for girls, they are the
conduits that lead the urine safely to its destination.

Just as we are leaving, a begging tzigane enters, his fierce
head bound in a great fringed scarlet shawl. There are
numbers of them in the region. Some days before in the
Russian town, squatting at the corner of the street, I had
seen a magnificent dark woman telling fortunes with a pack
of tarot cards, for a rouble, to two fair little Russian girls
with anxious faces. As she presents a lipiotchka to the beggar,
Tula says to him:

" You know, I wish I could afford a beautiful shawl like
that! "

Many of the Uzbeks are still away in the country in

gardens they inhabit in the summer. We find Djura, Riza's eldest daughter, at home, squatting in Turkish fashion under a tall columned veranda at the foot of a carved wooden pillar. Three children are playing in the yard which is shaded by a willow, against which a skinny cow is rubbing itself. But I see no place for a cistern, as is customary in native houses.

Djura, who is full of dimples and wears bracelets, silk trousers, and a black ribbon band round her head, makes us comfortable in a tall, cool chamber covered with sombre carpets. They are its only article of furniture, and sole ornament, so that there is nothing to distract one from the appreciation of their beauty. Again we find the customary symmetrical niches containing teapots, mirrors, napkins, and quilts. The special little table belonging to the 'saundall' stands over the hole in the floor reserved for embers; and in the corner is the square hole by which the water runs away.

Djura serves us with fried cakes, but will neither sit nor eat in our presence.

From the other side of the passage, whenever the door opens, the neighbours hasten to try and take a look at us.

Djura is no more interested than her sister in the modernity which expires outside her very door, incapable of passing the elbow joint of the passage that leads into each yard. She complains of the price of flour and 'kishmish,' the real daily bread of the natives. When the children are old enough for school, perhaps then she will realize all the changes she has gone in ignorance of.

As I leave, a glance at our laughing neighbours permits me to see an old woman smoking a chilim, and a young embroideress.

At the Kishlak

I run across the handsome, blue-eyed Yann, who says to me:

"Do you still want to go to a kishlak to see the men at work, the silkworms, and ride on a camel? We're meeting this evening at seven to go and visit one of my friends. That's better than going off with Riza to a village no one knows anything about."

At nine Maroussia and I are beginning to despair when Yann appears, followed by two Uzbeks with fine round, frank-looking faces, wearing leather waistcoats, and each carrying an enormous bottle of beer that holds nearly a gallon.

Both Maroussia and I knit our brows. " What does this mean? Is it a carouse you want to take us on? "

" Don't be afraid. Mura and his friend are absolutely trustworthy, you need have no fear. There's only just beer enough to put some life into us."

And Yann stops two ' isvoschiks,' who, loudly cracking their whips, drive us into the country at a good round pace.

" Mura, is it a long way to your home? "

" No, apa.[1] The time it would take to empty two tea-pots."

I have not the least idea what we may be going to. But the die is cast. At night, on unknown roads, once the carriages are paid off there is no drawing back.

Then the thick dust of a roadway to cross, a path up a cliff, high wooden steps, rungs, a terrace: then a door and we find ourselves in a spacious room.

An oil lamp, cushions, carpets: a girl, Mura's sister, brings in tea, hard-boiled eggs, and a tray of ' kishmish.' It is too late to visit the rest of the house.

Yann seems thoughtful. He does not want to tell us what takes place at an Uzbek marriage. Maroussia is in a bad humour, and rapidly tells me the reason:

" Yann has ruined our friendship. He has just told me that for six months now he has been able to think of nothing but me. Up till now he has always kept that pleading expression out of his face. That's why I suspected nothing."

Maroussia has already confided her point of view to me. She likes men and their company immensely, but detests them when they begin to want something from her: she doesn't

[1] Sister. Word by which women are addressed.

feel the least desire to get near enough to any one of them to affect him in any way. She said that very thing to her husband when they were engaged. Yet all the same he wanted to marry her, so that at least he might be able to live at her side.

"Your charming husband, Maroussia, is not very appetizing I agree, but Yann is handsome, and if he can't inspire you with desire, I fear it will only go on getting more difficult to make you yield. I think you must have set your ideals so high, because you are afraid you might be disillusioned, and thus destroy your present tranquillity."

Yann and Maroussia are arguing with each other.

I am worn out by my well-filled day, for I have already visited a farmyard outside the city on the road to Agalik where I watched the natives cooking the cocoons in great vats. The dead worms had stunk simply horribly. It reminded me of a shore strewn with shoals of fish, putrefying in the sunlight and swarming with flies.

And then I had paid a visit to the mausoleum of Hodja Daniar, at the other end of Afro Siab, an immense cylinder of stone five or six yards long, in the shadow of a buntchuk, the holy mast.

The legend says that the giant saint still goes on growing in his tomb.

Continuing my walk, I had a swim in the great aqueduct shaded by willows, before going on to the Observatory of Ulug Beg. This successor to Timur had determined the exact meridian of Samarkand, and it was on the calculations worked out by him in the fifteenth century that all the calendars of the Middle Ages were based. Here he made his observations of the sky. At the bottom of a deep trench shaped like the segment of a circle, a graduated stone rail supports a movable seat under the eye-piece of the telescope.

Despite the snoring of the young men, Yann and Maroussia go on talking all the time.

Waking is difficult. We are alone. It is late. Everyone has left. Yann and Maroussia are no longer on speaking terms, and we decide to return to Samarkand as quickly as we can. Farewell fields, silk, camels, broods!

As revealed from the top of our cliff, the countryside gleams with a crystal clarity that only a morning of Turkestan can bring. Thousands of miles from the atmospheric disturbances of the sea, the air is unbelievably translucent. I leave the guest room to throw a glance into the yard of the house, and see an old woman drying the pierced bedding of a cradle, and a bleating black sheep.

" Ella, come with me to visit the next house," says Yann. " No one's lived in it for two years now, but that doesn't matter."

Bare floors and walls, a window still standing, and a dark venthole, like a gaping letter-box, at the very foot of the wall.

" Yes, you're looking at the right spot," says Yann, following my eyes. " Just think how things happened. . . . There was a poor couple. He loved his wife and horse above all things. Wherever he took the horse, it was faster than others and won prizes and gifts. First they had no children. Then his wife gave him a daughter. The tabib takes a liking to the horse and wants to buy it; he offers a large sum, but unsuccessfully. The child is beginning to grow into a fine girl. Everything is perfect.

" But suddenly the child develops a white spot on her neck: leprosy, perhaps. In that case the family will have to leave the village. ' Tabib, examine my girl, what has she got? ' The bearded tabib pretends to fly in terror, but the father holds him back. ' Only tell me; I'll give you anything you ask.' ' Give me your horse, and I'll not breathe a word of it.' "

" She was three years old. They put her into that sort of cellar so that no one should see her. The mother is very unhappy, she feeds the child at night in order not to be taken by surprise. She fondles her daughter, then rubs her face to catch the disease herself, but without result. The child cries, wants to come out and be with her mother. They make her keep quiet.

" Fifteen years pass. The Revolution comes. The village gets to hear of the child, and the komsomols suddenly decide to investigate the old rumours. The daughter crawls out on all-fours. Her skin is a mass of wrinkles. She is terrified of everyone, like a wild animal. She does not know how to talk. They beg the father to tell how it happened. A Russian doctor examines the girl and says it was only a boil. They send for the tabib with the long beard and begin to question him. But to the father everything is clear: he picks up his knife and kills him."

We return through the bushes glittering with dew. This terrible story makes me think, yet again, that hear I am living in the heart of the Middle Ages. That fact must not be ignored. We are still in the year 1311, forty years behind the Arabian calendar of the hegira. At every step the fourteenth century rises to face the twentieth. Here, right has always been to the mightiest, and the notion of justice for all must be inculcated from the very bottom. At every step the force of habit opposes the will to do that the Soviets have brought with them.

CHAPTER X

The Trial of the Bassmatchi

I AM AWAKENED by the hardly credible sounds of horses' hoofs echoing on the stone paving of my madrasah . . . and make a rush to look out. Soldiers, armed and mounted, are supervizing the placing of chairs so as to face the Iwan-arch leading into the courtyard. It is the day, breathlessly awaited, for the verdict to be pronounced, in the trial of the Bassmatchi which has gone on for months.

From the vantage point of my window, perched in unstable equilibrium, I try to photograph the courtyard, which little by little fills with the populace. I would rather have chosen some different view-point, but fear lest my camera be confiscated again. I know . . . I'll climb on the roofs as I do every morning. But no: the narrow passage at the end of the courtyard is shut to the public and guarded by a militiaman.

I'll risk it. I manage to squeeze through to the foot of the dais where three judges are gossiping as they wait for the accused to be brought. I show them my camera, tell them I have a permit to use it, and ask if I may stay near them. They hesitate a little, then acquiesce. One of them is wearing a grey mackintosh, and a white cloth cap whose peak over-shadows the aquiline Armenian nose. The two others wear the Uzbek 'tiubiteka,' and chapans striped with green and lilac. Behind them, on the alcove wall, are the twin portraits of Marx and Lenin. From the vault of enamelled bricks a scarlet velvet banner hangs, on which is embroidered a man standing in front of a counter and holding the scales of Justice up to an interested onlooker. On the ground, at the foot of the great ogival arch, I see the enormous head of Stalin soaring in the sky of a 'Five-Year Plan' photo-montage.

243

A big carpet has been spread over the dais, in the middle of which is a table behind which the President of the Court sits: a spare man with his head jammed into a black fur bonnet, and wrapped in a black overcoat that makes him stand out sharply. On one corner of the table, covered with a length of red cotton, is a bronze bust of Lenin, the salient features, knitted brows, and bossy forehead, emphasized by the white light of the rain-washed sky. Strangely enough the President of the Court resembles him. He has the same piercing glance, drooping moustaches, and straggling goatee beard.

On the courtyard level a number of clerks are writing in Persian characters, their table covered with pink and gold brocade.

Then come the accused, brought in under escort, some forty in all, all natives, wrapped in their padded coats, patched and variegated. One man has bare feet, and his hands are crossed over his chapan covered with a design of roses. He sets down a kettle in front of him.

" There's Amrista," my neighbour says, " their chief ! "

" Which ? "

" The smallest of them, with the green skull cap."

Drooping shoulders, round spare skull, deep-sunken eyes, thin lips: his mantle wraps him round like a marionette, as he jokes with the crowd.

" He has been imprisoned twelve times already," says my neighbour with the splendid, casually bound turban. " He has always managed to escape, and cares nothing for the police. He said to them, ' Well, kill me; why should I worry? There are scores more ready to take my place.' "

Behind the roped-in enclosure reserved for the accused a row of women stand, anxious and immobile, shrouded in white ' paranjas ' fastened by black ' chedras ' of horse-hair: they are the wives and mothers of the accused. Unwittingly, their children play on the ground. Behind, comes a wall of male faces that gaze at the scene as at a free entertainment; specimens of every possible Asiatic admixture, from Japanese-looking faces to the type of blond Bashkir in whom Slav blood is mingled.

Two magnificent police dogs are held in leash by a militiaman. A judge reads the names, first-names, and status of each, first in Uzbek, then in Russian, monotonously, unintelligibly. To the left of Amrista, an old man, small, with a white beard fringing his face, stretches forward a skinny neck in an attempt to hear. His immense blue, astonished eyes are widely open, and he looks so innocent that one feels he could pass into heaven without absolution.

" That big chap, near you, is a tailor by trade, but he has killed eight people already."

During the day each of them worked at his trade: goldsmith, journeyman, street sweeper, café proprietor. But at night they came together, discussed the new laws, criticized the Government, created malcontents, and organized raids against the farms which had accepted Bolshevism, sabotaging wherever possible.

What I Learnt of Their Past

Under the name Bassmatchi, which means thief and bandit,[1] are grouped all the enemies of the Soviet regime: the brigands liberated from prison at the Revolution, the Nationalist counter-revolutionaries belonging to the party of Said Mir Alim Khan, the ancient Emir of Bokhara, and again the White Russians, Tsarists in the past. In non-Soviet circles, the word stands for a Nationalist rebel. So savage was the resistance put up by them that for a long time the Red Army was compelled to maintain large numbers of troops under arms in Turkestan.

The Bassmatch movement was born after the fall of the Kokand Provisional Government, which attempted to capture power in Turkestan after the Revolution. Following fifty years of Russian occupation, during which no internal organization had managed to lift its head, this sudden spirit

[1] From the Turkish verb basmak = to constrain, oppress, violate.

of resistance was due to a number of causes. There had been a great development in national consciouness since the fall of the Khanates. Then, the instinct to self-preservation was itself an urge to insurrection, because conquest by the Reds had inevitably brought with it conditions of great severity, wiping out the cotton harvest for a time, and, as a result of too-repeated requisitions, bringing famine conditions in its train. These organized bands, off-scourings of criminals at the beginning, were called on to aid the Government of Kokand,[1] and so became transformed into heroes for freedom, battling in the name of the native inhabitants.

At Tashkent, under the command of General Djunkovski, the White Russians, supported by British aid, organized a counter-revolution: but then the latter departed to aid the 'Soviet' Government of Ashkabad, which had set itself in opposition to the Bolshevik dictatorship.

At this period, during the first years of the Revolution, the thesis maintained by Moscow was that none but a Russian could be Dictator of Turkestan (*Pravda*, 20—6—1920).

This anti-Nationalist bias, applied indiscriminately to the whole country according to the adversaries of the regime, is what was at the bottom of the general uprising.

Of course, there were rebels before the Revolution, too, as I have explained in some detail in connection with the Kirghiz uprisings in 1916, when, to maintain its prestige, the then Government attempted to put the blame on the Turkish agents-provocateurs. But after the strict measures taken by the Russian General Ivanov-Rinov, at the time the mobilization order, calling up men aged from nineteen to forty-three, was commuted into work in labour battalions, a relative calm was established.

Numerous conflicts also took place between the Uzbeks and Turkmen in the region of Khiva, the pacification of which devolved on the Russians. In 1916, when Djunaid at the head of his warriors captured Khiva, he had the Khan of Khiva, Said Asfendiar Bahadur Khan, completely at his mercy. But

[1] According to the present Soviet version.

Djunaid had to evacuate Khiva when opposed by the punitive expedition of General Galkine. As a result he bore the Russians great enmity, even when they were Bolsheviks. In 1918, after the departure of Colonel Zaitsev, he recaptured Khiva and held it for two years. In 1924, with the help of the priests and merchants, he again recaptured Khiva : but the Red Army having finally crushed the Bassmatchi of the Pamirs, moved against him and forced him to evacuate the place.

A pact was entered into, which Djunaid respected up to the time when the execution of some of his partisans led him to show his teeth. It was necessary to declare a state of general mobilization, to pass a decree establishing the railway line a military zone, and convoke the Military Revolutionary Counsel before he would submit.

According to some, the submission of Turkestan to the Reds must have cost more lives than the whole of the Russian conquest of fifty years earlier.

Yet the Ferghana region had always been peaceful before becoming the cradle of the Bassmatch movement. Even the Soviet writers themselves describe it as the inevitable reaction to the anti-Moslem programme of the Soviet leaders.

The third Congress of the Soviets of Turkestan, in November 1917, refused to Moslems all right to occupy Government positions. As a result, a National Congress met at Kokand to try and remedy such a state of affairs. They had neither weapons nor money, but simply faith in the Communist Revolution. On that they rested their trust rather than in a protracted struggle against the Central Executive of the Russian Government. But one grievance against the Soviet power was that nothing was done to evacuate the Red Army that was living on the country. Stalin's own answer was: "Wipe out the Russian military forces in Turkestan yourselves, if you can muster strength enough with your proletariat and landworkers, and if the population considers them foreigners in the land."[1]

[1] According to the book by Vadim Tchaikim, *The Execution of the Twenty-six Commissars of Baku.* Moscow, 1922.

In 1918 Kokand was bombarded. The attempt at self-government faded away. But the many rebels sowed insurrection. At that time the Bassmatch movement had numerous adherents, for the unemployed found support among the bourgeois and the clergy. Their only idea, however, was to plead for special reforms which would render the Soviet programme more acceptable to the Moslems. In 1922-3 agrarian reform was brought to a standstill, the confiscation of the 'vakufs' (property of the mosques) was put a stop to, and Moslem schools were officially tolerated. Following on these concessions, four thousand Bassmatchi passed over to the Bolsheviks.

At that time there was no common National ideal, only a desire for autonomy.

Ferghana saw itself cut off from all relation with the rest of Turkestan. The insurgents grew discouraged and became blind tools in the hands of adventurous 'kurbashi,' or warrior chiefs, like Madamin Bek, an ex-convict serving under the Soviet flag. Kurshirmat, his rival, in command of all the anti-Soviet forces in Ferghana, accused him of treason and managed to slay him, but was himself forced to retire into Afghanistan in '23.

The Bassmatchi themselves have distorted the objects at issue and divide where they should unite. Every group seeks to seize power at the expense of the others. It would not have been difficult to suppress them at this time, but the constant pillaging by undisciplined Reds led to the creation of fresh rebels. The Emir fled into the mountains in 1920, and Ibrahim Bek, leading the insurgents, fought to support him.

But when Bokhara was Sovietized the Bassmatch movement took on new vitality, supported now by the intellectuals who feared to see all opposition vanquished. A number of secret conferences took place in which an attempt was made to give a political form to the movement. Autonomy, which represented a link with Russia proper, was out of the question; nothing less than National independence would satisfy them. This Committee for the National liberation of Central Asia, without money and without weapons, decided in 1921 to appeal for support to the British Consul at Kuldja, and to proclaim Turkestan an ' Independent Democratic Republic.'

The members were arrested, however, and at the trial the President of the Court found them guilty, basing his condemnation on the ' shari'ah '; his grounds being that the accused had appealed for aid to the infidel British, a race at enmity with the Moslems, since they were oppressing such holy places as Mecca and Medina.

By '21 the Reds had liquidated the White fronts and defeated the Bassmatchi.

Enver Pasha was in Baku[1] in 1920 as delegate for the African and Hindu Revolutionaries, but Comrade Zinoviev refused to call on him to speak. His association with Moscow then seemed regrettable to him, since he had heard of the excesses of the Red detachments. It was said that the Emir's treasures were being sent to Moscow, ' as a gift from the grateful people of Bokhara.'

In November '21, Enver appeared unexpectedly in Bokhara to see for himself what was happening there. At that time it seemed to him that under cover of liberating the people the Soviet policy in Turkestan merely continued that of the old regime. Those members of the Young-Bokhariot Party who were in power, like Faisulla and Osman Khodja, told him that they were the prisoners of the Red Army and had not obtained the promised independence.

Enver realized he could do nothing in Bokhara. Making a pretext of going on a hunting expedition, he left for Tajikistan, and from there sent his first message to the Central Government. He suggested that it should withdraw its troops from the region, and proposed organizing the establishment of a Republic of Turkestan in alliance with the Soviets and with a common foreign policy. " Then," he added, " aided by the Revolutionary forces of Turkestan, I swear to you I will drive the British out of India."

[1] At the First Congress of the Peoples of the Orient, September 1 to 8, 1920.

Enver was the son-in-law of the Sultan Caliph of Constantinople, and intimately connected with the Moslem intellectuals, but his name meant little to the malcontents with whom he was associated. He committed a grave error in assuming the post of Grand Vizir to the ex-Emir Said Alim, the despotic and detested ally of the Tsarist bayonets.

Neither the Ferghana nor Samarkand regions would render allegiance to him. Even the Emir Said Alim did not trust the one-time leader of the Young Turks, and suspected him of wanting to bring about the unification of the Turkish peoples of Turan for his own benefit.

The Bokhara Government decided to send a Revisionary Commission to Enver, with Osman Khodja as president, the ostensible object being to put down the insurrection. But in reality the Commission wanted to help Enver in his fight against Moscow.

Finally, however, Osman was forced to take refuge in Stamboul. Faisulla had intended to join him a week later, but a close watch being kept on him he was forced to remain.

Yet Enver remained powerful. In Turkmenia, Djunaid, too, was for him, but the Bassmatchi were incapable of conceiving of a Pan-Islamic Empire. A local province was the most they aspired to. Ibrahim Bek, a vassal of the Emir, refused to support him. Anyway, in the end Enver Pasha was hemmed in among the mountains of Tajikistan and slain on August 4, 1922.

Yet the insurrection continued to spread as the rivalries between the Bassmatchi chiefs grew more intense. The one thought of each Kurbashi was how to seize a region for himself, settle down as Bek there, and restore the ancient feudalism.

But with the occupation of Garm, the Reds won ground among the high mountains. It was then that the Emir addressed a lengthy appeal to the League of Nations and to those ' who love peace and respect justice.'

In '24 the Soviets were accusing England of fomenting trouble in Central Asia. Faisulla Khodjaief said then that the Bassmatchi were only undisciplined bands, no longer of any political significance. The autonomous Republic of Tajikistan was inaugurated in 1925, and four years later the country became a Socialist Soviet Republic, ranking equal with the Ukraine and Uzbekistan.

Up to 1931, Ibrahim Bek was at the head of the insurgent bands and invested with great authority. Deep in the Pamirs, in the region of Hissar, existed the tribes of the Lokai and Matchai, notorious for their rebelliousness. They were governed by all-powerful Beks, with feudal customs, who pillaged the country. Sometimes the peasants would revolt, kill the Bek, and fleeing, join the Bassmatchi.

The peasant, having paid his tribute to the Bek, thought he had earned the right to rob his neighbour in a similar fashion. Ibrahim Bek, although his father had been a rich miller, would often borrow horses from his neighbours, as frequently happens in this country. He was feared because he was an excellent shot. He rose against Enver and joined the party of the Emir, in whose name he issued proclamations throughout the region. The Tajiks were against Ibrahim Bek, an Uzbek Lokai, and partisan of the Emir of Bokhara who was a Mangite Uzbek. This struggle of the tribes was termed a class struggle by the Soviet powers. It was not till July 26, 1931, that Ibrahim was captured with his second, and a rider. He was led away to Tashkent, and should be imprisoned there still.

But I must return to the trial.

The accused rise, and all are led away into the interior of the mosque where they are searched. The onlookers elbow each other to see better, and the two small trees planted in the middle of the courtyard bend to the ground in an unaccountable manner, the leafy branches sticking out from under the arms of the spectators.

Is the crowd going to make a dash to liberate one or other of the prisoners? No, they stand looking at them. In pairs, and under escort, they pay short visits to the other side of the vaulted corridor at the end of the courtyard. . . .

It is cold and an unpleasant rain keeps falling. I go back to my cell to get a piece of bread. It is late already and I am hungry.

The Bassmatchi resume their seats again, shivering with cold and burying their hands in their long sleeves. Amrista must have malaria : he looks green under the falling rain. The fat chops of the stout, treacherous-looking tailor are quivering. All now have their heads bowed, letting them fall slackly, at the limit of exhaustion, their chins resting on their clavicles. All these naked, shorn necks, projecting out of the gaping khalats, seem rigid in expectation of the axe to fall. . . .

If the moment were not such a serious one, the sight of all these necks uniformly curved to their full extent would seem almost comic : it makes me think of those prayer meetings where everyone exaggerates the devoutness of his pose, in order to make his contrition seem by so much the more edifying.

On the dais, the man is still reading : an endless succession of syllables that follow on each other, muffled, guttural, strangely commingled, and terminating with sudden emphasis. . . .

A cry, a prolonged howl. . . . The women rush forward, passing under the cord. The nineteen prisoners whose names have been read are sentenced to death. The confusion is heart-rending.

Their swords drawn, the militiamen force a passage through the khalats and turbans, and again the little trees are mown down by the turmoil, and the women, forcibly torn away, are removed to a distance from their men.

Violently buffeted about, it is impossible for me to see what is happening, and I have to use all my strength not to get swept away. Impossible to get back to my place. A little after and the crowd begins to melt. For the last time I get a glimpse of the Bassmatch with bare feet, his chipped blue enamel kettle tucked under an arm : yes, to the very moment of death the human carcase demands to be fed.

THE TRIAL OF THE BASSMATCHI

In the empty courtyard the little trees miraculously stand erect once more; the chairs lie scattered about.

When I wake next morning, Lenin still meditates alone upon the table. The chairs are being piled up preparatory to being taken away. An Uzbek passes dressed in a thick black winter mantle, a white earthen teapot in his hand. His boots re-echo through the courtyard, now void and silent again.

In the newspapers I can find no slightest detail about the trial of the Bassmatchi.

CHAPTER XI

Bokhara the Fallen

THE TRAIN DEPOSITS me at Kagan, the Bokhara station, about one hundred and fifty miles from Samarkand. Thanks to an employee who by force put me at the head of the line, I got a place in the ordinary train. I was sad at leaving Samarkand, for I had got to love its animation; the swarming crowds where I felt so much at home, the flour market where it was almost impossible to advance, the roofed-in great bazaar at the foot of Bibi Khanum, the innumerable chai-kanas with their wooden platforms picturesquely set in the shade of some fine karagatch. . . .

Maroussia could hardly believe I was going, when I said good-bye to her in front of the huge school buildings on the Boulevard Vseoboutch.

My timid neighbour is an old Russian peasant woman, whose eyes never quit the piece of bread I am munching, and so I share what I have with her.

This Transcaspian line which stretches from Krasnovodsk to Tashkent, constructed in 1882, before the days of 'Five-Year Plans,' "was a piece of work almost American in the rapidity of its execution, apart from the fact that Russian life and methods show many striking analogies with the ways of Uncle Sam," wrote Rickmers in 1913.

But there is a lot of difference between Bokhara and either Russia or America, for the first thing I see are ruins and tombs. At the very gates of the city, surrounded by a ten-mile wall, the graveyards begin to stretch, or rather rise, I should say, for the little parallel tunnels are piled one upon the other.

Bokhara, famous for its hundred and fifty thousand inhabi-

254

tants, city of storks, stronghold of Moslem science and Islam's power; to which students from the world over gathered to the number of twenty thousand, in a hundred and fifty madrasahs: what are you now?

Then it took fifteen to twenty years to be consecrated 'Imam' or head of a mosque. In addition to the Koran, rhetoric, oratorical art, poetry, and logic, were part of the curriculum. The lectures began after the fashion observed in Yemen: raising the eyes, turning the palms towards the face, and lastly caressing the beard.[1]

Ruin was brought upon it by its cruel Emirs, who crushed the people beneath their taxes and murdered men for their own pleasure. The instruments used by the torturers can still be seen in the Museum. A keep was full of frightful insects: bugs bred specially for the prisoners' torture. When there were no men to throw to them, raw flesh was given instead.

Bread and Water

Surrounded by dirty tortuous streets, and in the centre of the city, I find a lodging on the first floor of the tourist 'base,' established in the courtyard of a madrasah.

There is a water tap at the corner of the square, where for a few kopeks the Bokhariots are able to fill their enormous, shining water-skins hung with braces. Bokhara, whose irrigation system is the last to receive the waters of the Zeravshan, had the worst water in Turkestan, and 95 per cent of the inhabitants suffered from fevers. During the period of floods, all the reservoirs of the city, the 'haus,' would fill with water, and the main reservoir then became the hub of the city. There one filled one's water-pots; there one performed one's ablutions, washed out ones clothes and tea bowls. The filth was amazing.

It was by way of the water that the larval form of the

[1] There were fifteen madrasahs in Tashkent, thirty in Kokand, and six in Samarkand in 1843.

Guinea worm (the richta) entered the bodies of the majority of the inhabitants. Richta means ' cotton-thread,' and the parasite established itself under the skin, at times attaining a length of over a yard. The barbers rid their clients of them by slow degrees, every day winding an inch or two of the creature round a match-stick. Great caution was needed, otherwise the worm broke and one had to start all over again.

But now the Labihaus in front of my madrasah Dinan Begui is dry, and there is no longer a corner that offers shelter from the suffocating dust. Picturesque crowds gather no more on the wet steps, but the water is healthy, and the richta no longer exists.

On the other hand, the difficulties of procuring food are such that the hunt after bread is the main event of the day.

I have the right to go and eat in the ' technicians ' restaurant where the food is good, but too dear for my budget, since it amounts to three or four roubles a meal. In any case it is a real struggle to get one's minute portion of soup or goulash, which is practically stewed bones swimming in sauce.

I therefore do my own cooking at home. I have a ration card, which theoretically should enable me to buy about fourteen ounces of bread a day. Regularly I go to the Co-operative, where, with some forty others, I wait for the loaves to arrive: for if one is not on the spot, one misses the propitious moment and arrives when all the bread has been sold. When my turn comes I have to argue with the shop-man, who often refuses to let me have any.

Gossiping and joking, the people wait: they impute no blame to anyone, and one feels they are now entirely philo-sophical. . . . At home they would imagine the country was going to pieces, there would be despair on people's faces accompanied by wild gesticulations. But here the expression on men's faces in no wise reflects the things they are saying to each other. I hear someone say:

" The ration has been reduced still further. Ten and a half

ounces for the manual worker, twenty-one for the technical specialist."

"They say that beginning from February we shall be eating Canadian wheat."

Your neighbour asks you to keep her place while she goes to buy a cabbage and an onion for her soup. . . .

I cannot prevent myself saying that on the other side of the world, grain is being used for firing locomotives, or cast into the sea. They think I am lying.

"Well then, if they are such lunatics, things must be in a hell of a mess over there," says an old man, smiling broadly.

A low murmur: the warm brown bread is being brought into the shop. Steam rises at every cut. The man cuts off the portions with a long knife which he dips into a pan of luke-warm water, the damp crumb clinging to the knife in long, glittering threads. The bread tastes sweetish and I think must contain a large admixture of jugara flour.

As they go off, one and all begin nibbling at the corners of their bread.

A kilogram of potatoes costs three roubles. In the vegetable market all I can see are carrots and onions. Rice, the staple food of the natives, costs six to eight roubles the kilogram. A little old man has six eggs in his hand which he will let me have for three roubles, but refuses to sell them separately.

If someone happens to pass holding a lipiotchka in his hand, people will stop and offer to buy it, at the same time asking where it was bought. But even in the time it takes them to reach the corner of the street where the vendor stood, all they see is the tiny salesman cleared out, already walking away down the street with his flat empty basket balancing on his head.

Beggars abound. They shiver and must suffer from agues.

I try to see what the rest of the people eat. Returning from the Ark, the ancient citadel or Kremlin, I note a 'closed' restaurant, reserved for the use of the workers at the generating station. After 5.30, however, when they have all left,

the cooks are willing to serve odd customers. For eighty-five
kopeks there is always a good soup, followed by rice or
macaroni.

Strolling past a house in course of construction, I hear the
contractor say to his bricklayer:

"I'll pay you to-morrow, the bank hadn't the money
available to-day."

"Keep my money! What can I do with it? It's bread I
need. Bread! That's what my children ask me for at home."

A moment's silence.

"What do you think I can do with ten ounces a day?
Most of the weight is water, and it means nothing at all."

At this the contractor disappeared, and came back again
with his own bread, which he handed in silence to the other.
What else could he do?

I pay a visit to the city Soviet, as I want to meet the Jewish
community of Bokhara, reputed for the purity of its descent
and traditions. I also want to visit a caracul sheep farm, the
fur of which is a staple export. I am sent on to the Committee of the Communist Party, but there is never anyone
there: they are all away in the kishlaks, helping to raise shock
brigades for the cotton harvest; for, more important than
anything, the figures set out by the Plan must be fulfilled.

In the Ant-heap

I find it impossible to tire of watching the life that flows
round me. There are two streets in which the native traffic
swarms as its densest. "Posht!"[1] cry the donkeymen and
'arbakeshes,' as they carve their way through the crowd,
where everyone is trying to either buy or sell something.

Crouching down, with my back to a wall, I hearken to the
ebb and flow of all this restless humanity. I feel I am at the
centre of an ant-hill, and realize suddenly how purposeful the
scurrying of each ant is.

Two sons of the desert, recognizable by their bronzed skins,

[1] "Look out!"

their slow, sure gait, look over a heap of 'kishmishes,' and taste the small grapes; then they call over a third comrade, wearing Kazak boots with high pointed heels and a Louis XV look about them. The price asked makes him burst out laughing: then they go off.

There are enormous turbans of grey wool, very useful for carrying a lamp glass, which tucked into a couple of skeins of wool is admirably protected from the pushing crowd. Then I find myself in a covered space, and here the crowd is most dense. Everybody grins when the yoked oxen of some cart push with their horns at the packed bodies.

Without a break, an apple seller yells incessantly to keep the crowd moving in front of his stall.

Two Afghans with black turbans are tempted by a piece of yellow satinette offered for sale by a Russian, who says to them:

" Measure my yards, just measure them: they are all there, every one! "

A well-meaning third party acts as interpreter.

Women are selling odds and ends that baffle description. Should a piece of Chinese porcelain or a ' tekinski ' [1] turn up, it is bought within ten minutes by the experts whom daily I see taking a turn round the market. The least scrap of ' tekiner,' the dark carpets made by the tribe of Téké, is worth a hundred roubles. Mostly ' kurdjuns ' are made of them, the saddle-bags that every native loads on his horse, his ass, or his camel. They tell me that the geometric designs they bear are always stylized representations of the yurt in the midst of some wide pasture-ground, the arik cutting across it, and the flowers and horse in the field.

In front of the open mouth of a chai-kana oven street boys are squattin, warming their hands. Selling shirts, some squawking women stand over their heads, one with a gold star in her nose.

A beggar passes, puts some embers into a skimmer, burns a few leaves in it, and proffers you the perfume.

[1] Bokhara rug.

No one has any idea what my Leica is, but whenever I handle it, people rush up and want to buy it. The commercial instinct is very active in this decayed metropolis. Everyone one meets is nibbling something : almonds, ouriouks, or grapes taken casually from some stall.

A lorry rolls by, leaving behind it an unusual odour of petrol; the smell is astonishing to nostrils accustomed to the dusty effluvias of urine. But really to enter into the lives of the ants that surround me, one must do as they do : buy or sell. I roam around therefore, with my hands in front of me, offering a hair clipper, which I had once brought to take on a long cruise under sail. I ask twenty roubles, but am prepared to come down to ten. I have also a knife and a ten-franc watch bought at Woolworth's.

The usual sharks, in their determination not to let a bargain slip by them, hurl themselves on me the moment I enter the alley that resounds to the hammers of the tinkers.

A man with a reddish beard, painted eyes, and reddened nails, fingers the edge of my blade disdainfully. . . . Still I do well, for I take myself off with a total of thirty-five roubles, and buy a water-melon for four of them.

I have hardly begun to finger a pair of flannel trousers being waved about by a burly Russian, when he shouts brutally, as they all do, in fact :

" But take it! Why don't you take it ? " as though it annoyed him I should be so stupid as to let such a bargain slip for a mere thirty roubles.

At times I stop suddenly, on the point of stretching my hand out to some man, in spite of his turban, so strong in me is the feeling that I have known him for years. No doubt he is a Tajik : and I sense the same blood in us both.

In front of a chai-kana a painted native girl, with vulgar prominent teeth, is drinking alone. At her feet the skull cap vendors are almost suffocated by the crowd whenever a telega rolls by. The butcher roars out loudly, assailed in the midst of his cuts of scarlet camel flesh.

There are many who can say with the passing dervish

whose sole ornament is his calabash: "My glory is in poverty." A nougat merchant whose hands feel cold, buries them in his armpits. His nose is full of yellow liquid.

A woman is pinching both sides of her olive-coloured kerchief between her moist lips. Ancient women with pallid eyelids and brown scabs at the corners of the mouth hold wooden bowls out. Rain falls and reanimates the colours of the padded shoulders of much worn khalats. . . .

To get through the crowd, people rush forward into the wake of some passing ' arba '; on one I see a family round someone dying. His eyes are turned up and water is running over him. . . .

All, all, and everywhere, are but living corpses, battling with existence with more or less success. . . . I, too, motionless and watching. It is all a question of the more or less!

The Odour of Death

The population has dwindled to forty thousand inhabitants. For one house that still stands three are collapsing, for the house dies with the head of the family. Each builds its own dwelling.

There are tombs on the roofs. "Some holy man has merited the right to be interred there, and maintain his place among the living, thus avoiding the cemetery among the sand-dunes: that terrible equality into which Moslem death and all death precipitates the living. Rags and tufts of hair flutter from the barred window." (Henry de Monfreid.)

Everywhere there hangs the vague decaying odour of ancient unaerated sand: the smell seems more intense in the vast cemeteries, where the feet sink silent on the loess paths. It is a sea of mounds, completely identical, through which I steer a course towards a clump of trees, glowing with every autumnal colour. The wind has piled masses of dead leaves in the courtyard of an abandoned mosque. Round it is a colonnaded peristyle.

I find the same odour again in the Chor Minar mosque,

with its ruined cells like black and empty eye-sockets. The entrance passes under a group of four minarets, each with a turquoise helmet, each surmounted by a nest of storks.

A drunkard falls down in the street, and whenever he tries to rise, the women, with their variegated kerchiefs, laugh hilariously.

In another cemetery tombs are being demolished in order to lay bare the mausoleum of Ismael the Samanid, slowly being silted up by sand. From the alveolae piled high issues a chill air that smells of rotten earth, and also somewhat of the dead silkworms of the heaped cocoons. Decomposed bones and stuffs lie about among the ruins. The dead are not crushed under the earth, but vaults are built over them.

The mausoleum of Ismael, the oldest monument in Turkestan, dates from the tenth century; it is a small hemisphere resting on a cube of colourless bricks, which at times project and make a geometrical design.

But the tomb of Chetchma Ayoub—the Spring of Job—is much stranger, for it is a simple cone of projecting bricks which rises, solitary, above the surrounding anonymous tombs. It is said that Job, having reached this spot, bent down to drink, and that as he did so, a place for shelter burgeoned round him.

Yes, death is everywhere: in these numerous abandoned madrasahs where enamelled bricks strew the earth, in these great cisterns whose dried-up terraces look like strange arenas, and in the abandoned patios.

But what still survives, moves one more deeply than anything in any other region of the world. Unforgettable is the amazing flowery freshness of the façade of coloured tiles of Abdul Aziz. Purity of line, elegance of proportion, riot of colour, in this posy is contained all the beauty of the madrasah with the lovely sounding name; its open, laughing courtyard, its two chambers with frescoes of purple and gold, and its stalactite ceilings.

Opposite it, the austere Ulug Beg with its narrow courtyard, its high walls framing the silence, inspires to meditation.

What mystery lies in the classic proportions! The lofty Iwan-arch lined by a row of spiral columns, moves me to veneration. Built in the fifteenth century, two hundred years before the tottering Abdul Aziz, it still stands solid and demands no prop.

But where the grandiose is concerned, the Kalan mosque—which means the great—has no compare.

From the height of the hundred and seventy feet of the Tower of Death which flanks it, and from which the Emir caused those condemned to death to be flung, one looks down upon the immense courtyard, the turquoise cupola over the sanctuary, and its central pediment facing the little pavilion for ablutions.

During festivals a colossal red carpet used to cover the stones of the pavement. How magical the effect must have been against the lovely silk brocades worn by the great ones of the earth!

Those Who Passed

Since the Khalan dates from the eleventh century, from my point of vantage I could have seen Jenghiz Khan in 1220 go into the pulpit—having just taken the city with one hundred and fifty thousand men—and proclaim himself the Scourge of Allah. I could have seen him command sages to give food to his horses from the wooden cases in which the Korans were kept.

On each side of the courtyard a triple-vaulted arcade stands, supported on enormous cubical pillars. It is dark under them, and an oppressive weight, as in some Romanesque cathedral, seems to bear down on my shoulders. The altar, mirhab, is only an oblong of designs in enamel.

The light is of so rare a quality that it demands pure, simple lines to strike upon; stained glass and sculpture lose all point in it.

Outside, on the vast open space at the foot of Chir Arab, the largest of all the schools in Bokhara, stands the shouting,

swarming crowd of a sale by auction. Raised on either side
of the doorway, two auctioneers yell out the bids. Mantles,
chapans, cushions, sewing machines, kerchiefs, pieces of silk,
knives, boots, every sort of thing is being dealt in by the
active multitude, that looks so minute, at the foot of the
immense façade whose wall is hollowed into two tiers of
niches.

Vambery, the intrepid traveller, disguised as a pilgrim,
visited Bokhara in the days when the Emir punished with
death every European entering the city.

Wearing a turban on his head, and with the Koran hanging
from his neck, he must have passed through some such crowd,
with the people begging him to breathe his holy breath on
them, and give them some of his powder of the house of
the Prophet, brought back from Medina, sovereign against
diseases.

A striking contrast! The great square in front of the Ark
is deserted: but above the monumental gates, the Emir's
palaces are now a Technicum for training teachers. The haus,
still full of water, lies at the foot of the Bala Khan mosque,
which is now the club of the workers. It is an immense
gallery, entirely of carved wood, the ceiling supported by a
double row of tall wooden columns, which, narrowing as they
rise, stand like the trunks of parallel palms.

It was here that in 1843, and with Bible in hand, another
European entered the city: the Reverend Joseph Wolff.
" These poor, darkened souls devoutly touched my book," he
says. His object was to discover the fates of two fellow
countrymen, Stoddart and Conolly, permitted by the Emir
to enter Bokhara on a commercial mission.

They had been guilty of a certain untactfulness, and the
court intrigues so poisoned their case that the issue at last
proved fatal. Thus Wolff's visit was a somewhat risky one.

" His Majesty the Emir Nasir Ullah Bahadur," he writes,
" was seated in the balcony of his palace looking down upon
us: thousands of people in the distance. All eyes were bent
on me to see if I would submit to the etiquette. When the

Shekaul (the Minister for Foreign Affairs) took hold of my shoulders, I not only submitted to his doing so to me three times, but I bowed repeatedly and exclaimed unceasingly: ' Peace to the King, Salamat Padishah ! ' until His Majesty burst into a fit of laughter, and of course all the rest standing round us."

Wolff was dressed in red and black, for he wore his gown wherever he visited the Emir. The Emir asked him to explain the reason for the particular colours.

" The black indicates that I am in mourning for my dear friends, the red that I am ready to give my blood for my faith."

This Nasir Ullah was a terrible man : he had killed five of his brothers in order to mount on the throne. Nasir Ullah was like a starving dog for blood, because he had had a Kazak wet-nurse, and the Kazaks were called eaters-of-men, being accused of feeding on corpses.

The Emir also remarked wonderingly :

" I can kill as many Persians as I like, and no one bothers. But I have hardly laid a hand on two Englishmen, when a person arrives from remote London commissioned to look into the matter."

At this period the city numbered one hundred and eighty thousand inhabitants, and every house had its own Persian slave.

All this past grandeur is utterly dead. At the moment it is only cotton that counts, and the mullahs who express their hostility to the throwing open of the ' chedras ' get themselves beaten by the women for their pains.

Can cotton resuscitate Bokhara, that fallen city ?

CHAPTER XII

Towards the Amu Daria

W HERE IS THE 6.30 bus?" I say to the employee at the terminus.

"I don't know: the second driver has not turned up yet."

"And the first?"

"He left in the night with his bus empty."

There's not a chance of the train at Kagan waiting for me. What a nuisance! In spite of all the driver's weight on the accelerator, the lost time cannot be made up.

It is no longer a cloud of dust that the lorries raise immediately the surfaced road comes to an end, but a dense sea of fog. At times a string of terrified camels emerges from it, walking askew, and sidling away like waves when cut by the ship's bows. They are wearing muzzles of coarse cloth, upon which their breath gleams as it turns into frost: while above their noses a tuft of wool rises upright into the air. Is it because they need a sight to help them to walk straight? The two swelling sacks of the load meet on the camel's back and hang to the earth on either side, enormous grey circumflex accent marks, moving onwards, at even distances and with an equal rhythm.

The foliage of the cotton plants is stunted and turned brown by the frost. On the horizon stretch yellow trees under a delicately tinted blue sky.

At the side of the road the heaps of round paving stones have a coating of powder, Rachel shade, like the cheeks of an actress going on the stage.

We have missed the mail train. It is barely seventy-five miles to Charjui on the Amu Daria, and to avoid a long wait I make do with a 'Maxim' on the point of leaving. In each of the goods wagons tattered Kazak families are camped, killing time by searching each other for fleas.

A railwayman tells me that a passenger coach has just been coupled-on, and that I shall be more comfortable there than with the Kazaks. I find myself opposite a man with greying hair, silent up to the moment when he sees my water-tight watch, upon which he asks me where it was made, and we begin to talk. For real loquacity give me someone you have never met before and whom, in a few hours, anonymous to all eternity, you will never see again.

Touching on the great deserts that surround Khiva, I had heard stories of brigands, who, mounted on swift unshod horses with large hoofs well adapted to the sand, time and again escaped their pursuers led by the Reds, soon decimated by the hard life.

Could it perhaps be Djunaid, continuing to make his raids, impregnable in the depths of the waste expanses? Khiva, that isolated city, difficult of access, where possibly the Soviet power prevails less than in other places, attracts me. Besides, the curator of the antiquities of Bokhara, a man of great erudition, the walls of whose dwelling were lined with scientific works, had told me of a strange city, the ancient Mongol capital, situated near the shores of the Sea of Aral, destroyed by invading sand, and where, still standing, might be seen monuments that date from the eleventh century.

I therefore tried to find out how to get to Khiva, and whether there was a passenger service along the Amu Daria. The air route Charjui-Khiva was too dear for me. But the curator in Bokhara had counselled me not to undertake the voyage to these savage regions.

In the town there was no information of any kind to be had from the railway station. For two hours on end the clerk had tried in vain to get the station-master on the telephone, and he, in the end, could tell us nothing. (Oh, what a science this telephoning has become: the skill it needs to turn the handle that rings the exchange, twenty-three times one way, and then suddenly reversing the action, to end up with seven turns backwards. When there's no reply from the office, the thing to do, of course, is to blow energetically down the mouthpiece.)

" Do you know how one can get to Khiva? " I ask my neighbour in the train.

" By aeroplane in four hours, twice a week."

" And otherwise? "

" I don't know."

" Is there much cotton also in the Khiva oasis? "

" In Kharezm, yes; more and more."

" But what induced the natives to grow cotton? "

" They were encouraged to do so by being offered all kinds of advantages: but they practically have to do so if they want to be in a position to buy anything at all from the Co-operative stores, which control all grain and manufactured products. Indeed, they are often told what proportion of the land they can plant with barley, rice, maize, or fruit trees."

" But is there anything to be found in the Co-operatives? "

" Often the ones most distant from the centres are the best stocked. That's good politics. My sister came to live at Turt Köl, and brought some soap from Moscow that she had managed to buy at five roubles a cake, after hours of searching. When she got here, she found she could get as much as she wanted in the market at two roubles a time. It's chiefly corn that is lacking here, for what is sold in the bazaar is hellishly dear."

" Where is this Turt Köl? "

" It's the capital of the Karakalpaks on the Amu Daria."

The train stops in the midst of a waterless waste. Massed near the railway line are camels, and bales of cotton are being unloaded and then weighed, while mounds of corn lie open to the sky.

From the Kazak wagons comes a muffled knocking, which is repeated all down the train. Intrigued, I discover that the women are pounding grain in mortars, and making their own flour.

The children ask to be lifted out on the ground. They

have a quarter of a shirt over their shoulders, and scabs on their heads. A woman rewinds her white turbaned head-dress, the only article of her clothing which is not in shreds, and I see her matted hair and long silver ear-rings. Her baby, hanging to her gown, supports itself on thin sticks of legs, whose knee-bones stick out prominently. There is no flesh on its little backside, which looks like a wrinkled bladder hanging in numerous folds.

Whence do they come? What are they going to?

Charjui

Now only desert surrounds us: sucked up by the sand, the last trickle of the Zeravshan, father of Samarkand and Bokhara, disappears fifteen miles before reaching the Amu Daria, the great Oxus that issues from the Pamirs.

The desert encroaches at the rate of a little more than half a mile a century. The water recedes not only because new ariks are added to the system, but because the western winds pile up large symmetrical crescent-shaped sand-dunes, the 'barkhans.'

Attempts are being made to acclimatize special forms of vegetation in order to check this encroachment, which in places proceeds at the rate of fifty to sixty yards a year.

The irrigatory system has not only to water the fields, but, even more important, to wash out and carry away the salts that impregnate the ground. Then the earth is rendered fertile by the loess dust conveyed by the wind.

It annoys me to think of just stupidly sitting in the train until it gets to the Caspian and Black Sea, and so I get out at Charjui with the object of trying to book a passage down the Amu Daria.

My luggage deposited in the cloak-room, I begin to make inquiries. The station-master sends me to the shipping office, which I find shut though it is barely four. In front of the door two women sit on their packages: one crying.

"I can't stand any more: to-morrow I shall go back to Samara."

"Why, no!" says the other. "Now you have come so far, the worst is over. Novo Urgenj is quite near."

Quite near? When the boat takes eight days, and as for motor-lorries and the 'hydroglisseur,' there isn't a free place available for the next ten days. As for travelling by aeroplane, no money on earth would buy a passage.

"I want to go to the docks; where are they?" I say to them.

"Five miles from here, over there, on the other side of the island. Perhaps we'll go too?"

But I leave them behind, and their slowness and indecision, as I follow one of the railway lines through the outskirts of the city. There, below me, the Kazaks of the train have collected in small groups, and are beginning to set their tents up, a hundred of them, dark and sombre. What is going to become of them? Have they escaped from some totally abandoned region? Will they perish of hunger? And then I ask myself whether all that is being done to improve the common lot may not arrive too late to save the country, though I know that in Asia human lives count as nothing.

The line ends among vast warehouses, near a shipyard, where I see metal barges on the stocks. A dyke crosses a narrow canal, and I pass over it to a marshy island dotted with sparse reeds.

At the Haven

A floating pontoon lies by the sandy bank, and there I find the harbour offices. Casks of oil, bales of cotton, and three large modern tents in which live numerous Russians, lie facing it.

"Good day, comrade ticket-seller, when does your next boat leave?"

"To-morrow at dawn, but everything is full, both cabins and deck."

" Are there boats on the Sea of Aral, and have you a service going there? "

" We have cargo boats on the Aral that go from Kantousiak at the mouth of the Amu, as far as Aralskoie More. But from Turt Köl and Novo Urgenj there is only an unregular service and kayuks."

Every moment prospective passengers unsuccessfully try to book place for the morrow.

" Comrade, my wife is very ill, she cannot possibly live through a long stay in this place."

" Comrade, look, here's a telegram from my dying father in Turt Köl."

" No! we cannot take another person. We have booked a hundred and forty already in place of the regulation ninety, not to mention ten tons of freight."

" Comrade," I say in my turn, " look at my papers, I am a journalist, and have come a very long distance to visit your region. But now I am pressed for time and am only too willing to dispense with a cabin."

" Very well then, be there at six to-morrow morning. I shall be seeing the passengers on board. Thirty-five roubles to Novo Urgenj, on deck."

Sometimes it is indeed a privilege to be a foreigner.

My stuff is at the station. I go back to get it. The cloakroom is shut, for the man has gone away for a meal. I resign myself to wait. Night falls. I spot an isvostchik and ask him what he would charge to take me to the haven.

" No, miss, I don't go that way at night : there are Bassmatchi about, and I want to keep my horse."

The chafferers near the station have not even lipiochkas to sell. There are only green melons at a rouble a slice, but their deliciousness baffles description, the white perfumed flesh is so delicate, sweet and refreshing, and melts in the mouth! It was these same renowned melons that, packed in mountain snow, were brought to the Caliphs of Baghdad, Mamun, and Watik, in hermetically sealed tin boxes.

I go forward slowly, for my load is a heavy one. At the

gateway into the docks a watchman prods my sacks and assures himself I am no incendiary. I stop for a brief moment in a nook, where the breath-taking odour of tar inundates me with new strength.

Men are at work on the barges: the air is filled with the fantastic and dazzling blue light of electric welding.

Then I have left them behind, moving onwards into the empty darkness, and stumbling in the deep sand of the track.

There is no hurry: all the night is in front of me. Suppose I rest again? What's that? I heard someone spit! Someone is coming after me! I hope he doesn't see me! No, frightened himself, he steps back!

"Comrade! Taking a rest?" he asks, only partially reassured.

"Yes, I am going to the haven, but my sack is heavy."

He laughs at his fears, gives me a hand, and we arrive at the water-side of the wide northward-flowing river.

He is in charge of a little cutter, and I unfold my sleeping-bag on the planks of its gently rocking hull. The sound of lapping water against the planking on which my head rests fills me with mad joy. Once more I have found my ever faithful friend, the running water, with its smell, its movement, its caprice. Forward, sitting in their minute quarters, three men are drinking tea.

They must be talking of past adventures, for I hear the words 'Rostov, Baltic . . .' and I begin thinking of all those men who at outlying posts in France, in similar fo'c'sles, swap stories with each other of ancient voyages to Mauretania and Iceland.

On waking, I see a rope moving over my head and sit up. A kayuk has glided up to the side, a huge empty barge, in which is a native pushing it off with a pole, while its prow is adorned with a horse's tail. On the banks the crew tows against the current, every man wearing a great black busby.

The water is the colour of *café-au-lait*, and into this my friend plunges his kettle to be filled. At the foot of the bank people wash their hands and faces.

CHAPTER XIII

THE "PELICAN'S" STORE-ROOM

THE *Pelican* that is to bear away the elect arrives. It turns out to be a paddle-boat.

We are hardly under way before we pass beneath the immense railway bridge built thirty years ago: twenty-five arches, each two hundred and thirty feet wide.

The current is rapid—five miles an hour—and navigation difficult because of the shallow water and shifting sandbanks. Poles stuck in the river-bed mark the channel, and the bearded pilot, a blond Tartar, remains constantly on the poop.

During the floods, after the April rains and the melting snows of June, this great river, nearly nine hundred miles in length, is chocolate colour. It is then some two miles wide, with its greatest depth sixty-five feet, in a place where the river narrows to three hundred yards. Even before the Revolution there were boats plying here similar to those on the Volga.

Something goes wrong with the engines: an anchor drops. The sound of hammering comes through the skylight of the engine-room: then we start again.

One of the passengers, an engineer named Lavrov, accompanied by two students with whom I have entered into conversation, invites me to eat some cold chicken on his bunk. He is in charge of the work at Tiuya Mouyoun, where a colossal barrage has been planned. He greatly admires my six-bladed penknife that was bought in London.

As night is falling, the *Pelican* swerves round, with its bows to the current, and comes to a stop, digging its nose into the crumbling banks. Before retiring for the night, we go ashore to stretch our legs among the rank vegetation, some of which burns and crackles in a great fire.

The deck, the bench that goes all round it, and the paddle-box, are all occupied by sleepers; but I spot the store-room of the ship's steward and install myself on his roof, and am thus able to look down on the crowded decks.

On shore the red smear of the reed fire is a bleeding wound that writhes and shudders in the flesh of night.

Only the three wires of the wireless antennae separate me from the stars, like a fragile parapet on the edge of an abyss that is one mass of glittering sparks.

The *Pelican* has been *en route* some time when the chill morning wind awakens me. From my eyrie I see kayuks sailing against the current, with their great square sails belly-ing in the wind, the part of the sail near the yard much darkened by exposure to the weather. It makes me think of the sails of the *Santa Maria* as shown in old engravings.

As we pass them, I see bales of cotton, the twenty teapots of the crew in a line along the freeboard, and their busbies hanging from cleats in the mast, like so many scalps. Stand-ing in the bows is the look-out, and an enormous oar does the work of a rudder.

But often the kayuk is a long way out of the channel, keeping to where the current runs least strong.

From my position I need not see the deck. My gaze soars away into the immense horizon. Nothing prevents me imagining I am some wealthy tourist who has fitted out her yacht to take her to Khiva, the Khanate which, longer than any other, preserved its independence. It is the Oxus of the Greeks I am navigating, the Oecous, Okous-Sou—the ox's water. At my command my men have started my engines up. The muffled noises of my crew come only to me dimly. Soon the steward will be saying: "Breakfast is ready, Milady!"

For stewards always talk in English, and there will be eggs and bacon, toast, and . . . but let that go. . . .

In actuality I set up my Primus in the mechanic's cubby hole, and boil a little river water for my tea. I am very grateful for the hospitality, for I save the two or three roubles it costs to pay for the soup which the cook serves to the public, and then, too, it is forbidden to cook on deck.

An even-tempered man is Vassily Ivanovitch, dressed in a shapeless blouse, with a cigarette-holder stuck in his teeth, and a greasy face like that of every mechanic on earth. His cabin is clean.

" What a job ! Eight months now we've been forcing this wretched coffee-mill for all she's worth. I don't know how she stands up to it. But we won the bonus, for we got more voyages to our credit than the *Kommunar*. What a crowd there is on board, and to think that on the return journey we never have more than ten."

A mighty roar : the ' hydroglisseur ' bounds along the water at forty miles an hour and disappears : what do the camels on the bank make of it ? Six hours later it will have reached Turt Köl. We shall get there in six days, that is if we don't run aground.

The landscape is reduced to a mere assemblage of horizontal lines; the dun-coloured stroke of the sand, gold of the grass, blue of sky. How is it that the brown water seems such a limpid blue when the sky is reflected in it ? The round backs of sandbanks emerge.

The western shore turns into a cliff, upon which identically repeated barge-haulers follow each other at equal distances, twelve or fifteen of them with a twist of the rope caught round the shoulder, the body leaning so far forward that the arm not in use reaches to the ground. All move with the same foot, a long step followed always by a short. Far behind follows the kayuk, towed from the top of the mast.

Behind them the sky is an ochreous blue turning to vermilion : it is sunset.

A violent shock : the boat stops. We have grounded broadside-on to the current, which seems to laugh at us as it gurgles against our hull and scours a bed for us to lie in. There is barely a foot and a half of water under us, but by strenuous work with the poles, with everyone taking part and nearly bending double in the effort, we push ourselves off again and gain the shore. It seems to me the waters of the Styx must be dense and fluid in this way.

"To-night we shall have to set a watch," says Vassili. "There are Bassmatchi round about here; they have attacked and robbed the regular motor-coach and kidnapped four Russian women."

"Oh! if only there were an attack. How useful my front seat would be!"

But dawn begins to glimmer and nothing has happened. All I can see is the black band of the earth between the paling sky and water. As soon as we begin to advance the cold is piercing, and hurriedly I tuck in my hands, after hiding my head under the flap of my sleeping-bag.

Then to the east the horizon begins to shake out long, rainbow-coloured streamers. And when this play of colour is over, the earth is lilac between gold sky and water.

There are black camels at the foot of the smooth suède-like dunes. On the opposite uninterrupted bank the grasses look like the stiff bristles of some great unkempt brush.

We spy some yurts like brown mushrooms in the brushwood, and land in the hope of revictualling ourselves. It is a mad stampede, everyone wanting to be first. There are melons at four and five roubles apiece, and an immense Turkoman wearing felt boots, with a black sheepskin hat on his head, cutting up the carcase of a ram and spitting the pieces on a picket stuck in the earth. The women are draped in scarlet calico that spreads over their tall, tiara-shaped coiffures.

We pass a large tug and two iron barges.

I gaze at the furrows which the wake of our boat spreads over the surface of the water: the colour is like a piece of taffeta that changes from buff to blue, crumpling at moments in the eddies.

Before us, sky and water are indistinguishable from each other, and we drift on towards a line of sand that looks like a shelf set in walls of sky.

Then we anchor off Dargan Ata. The township, settled by

Russians, is three miles away in an unknown direction. With Lavrov, I go on board a motor-kayuk ascending the river, and we eat a couple of pheasants in company with a hydrographer returning from Tiuya Mouyoun. Bad news: a man has just been killed there by a Bassmatch. The same thing has happened too in the white building on the opposite shore. It is a ewe-breeding Sovkhoz.

The hydrographer has spent a winter in the Syrt, and tells me that there were many Kirghiz then passing into China.

On the *Pelican* one of the students is down with fever, but has no quinine. I give him some. Our pilot hears of it and asks me for some too. He gives me some bread in exchange, for I have not been able to buy any since Bokhara.

Kayuks

I wake to voices crying " Fish! " A net is being hauled up on the beach, with an enormous struggling fish in it. The beast is white and green and has a round snout: its local name is ' sohm ': it belongs to the order of silurians.

A kayuk lies stranded in the middle of the river, and all its crew is in the water heaving with their backs against the clincher-built side. Another kayuk passes with the men in it rowing upright, their backs to the prow: the flats of the oars are simple boards nailed to long poles. From a distance the black head-dresses of the men, their ' chugurmas,' look like black pinheads.

But most of the traffic is under sail. Sometimes the eyes will see a score of them, of all sizes, lined out along the liquid road. Where the river makes sudden turns, they seem to have got quite out of hand and to be wandering over the low-lying land.

When the sail has to be hoisted the kayuk draws inshore and the sail is spread on the ground. The men climb up the mast, and hang in a cluster to the halyard, whereupon the great-yard rises into the air, carrying the open sail.

With a good following wind, these kayuks can travel against the current almost as fast as the *Pelican*.

At the stops, the Uzbek sailors live on the poop under the open sky. The simple, but grandiose scene, seems to me to belong to the legendary past of the *Thousand and one Nights*. From the prow, adorned with the tail of a horse—protection against ill luck—a deck descends in two levels towards the big round oven of earth. The men squat in a semicircle on this platform, their backs against the sides, wrapped closely in their padded cassocks, with the long, undulating curls of the huge chugurmas round their heads, and each with a teapot near at hand.

The cook bustles about his hive-shaped oven; on top, in the large cast-iron boiler, cooks the dough for lipiotchkas; underneath, branches stick out of the furnace. Armed with enormous tongs, the cook extracts a copper pitcher from the embers by clasping it round the neck, and inclines it over the teapots that are passed to him.

Motionless, without a gesture, or a word, and with the dignity of caliphs, each waits for his teapot to be placed in front of him. At the bottom of each bowl a brown sandy deposit remains of undissolved cocoa powder.

Vassili allows me to have half his copious ration of meat-soup, macaroni, or potatoes. But he loses my pipe that a great navigator, now in the Antipodes, once gave me. I am bitterly angry with him, and promise him six new ones if he can only find my lost one.

" Last night," he says, " I put it in the pocket of my blouse as I was going to Dargan Ata : but there was a hole in it, and it must have slipped through. . . ."

I had lent it him in return for his hospitality.

We were approaching the ravine in which Tiouya Mouyoun is situated, and Lavrov suggested I might land and spend a few days seeing the work they were doing, for the scheme envisaged the irrigation of some seventy-five thousand acres. There were also Turkmen encampments that might be visited in the vicinity. He even offered to provide me with bread and flour, an offer not to be despised. When Lavrov was going ashore, therefore, I was close upon his heels. But not till I was actually on the gangway did he say:

"No, it would be better if you did not come!"

What a strange person! Could he have changed his mind when he saw that I would not sell my penknife to him at any price?

Setting off on an exploring expedition among the overhanging vegetation of the Holy Isle at which we had put in, and giving a wide berth to the bonfires, the songs and the accordions of the passengers, I chanced upon a hut of reeds, and by the light of an oil lamp perceived the dignified faces of numbers of Turkmen, most arresting under their black bonnets, who fell silent when they saw me. Could it have been a gathering of Ali Baba's Forty Thieves, or, better, Shamans preparing something magic. I sensed that it would be better not to stay, and returned again to the roof of my store-room.

A friendly woman, going home after a holiday spent in the Caucasus, had offered me some bread: when I met her again she says:

"During the night someone stole my loaf. But if you go ashore at Turt Köl you can get some there, for they have everything one needs."

Astonishing words, heard for the first time, which amply explain the rush to the country of the Karakalpaks.

A little conical mountain near the shore is attributed to Jenghiz Khan. When he reached this place, his men had each to pour a hatful of earth out on this spot. Returning from their conquests they had to repeat the same gesture, whereupon the Inflexible Emperor, comparing the two heaps, was able to estimate the number of warriors he had lost.

CHAPTER XIV

TURT KÖL[1]

TWO TENTS IN a cotton field: such is the port. It is impossible to put anything up, for the river eats into the cliff and huge blocks of sand collapse with muffled thuds.

An arba puts me down in front of the Goverment building in the main square, over a mile away, and I go in to find out where I can stay.

" But there must be a tourist 'base' of some sort; we voted a subsidy."

" Can you tell me also the best place to find a reliable caravan going to Astrakhan or Orenburg? "

" But from Kungrad or Tashauz, it's at least thirty to forty days to Orenburg, and you'll freeze on the way. I advise you not to try it. You don't know what it is to be on a camel in thirty degrees of frost."

In another office, situated in the same immense square, the president of the Society for Proletarian Tourists, a young Karakalpak with moustaches, goes into transports of joy at the sight of me.

" You are our first tourist. Comrades! A tourist, a tourist from Paris, from France! "

" What's that, a tourist? " asks his secretary.

" It's . . . but you've got your papers? You write in this book . . . Ella . . . no, not there. . . . That's where you put the destination. . . ."

The secretary accompanies me to the Dekhan house, that is, the peasants' hostelry.

The master is out: his little girl tells me there is not a foot of space available anywhere. And indeed the dormitories are packed. There is a housing crisis. Turt Köl, Petro-Alexandrovsk in the past, numbers twenty thousand inhabitants.

[1] Four-lakes.

I go back to the office, storming.

"You don't care a hang for your tourists! You've made no arrangements at all for putting them up. What's the point of making me waste my time fruitlessly. Sign some coupons for bread, sugar, tea, oil, and rice for me, and I'll leave immediately."

Whereupon a Russian employee, calm and collected, says: "Come with me: we'll find you room at home all right."

When we arrive his wife is waiting, the soup is ready, and his little girl is back from school.

For ten days I shall be the guest of this charming family, where the woman makes a practice of drying bread crusts in the oven, to send them in a box to her student son in Tashkent. I shall stay ten days, because I have decided I must develop my delicate films. Suddenly I am afraid they may spoil after six months of constant changes of temperature. But there I made a mistake.

I get some developer from a friendly architect passionately keen on photography, and whenever the dark room is available pass my evenings at the House of the Commune.

There is no running water, however, in which to wash the films, for the ariks are all dry at this season, and I have to go to the well which still contains water from the Amu Daria. It is excellent, if the sediment is allowed to settle, but the water from other wells, though clear as crystal, contains salts which would utterly ruin my negatives.

Fortunately, the moon illumines the ditch and its slippery edges of damp clay.

But now it turns cold, with the setting in of the gales from the Kizil Kum, the desert of Red Sands. The leaves are torn from the trees, and the people go muffled up. Every fifteen minutes I break into violent gymnastics to get myself warm again.

It was then that, falling a victim to my own anxiety, and agonizingly afraid of seeing my negatives spoilt, I ruin the spool recording my ascent of Sari Tor; views I could never have taken but for an epic concentration of will. Rarely has my silliness seemed to me so painful a burden to bear as on that day.

Under the Soviets

For important festivals celebrating the Revolution, a platform is put up in the square, while a triumphal arch bears the words, " Prepared for Labour and Defence," under the side view of an airship *Voroshilof.*

Bearing banners and bannerets, delegations pass by from schools, offices, and kolkhozes, each accompanied by a host of people. In the midst of the dark winter overcoats stands an interested group of native women, swathed in the white veils that fall from their heads.

The event of the day stretches ten miles, and is a procession of two hundred and fifty arbas, and fifteen hundred camels laden with cotton, for which wheat will be given in exchange.

The President of the Republic is an intelligent Karakalpak, whose speech, amplified by loud-speakers, is brief and to the point. He says: " We have barely touched the fringe of Socialism, yet already its results have been remarkable: we must persevere, that is the only way to vanquish the general ignorance."

Russians and ' Nationals ' mingle in the crowd. It is almost impossible to guess what is going on behind the narrow eyes of the latter. The wind blows the white beards of the old men about; the young are beardless and look well set-up and clean. The different kinds of head-dress would merit a detailed study. There is the ' toppo,' close fitting, the corrugated crown of the tiubiteka, the enormous ' chugurma ' a sort of weeping willow of curly hair, the ' kabardinka ' of grey astrakhan with a velvet top, and the immense round caracul brim of the ' papakha,' tight and spheroid like a big cabbage. There are many dark faces also under pale felt bonnets, that look like inverted tulips with three petals of thick fur turned up at each side and in front.

The sand begins at the very gates of the city, at the foot of the crenellated wall.

A camel stands motionless near a yurt, where to my great pleasure I am invited to drink tea.

The samovar sparkles in the sun, and the woman wears silver rings on her thumb and first finger, between which she holds her bowl.

Her robes are dazzling white, and a yellow silk kerchief covers her white hair. Her full, perfect features make her seem to me like some incomparable greengage.

The skull cap worn by her son is sewn with gold thread and adorned with bells and a tuft of feathers. Fearful, he refuses to let himself be photographed, and his bearded father has to hold him forcibly. At the back of the yurt glitter three coffers strengthened with plates of brass. The yurt is a rich one, lined with embroidered koshmous.

Then a young relative comes in, a Communist, studying at the Educational Technicum, deeply interested to find, from the maker's name on my watch, that he and I have the same alphabet. When he leaves, he takes all the bread cards of the family with him.

A Karakalpak Meeting

At times I interrupt my photographic work to see what is happening in the large adjoining hall. A meeting of the trade unions has gathered together the young 'Nationals' of the city.

An enormous amount of noise goes on during the speeches owing to private conversations and the incessant coming and going of people. At the end of every speech and its translation, a few bars of the *Internationale* are sung, as well as whenever the name of Stalin is mentioned.

My neighbour tells a Karakalpak to stop smoking, but in front of us a Russian calmly continues to puff at his cigarette wrapped in a piece of newspaper.

Those who have brought their oratorical feat to an end sit

down again, controlling with difficulty the immense satisfaction with which it has filled them.

The red kerchiefs of the Communists are extremely
becoming to the little Karakalpak women with their Japanese-
looking faces.

Those Who Come from the Desert

In the market there is an abundance of meat hanging
from the butchers' brackets, the price of which is not more
than five roubles a kilogram. Butter costs eight roubles a
pound, and three lipiotchkas can be bought for a rouble.
Potatoes cost thirty kopeks, and there are piles of enormous
white onions, heaps of melons, tomatoes, peppers. Turt Köl
is indeed a land flowing with milk and honey.

Fish is being fried, and the very smell makes one hungry;
there is the shashlik griller draped in a sleeved overall, surrounded by spectators; powdered green tobacco is being
sifted, so that the air is difficult to breathe and irritates the
nostrils; and all the work is done on the ground, sitting back
on one's heels.

A line of men wait in front of a Co-operative depot for
goloshes and matches. In the midst of the black caterpillar
formed by their bonnets, a Kirghiz with triangular eyes
introduces a note of white with his pointed felt hat. The
native women have their head-dress raised remarkably high,
on a sort of scaffolding, the turban wrapping it round: at
times a silver marguerite is stuck in their nostrils. They greet
each other by putting their hands in front of their mouths,
and then placing them in the hollow of each others' backs.

The old people walk holding each other by the hand.

At the lipiotchka maker's the cakes of bread pile up in
hundreds. The oven takes up practically a third of the dark
room. The mouth is quite the height of a man. A young
Persian, with black eyes and rapid gestures, inserts his arm up
to the shoulder in order to stick the dough against the walls:
he wears a sort of stuff tiara, and protects his face from the

heat by a handkerchief passed under the chin and knotted over the head.

The yellow-eyed baker is a Tajik, his other bearded workmen Uzbeks. In the back room, on a tripod set on the earth, onions are stewing, covered with a fine faience plate, peacock-blue.

But beyond the wood market, with camels laden with gnarled roots of the saxaul, their legs like an ✕, what surprises one most is the innumerable unharnessed arbas, a jumble of flat spokes and gigantic wheels; and the asses, horses, camels, that make the vast stables of an Asiatic metropolis.

A loud, raucous wheezing comes from the camels, whose nostrils are being brutally hurt: to make them kneel the men drag down the rope that hangs from their noses. Covered with down the young suck at their mothers, their humps hardly more than two tufts of brown hair. Cameleers and arbakeshes squat on their heels, talking or chaffering near their grainsacks, while the great wheels of the arbas mirror themselves faultlessly in the unrippled surface of a lake of urine. Patres familias pass, with an infant carried on their hands which are crossed above their buttocks. . . .

And there, magnificent and alone, and pounding the earth with chained feet, two lords of the desert stand surrounded by an admiring crowd, the muzzle of each covered with a thick frothy lather of whipped cream. From the head of the soaring dromedary rise two proud aigrettes of wool, one over the unpierced nose, the other over the forehead. From the bridle four rows of faded tassels hang along the neck. Above the knees are bracelets of little bells; and a larger bell hangs as a pendant from the collar.

The other beast is a bulky, enormous camel, which from time to time throws up its mighty neck like a swan: then gargles noisily, and casts into the air jets of froth that fall back in white flakes upon its ruffle.

A fine rug lies over each saddle, and from the cantles rises a tall plume. Other tassels dangle from the traces underneath their bellies.

And beyond is the wind whistling through cold, deserted avenues. Filthy and narrow streets are ' alive,' and that keeps one warm, I find, but in the wide, dirty avenues one seems to have strayed into some dreary suburb. . . .

Arrested

I telephone twice to the port. The early arrival of the *Kommunar* bound for Kopalik, the port of Novo Urgenj, which is an unavoidable stage on the journey to Khiva, is announced. I am anxious to leave as soon as possible. If this cold continues the Sea of Aral will freeze soon, and all navigation will be over for the season.

I take myself to the building where the State's motor-cars are garaged, backed by a paper which grants me the privilege of being driven to the port. The chauffeur refuses to have anything to do with it, and leaves me to my devices. The paper lacks a signature. I rage—for time is precious.

I rush back to the Sovnarkom, root out the secretary whose signature I need—a man who can hardly keep awake, he has so much to do, with a three-day growth on his face, though by nature as spick and span as an Englishman—and get to the river too late.

" Don't bother," says the booking clerk. " Any moment now a sloop may be leaving."

" Good. I'll stay. You'll let me know ! "

Whole families are camping out under the passengers' tent. The cold is so intense that it has forced everyone to disappear under their blankets. I tear some jugara stalks from the field outside to insulate me from the cold ground.

Then I make some tea. As I am buttering my bread my neighbour holds out a hand, and taking some of the butter melts it in her palms before rubbing it into her hair ; a primitive brilliantine, which, it would seem, acts as a preventive against lice. Her baby cries. These incessant infant cries, so identical with each other ! It almost seems that the same baby is crying wherever one goes. To make it stop, the mother makes a noise even louder than itself, and slaps it energetically. Every nose has a drop hanging from it.

Near some large anchored kayuks the sailors have made a conical tent with one of the sails supported on oars. They offer me tea and I warm myself at their fire. An ancient dame with an elaborately bound turban squats at my side; it is no longer steam that rises from her bowl, but a tiny cloud. The men look like youthful brigands.

The night is arctic, and the sides of our large tent clap sharply in the wind. Benumbed by the cold, I rise late. Seeing me walk into the office, the employee cries out:

" Why, I forgot all about you: a small motor-boat has just left. But Danieletz is here, the harbour-master at Kopalik, and he is leaving any moment now."

A motor-car drives up to the office, and a man gets out who says to me: " You are the foreigner from France. Follow me immediately."

There is no time to protest for the car starts off at once.

" But all my things are lying about; my stove and, what's most important, my camera."

" I'll telephone to the port to have everything collected."

What am I guilty of? If the man wants to have my things collected, it means I am not going to be brought back at once. I begin to be afraid. . . . If some department wants to earn a little kudos, it will be easy for them to find some photograph I should not have taken: the Bassmatchi or pictures of aeroplanes. And all the notes I left lying about! Have I at least destroyed the records of my visits to the exiles?

" What a baby I am; it's my lack of experience that has got me into this hole! "

Then follow explanations.

" Why did you not register your arrival at the office? "

" But the S.P.T., with whom I did register, is responsible for me. And I was in your office every day almost: why did no one ask me anything? "

" We thought you were spending the winter here. Your passport is in order. You'll be taken back to the port."

CHAPTER XV

KHIVA

A SMALL MOTOR-BOAT starts off at last, and eventually deposits Danieletz and myself on the bank, some twenty miles down the river, before it vanishes into a channel. We wait. A minute kayuk, crammed with men and merchandise, passes. Danieletz, a typical burly seafaring man, hails it imperiously. We are taken on board and glide away, swept along on the current.

"With luck, and if the cold breaks, you should be able to reach Kantousiak in time. On the Aral Sea navigation is impossible after November 22nd or 24th. In five days the *Lastotchka* is due to sail down the Amu: that's your last chance."

At Kopalik, a vast depot where sacks and bales lie open to the sky, I hire an arba for ten roubles and am driven to Novo Urgenj.

The deep tracks lead through a monotonous desert. It takes almost three hours to do the seven miles and a half.

I get off at the house of the postmaster, an Uzbek met on the *Pelican,* who had kindly invited me to visit him. I am very glad to be able to dispense, thanks to him, with the caravanserai, where one has continually to watch one's belongings.

In his one room we live in the Uzbek manner, eating and sleeping on the ground. Two babies play round the timid young wife who knows no Russian. She wears silky plaits, and her long trousers are tucked into fine leather boots.

She eats when her husband has finished, and waters the floor with the tea left at the bottom of the pialas. The big stove roars as it burns up the compressed cotton seed, thin cakes that break like brick. The man, lord and master, sleeps in the bed.

Next morning the mail arba leaves for Khiva, and I settle down on top of the big leather postal sacks in preparation for the twenty-two miles in front of me.

Immediately we have left the important centre of Novo Urgenj it is all flat buff and yellow loess.

The farmyards, with large geometrical designs carved in the pisé walls and their pretence of large round columns widening at the base, seem strangely African.

The ariks are all dry, and numerous working parties are cleaning them out. Nearby, some ' chigirs ' have been dismantled. This is a mechanism like a noriah, which raises water in pots that surround a large wheel. An ass walks round a circular platform, drawing an arm, and is able to raise some ninety gallons of water a minute. The great wheel and the broken pitchers were lying on the ground.

It is an exciting moment, when, in the deep ruts of the road, we are about to pass some arba. Which will give way to the other? At times, the vehicles stop nose to nose even, then the one most in a hurry swerves off to the embankment. We stop to water our horse, and the ground round the well-hole is invisible under an ice carapace. A centuries' old karagatch shades a mazar, a burying-place: there, three small mausolea rise over the tombs of the vulgar, their cupolas surmounted by green, glittering glass balls, like the truck of a mast.

In the middle of the day we stop to drink tea by the roadside where silent arbakeshes squat in front of the hearth of the chai-kana.

The arid autumn is melancholy under the blanched sun! In the fields they are picking cotton from dried, leafless stalks.

An immense smoking brick kiln, wireless masts, walls: Khiva at last. In the post office yard I go up to the young postmaster, a Russian, and say to him:

" I should like to go to the curator of the museum to ask him to put me up for a couple of days. Is it far from here? "

"Yes, pretty far. . . . But he's an Uzbek who knows no Russian. You would do better to stay with us. . . .

A proposition which I accept immediately. His wife is energetic, hustles him about, and deals with the baby and our tea at one and the same time.

A post office employee enters, a German with a pointed beard and blue eyes. In reply to my astonishment, he says:

" We have a German colony here at Ak Metchet that has been in existence over fifty years. Originally we came from our Republic on the Volga. In that great building facing us, the hospital, there is my brother, an accountant ill with jaundice. His little girl has pneumonia, and perhaps you could take a photograph of her: we should then have some token by which to remember her should she not recover. My brother has also studied theology and sometimes takes charge of our prayer meetings: we are Mennonites."

We cross the street. In the hospital yard there is a small Co-operative depot for the use of the staff. Our credentials are checked twice carefully, then we are allowed to penetrate into an antechamber, where we leave our coats and don white overalls.

Herr Quiring is in bed. I see a refined face with drawn-out features and moustaches, and an emaciated high forehead that makes me think of Romain Rolland. The sad little girl, whose face is framed in short fair hair, hardly replies to me, Her mother, young, with splendid teeth and a happy expression, grave grey eyes, and a wide brow under the diadem of thick fair plaits, is nursing them both.

" We Germans cannot complain," she says, " we have good jobs and earn good money. You should visit our colony nine miles from here."

" Mammy, when shall we see the photographs? "

" We must wait till the young lady has finished her long journey, far away, farther than Berlin even! "

The mother dresses the child and ties a bow in her hair with a piece of gauze in place of a ribbon. The child smiles at last, when I say with my camera raised:

" Show me how much you love your mother! "
Then she puts her arms round her mother's neck and hugs
her very tight.

Exploration

To avoid a new arrest for the offence committed at Turt
Köl, this time I announce my arrival to the O.G.P.U. before
starting to wander about in Khiva, city of nightingales.

Inside the walls of the Nourlla-Bai, where only important
persons dwelt, is the relatively modern house of the last Khan
—now a public library, with dark rooms of painted wood—
surrounded by impressive avenues of black karagatches.

On a pedestal, dazzling white among the trees, stands a
bust of Lenin. Facing him, a loud-speaker is fastened to a
pillar.

The harem is a battlemented fortress surrounded by tur-
reted walls. The numerous courtyards, with tall balconies and
loggias supported on elegant wooden columns, now serve to
house the Pedagogic Institute, where once the eighty wives
of the Khan sat aimlessly about.

I cannot help wondering where Captain Burnaby was
lodged: that strange phenomenon which the whole town
flocked to see because he ate with a knife and fork. It was in
the middle of the last century. A Khivite who tried to imitate him pierced his cheek with the fork.

We must remember, however, that even with us this instrument has only been in use since the time of Louis XIV.

At hazard I wander through the tortuous secret alleyways.
As in Bokhara, the dominating impression is one of general
decay, but with a grimmer, less civilized quality.

Here is the enormous unfinished minaret of Madamin
Khan, a truncated cone glittering with slabs of faience in
bands of diagonals one above the other: it stands at the corner
of the celebrated madrasah, which deserves a visit. Over the
guarded door, however, I read the word ' Domzak,' which
means prison, and nothing I can say will get me in.

Madamin Khan, enemy of the Tsar, was betrayed by a Turkmen in 1855 and stabbed to death. His head was taken to the Shah of Persia with all the ceremony reserved for the Achemenids, who count as first among the Samanids.

Slavery was abolished in 1873. It is reckoned that throughout the whole oasis of Kharezm—or more exactly Kharzem, from ' khar ' abject, and ' zena ' tribe—there were roughly fifty thousand prisoners of war in a population of five to six hundred thousand inhabitants. The market price of a Russian, sound in wind and limb, was then eighty tillas (about 13s.), and there were five thousand such Russian slaves. The Persian women were, however, considered superior to the Russian.

In the courtyard of a sombre-looking madrasah dyers are at work, their rectangular vats fashioned from one huge piece of leather. Arrested by a muffled rumble, I look through a loophole in the wall of a house, and see a little ass with bony cruppers and blindfold eyes, walking round a room and dragging the millstone after it, which thus grinds the flour.

From the top of an immense smoke-stack minaret which I mount in the company of three schoolboys, I discover to the west, beyond the oasis, ' Black Sands,' the Kara Kum desert. This end of the town looks like a draughtboard: the white squares of roofs being interspersed with the dark squares of the small yards.

To the north, however, rise chiefly mosques and madrasahs.

At my feet glitter the golden bricks of the mausoleum of Paluan Ata, the ' Mighty,' in Persian; a very learned master in the art of wrestling, who had spent long years of study in India. In front of the entrance Iwan is a symmetrical court-yard surrounded by cells, a well, a tree, and a large cat. But all round, heaped up at hazard on the roofs, with even a tree hung with votive rags growing among them and standing buntchuk poles, lie tombs scattered like wooden billets bleached white by the dust.

Again a madrasah, this time occupied by an artel of Armenian weaving-women, their kerchiefs tied over their flat skull caps. How sorry I feel for them. All through the day they sit in front of their looms that lie over pits dug in the very earth of each cell, their fingers violet and stiff with the biting cold. The walls re-echo to the thuds of the comb. One of them sighs, and takes up her song again as I leave.

But what surprises me most is the Dashe Ulu, the stone house, the ancient harem of the Khans. Two of the chambers now comprise the museum, and there the bric-à-brac left by the princes has been piled. Though there is no huge porcelain frog wearing a top hat as at Shir Budum, the summer palace of the Emir of Bokhara (it makes me wonder what sort of wag could have made such a present), there are weapons, clothes, signed portraits, and instruments of torture.

All the walls round the great main courtyard, in the centre of which is a well, are covered with panels of enamelled tiles. At the level of the first storey eight verandas of carved wood succeed each other. By a vaulted passage that still smells of the wood that was sawn indoors, one comes to a first court. Three of the façades are pierced at the level of the first storey to allow for a carved and painted balcony. The fourth side is one immense peristyle two stories high, whose painted coffered ceiling is sustained by slim wooden columns swelling at the base.

All the walls here are covered with motifs in enamel, conveying an impression of refinement and opulence that is not easily forgotten. In an instant the eye grasps, as it were, the whole sober riot of decoration that makes of it some palace of the *Thousand and One Nights.*

In the midst of this courtyard with fifty-foot sides, a circular platform rises at the head of four steps. It is the spot where the yurt was set up for the accommodation of distinguished guests. In the Middle Ages, too, the Uzbeks lived in their yurts in the cities that they built.

A second courtyard, equally as astonishing, leads out of it, and I stand motionless, deeply moved to have been able to contemplate such beauty. Cover palace walls with panels of the loveliest brocades of the Empire period, surrounded by narrow borders that match them, and you will have some feeble idea what these walls disclose in the deserted courtyards that re-echo only to the cooing doves. Beyond any doubt, " Luxury to the nomad Mongol meant the embroideries and textiles with which he lined his tent. When he settled in the towns, all he asked was that his palaces and mosques should create a similar effect with facings of ceramics." (René Grousset.)

CHAPTER XVI

The Germans of Ak Metchet

ASTRIDE A BICYCLE, I career madly through the streets of Khiva; almost knocking into the hammering tin-smiths, terrifying the children, and issuing like a whirlwind out of the 'suk' covered with ruins, while performing miracles of balancing to keep out of the deep ruts. The crowd looks on admiringly, and I am as proud as though I were the genius who had invented this form of locomotion.

There are three bicycles in the whole of Khiva, and, unhoped-for opportunity, a Russian employee in the post office has been so far condescending as to lend me that rare object. The whole staff collected under the heads of Lenin and Stalin to see whether the foreigner really knew how to use it.

I fly past a band of schoolboys under the charge of two native women, pass through one of the gates of the city, and start off southwards towards Ak Metchet, the second oasis, where the German colony is to be found.

At the post office, I had been told:

"You know, they keep a set of special holidays of their own: all of a sudden they will turn up in their Sunday best. Every three days they come to market with their butter and fruit."

"And when they first came to these parts they had to promise the Khan they would raise no pigs for fifty years."

"They're pretty lucky! They get sacks of rice and medicines sent them from Germany."

Dried-up fields, fortress-like farms, tracks made difficult in places by the stuff cleared out of the ariks. I pedal for a long time. Twice it seems to me I have reached my objective, and then I see trees, far, far off beyond the desert.

In the thick sand of the desert, the sand silts up my wheels and wastes my energy. At times they skid. The only way is to keep on as fast as I can, till I can stay on no longer. Great stretches covered with salt almost make me think it is fresh snow. I arrive, bathed in sweat, rejoicing at the thought that in a few moments I shall be talking to Europeans, and make my way towards a prosperous-looking farm surrounded by yellowing poplars, with white curtains in the windows, where I hear:

" Maria, wer kommt dort? "

In German, I ask a young man where Otto Theuss lives, prepared to be met with excited and astonished cries. Not at all: reserved, grave, and blond under his furred bonnet, he points out a group of dwellings, only the farmyards of which can be seen. Cows watched by an Uzbek herdsman drink from a roofed-in spring. Two young girls take charge of me, timidly. A bucketful of water, white hand-basin, a piece of soap, a hand towel are brought me. The kitchen table and brick stove are every whit as trim and neat as the corners of the house.

" Oh, yes," they tell me, " that makes a lot of work: we have to repair the pisé every year. It cracks and crumbles, then the rain gets in."

In the room—the girls take off their clogs before going in —is a big table and benches, an earthen stove, Bible texts on the wall, a country dresser, and two spectacled aunts knitting away in straight-backed armchairs. On a side table is the *Vossische Zeitung* which takes eighteen days to make the journey.

The aunts make no attempt to conceal their astonishment.

"You came by bicycle? And alone? Weren't you afraid?"

" Ah, you've come from Kirghizia? So did I. I came from Aulie Ata where conditions were becoming too difficult for us. Some of our relatives are coming from the Volga. At present there are three hundred and forty in the colony. It makes rather a squeeze to find room for them all."

"Yes, I read in Ali Suavi that Khiva is so remote from anywhere that it always has been a land of refuge: but tell me, doesn't the excellent way in which you run your colony set an example to your neighbours, the Uzbeks?"

"It makes no difference to them: they don't need any of the things that are so indispensable to us. There was a Turkmen who lived with us here for two years, an intelligent lad, and in the end he was talking our 'Platt-Deutsch' like one of us. Do you know what he said some days before he left? 'You are a strange and complicated lot of people: why does a person have to waste his time three times a day, washing fifteen plates, and knives and forks, when only one dish is necessary!'"

Supper is ready and we sit down to it. Otto Theuss utters a short prayer, in which he has the kindness to include the foreign visitor.

Here age alone matters. Even the married sons talk in low voices, with a wary eye on the father. I seem a child myself again and count ten every time I want to ask a question, as I slowly chew my food in order not to finish in front of the others. We eat boiled eggs with buttered rusks and coffee with milk in it. There is honey for the older members. The faces round me are frank and open, clean and freckled. The square foreheads reveal the obstinacy which saved the band from perishing fifty years earlier. The women have their hair parted in the centre and their plaits pulled back in a bun on the nape of the neck.

"Yes, I've had a good journey. I found living conditions at Kara Köl and Turt Köl the best of any: but then they were the towns furthest from the railway line."

"The news we read about Europe in our German newspapers is hardly reassuring."

"Yes—one would think human beings were mutually inciting each other to commit great wrongs."

"Every day we praise God that we have not forgotten His precepts."

Otto Theuss is small, with blue eyes and a red moustache.

His long skull is bald. The impression one gets of him is of a creature predominantly practical and decided. I summon up courage at last to confess how ignorant I am as to what the Mennonites are.

" Our sect was founded in Holland by Menno Simons at the beginning of the sixteenth century: it grouped together those who believed in the doctrine of the Anabaptists, and were opposed to violence, war, and the temporal powers. Almost immediately we had converts at Zürich and at Bâle. There are half a million of us in the world. These are our precepts: never touch a weapon, never take an oath, because our yes must be yes; and receive baptism only after truly comprehending and believing.

" There was an occasion when the King of Poland had us brought from Friesland to come and drain the Danzig marshes. Later, after the revolution of 1848, military service was made compulsory for every male Prussian. Then we demanded asylum from the Tsar for about a hundred of our families. We already had Prussian colonies in Russia, but, thanks to the railway train, the last to arrive were able to bring many things from home with them.

" According to our writings, we knew that our migration towards the East was not yet finished. In 1881 there was a proclamation making military service compulsory throughout Russia. Then, under the protection of General Kaufmann, the Governor of Turkestan, and with the promise of new land and guarantees of liberty and conscience, we left the Volga on July 3, 1880, to journey to Tashkent. Ten thousand of our people also set out for America.

" It seems that at that time a sheep was worth one rouble thirty kopeks in Uralsk. But the journey was very arduous. We could only cover four versts an hour. At Aktioubinsk there was no more oats for our horses. To cross the desert we had to take our carts to pieces, and get the parts transported on the backs of four hundred camels. Look: the uprights of this door are made of cart shafts.

" We passed the winter near Tashkent, and some of us

settled down in Aulie Ata. In 1881 Alexander II was assassi-nated, Kaufmann had a stroke, and nothing had yet been set down in writing regarding us.

" We made up our minds to crave asylum from the Emir of Bokhara, and set off again, passing through Samarkand. Some of us saw strange customs being practised in the yurts: they were amazed to see camel flesh being eaten and that only one bowl did service for a whole gathering. To cut up a sheep, they first blew into the skin through a hole in one of the legs, and so microbes were spread.

" The local Beks were not of the same mind as the Emir, and to make a long story short, it was Asfendiar, Khan of Khiva, who gave us a grant of land.

" The Khan wanted the services of our carpenters, some of whom were very skilful, to polish up his floors and wood-work; through them he learnt that the Turkmen had robbed us of our cattle and horses. He sent some dziguites to protect us. And it was then that we were granted Ak Metchet where there were already a hundred and thirty-nine apricot trees."

The Khan and his dignitaries were Uzbeks: sometimes they took advantage of their superior situation higher up the Amu Daria, to cut off the irrigation waters destined for the Turk-men. That was the reason the latter made their raids.

With the Schoolmaster

Everyone has left already by the time I wake and I break-fast alone. A young girl conducts me to see old Riesen.

The fronts of all the low houses form four sides of a large square, similar to those one finds in Prussia. A walled front garden, with a couple of poplars before each gateway, is brightened by the white of the window frames.

" What are the Christian names most fashionable now in Germany?" she asks. " If you knew how we should like something different from our Gretchens, Louisas, Evas, Rosas, Dorotheas. . . ."

" Have you any Brigittes and Marlenes?"

Emil Riesen, the aged schoolmaster, bearded and toothless, with fine grey eyes, has a whole world of memories in him; everything in fact that happened in their primal saga.

"Our beginnings here were very difficult. We got here with absolutely no money. We sold little lanterns of our own manufacture in the market, at eighty kopeks each, and then socks and blouses. One of us mended the Khan's phonograph. He liked transfers very much and so we stuck them on all the articles of furniture we made for him. As I knew Uzbek, I was always responsible for negotiations with the officials. At the time of the coronation of Nicholas II, Khan Said Muhammed Rahim took me as interpreter with him to Moscow, where he rented a palace for three hundred roubles a month. When the Tsarina asked him what he thought of Moscow, he said he felt more comfortable in his rabbit-run at Khiva. All things considered, he was merely an intelligent peasant; quite different from Ispendal, who ate with our implements and could have met the Tsar on terms of equality."

Riesen showed me a number of photographs depicting the dignitaries of the Court all clad in splendid khalats of brocade.

"The Khan liked us better than his subjects and presented us with khalats when we had to appear at his Court. He was prepared to pay me heavily if I would become a Moslem."

"But this photo? It's an American farm."

"Yes, that's where my sister lives in Kansas: yes, I spent six months there after I was deported from Angora. They accused me of spying for Germany, but the fall of Kerensky set me free."

While we are gossiping together, his wife, a meek little mouse, fills my haversack with aniseed biscuits, and by a gesture encourages me to go on emptying the plate set on the table.

At the neighbours', women are spinning with a large spinning-wheel.

In the centre of the square stand two cubes of pisé, trim,

and with white windows: the school and the meeting-house. The latter, set thus in the midst of a Soviet republic, is touching in its sun-bathed simplicity. Rows of chairs, divided by a gangway, lead to the foot of three steps, where a black pulpit stands out against the whitewashed wall. On the pulpit, I read: " Herr! Hilf mir! "

A harmonium, a fine candelabrum, and that is all.

" We have no pastor, but several of our lay brothers at frequent intervals are called upon to read and expound the Bible to us, and this they do in turn."

There is a comforting warmth in the classrooms when one goes in from outside. Girls on one side, boys on the other: maps, a globe, a blackboard between two windows. There is also a steamship of the Hamburg-Amerika line.

All rise when we go in; then a hymn is sung and the reading lesson—a Bible story—is resumed. The same books have done service for twenty years. Fingers follow the words, but Elisa is caught in the very act of not attending.

Like that of every Mennonite in Ak Metchet, the face of the schoolmaster seems instinct with scrupulous honesty. What does the future hold for this colony where the community comes to the aid of each of its members?

To think I had to come into the depths of Turkestan to comprehend the power that lies in cleanliness, and the discipline of a faith. . . .

CHAPTER XVII

A RACE WITH THE ICE

I TELEPHONE FROM Khiva to Danieletz at Kopalik, but the *Lastotchka* has not come in yet. In spite of all my hustling, it is nightfall before my arbakesh gets me to Novo Urgenj, and I sleep at the postmaster's.

In the morning, as I am about to leave, I find it impossible to get hold of my host, who has disappeared with my knife. I had refused to sell it to him, because I needed it myself, and because he would have displayed it to his friends and boasted that it was a present from the foreign woman to keep in memory of her favours. He was furious with me, and utterly refused to talk to me from the time when, exerting all my strength, I had managed to tear myself away from him.

Anxious as I am not to miss the boat, I run through every chai-kana of the city in search of him, but with no success. In despair I lodge a complaint at the police station and leave my Moscow address.

However, just as I am climbing the spokes of the arba wheel to take my seat, the postmaster suddenly appears, whereupon I begin upbraiding him.

"But I thought you had made me a present of the knife. Here it is: why make such a fuss?"

My arbakesh walks in front of his horse, tempting it with an armful of clover, which he doles out stalk by stalk. Then the same scene is repeated with dried jugara stalks. Finally, the man asks if I have any bread left in my sack. I give him some and he chews it slowly.

At the haven I find there is still a long wait in front of me. I take up my place well in front of the pontoon on which the offices stand, and settle myself by a windlass. On a bench in

one of the cabins I see an enormous dish of pirojkis. A lad
enters, helps himself, and goes out: then a man does the same,
and after him two fair little girls. . . . I cannot resist the
temptation, and do likewise.

While I am still licking my lips, the woman whose potato
cakes I have stolen, returns. She has blue eyes, slow movements, and a dark kerchief on her head.

We talk together while I wash out some socks and shirts.

" My husband is a doctor in Kopalik. But I have malaria,
and the least thing tires me. Here, eat if you're hungry,"
she says, holding out the plate.

I dare not confess my petty larceny.

" You must stay here to-night, on that bench, till the boat
comes. It's far too cold outside. My son can make a bed for
himself on one of the office tables."

They strongly advise me not to go downstream, for that is
towards the north, and the river may freeze at any moment.
I have only four or five days more in which to get to Kantusiak, so I give up the idea of visiting Kunia Urgenj, the
sand-buried city. I must find a boat as soon as possible to
take me across the Sea of Aral: otherwise I shall have to
retrace my steps, and that, nothing would induce me to do.
To the west, the route to Astrakhan leads across the desert
and is by no means safe, for quite recently a caravan of five
hundred camels, transporting sulphur, had been attacked and
destroyed.

In the minute cabin there are five of us in all, in addition
to two small dogs and a cat. Two benches facing each other
support the bed, on which both parents and two children
sleep. Truly, only the poor have such large hearts towards
the passing stranger.

The *Lastotchka* comes in three days late, with four passengers on board wishing also to proceed to Aralskoie More.

The die is cast. I embark. No return will be possible, for
the last boat has departed upstream before the river
freezes. . . .

I establish myself in the fo'c'sle of a dismantled boat,

towed alongside the *Lastotchka*, which is crammed with passengers. There are a dozen of us lying on two tiers of benches. We are practically in darkness. The windows have boards nailed over them, and a sheet of three-ply separates me from the abandoned engine-room. Silence reigns. We are on the raft of resignation, and soon I understand why.

With our dead weight the *Lastotchka* loses speed, and has difficulty in answering the helm. We are passing through some rapids near a promontory, taking them at a slant, when suddenly we feel a shock, and find we have run aground. The aft hawser breaks, and the boat towing us is powerless to float us again.

The night is glacial: we spend it deep inside our blankets.

In the morning we find the water has kindly swept some of the sand away, and at last we are pulled off. What a relief it is to see the beacons disappearing behind us!

A short respite. We are in tow astern, the helm lashed amidships, when, swept along by the current, with two successive shocks we touch bottom; the tow-rope snaps, and we stick where we are. The *Lastotchka*, turning to come to our aid, grounds too. We wear ourselves out, bent almost double over the long poles: we think we are moving, and it is only the boat slewing round. Discouraged, we give up.

It is terribly cold in the night. Fortunately, some of us have managed to break open the engine's paraffin tanks, and so we are able to feed two large Primus stoves, which throw out a good heat, and on which tea is boiled. We spend the time dozing until our noses, hands, and feet begin to feel frost-bitten; then we wake and massage them violently.

Two men tear up the floorboards, put an iron plate over the greasy bilge-water, break off the hand rails on deck, and make a fire which reanimates us again. Jackals howl in the reeds on the banks. There are tigers also in the region.

The only possible occupations are spitting, and rolling cigarettes in pieces of newspaper. A trade begins in loaves of bread. An old silent couple have nothing to sop in their tea, and I give them some buns I bought in Turt Köl.

Three fishermen pass in a flat canoe, a 'beidarka,' and proving our saviours we set off again full of hope.

Wrapping myself in everything I possess, I take charge of the helm, a piece of broken iron, determine at all costs to avoid a second and possibly fatal grounding. Then Tadji Murad, a sailor on the *Lastotchka*, comes to relieve me.

In the night I sell a kilo of rice to a sharp-witted young couple journeying to take a census of the Chimbai. Their task is by no means an easy one, for the natives, in apprehension of the taxes they may have to pay, conveniently forget the members of their families; and on the other hand, when they are told the numbers are wanted in connection with the distribution of commodities from the Co-operatives, declare every relative they ever had, including those dead.

A moustached old grouser had been at the head of a squadron sent out against the Bassmatchi of Kunia Urgenj, and relates how his men died off in the desert through lack of water. The Bassmatchi, it appears, are uncapturable: for the large hoofs of their horses, which have never been shod, do not sink in the sand. He explains that Kirghiz in Tajik means nomad of the steppes, and attaches no faith to the etymology 'kirk' forty, and 'kyz' virgins. The legend relates that a rich man had forty daughters: and as the kalim for purchasing them had to be in proportion to his riches, no suitors presented themselves. As a result, he abandoned them in a wood. Then the brigands appeared, who asked them who they were. "The forty virgins," they replied.

I am lazing in my sleeping-bag next morning when Tadji sends us crashing into the bank at full speed. For a moment I verily believe the creaking hull is going to be crushed like an egg shell. Caught in a violent race, the helm had refused to answer. Ready to lose my teeth, if need be—they chatter so with cold—I insist on staying at his side: I refuse to perish in the icy river, powerless in my thick clothes.

Here, we were in the vicinity of a famous place of pilgrimage, the mountain Sultan Baoua.

Kipchak has been on our tongues a long time, and now it

announces itself by the immense 'kurgan,' looking like a battlemented volcano. We stop for a short while, which gives me just time to hurry to the wireless station past a dusty cemetery, and discover that Kantusiak has not yet announced itself closed to navigation.

The abandoned houses by the waterside make a dreary landscape. Soon they must crash down, for the cliffs on which they stand are being undermined by the river. There are camels on the banks, and casks of oil. In the midst of the huts of yellow earth the 'Domzak' alone is whitewashed.

We glide past lagoons that are already white with ice.

Suddenly both hulls ground together. Fate! No one seems to mind. With turned-up trousers and bare feet the Captain-Commander brings over a tow-rope stiff with ice. The water is the same colour as his bony brown knee. He is a native of the region, able to get the best advantage out of the caprices of the ever-present, ever-uncapturable water. He makes us slew the boat round, and the current strikes against our bows. Then we run to and fro over the deck to work the keel lose. In the water the commander bends nearly double to get us to lie right . . . then we dart off like an arrow, and the jerk given by our tow-rope to the *Lastotchka* sets it free too.

The Earthen Way

Khodjeili is a large port. Here begin the ramifications of the delta. It is still a hundred and twenty-five miles to Kantusiak. We are welcomed by our travelling companion, the young Kazak komsomol, who had been left behind involuntarily at Kipchak. He had bought a horse a catch us up, and it still trembles on its legs that are coated with sweat. Everyone made fun of him, for he knew hardly any Russian, and so could not reply to the traps set for him on the subject of Communism.

The passengers go off to the city market some two and a half miles away. I go to the wireless hut at the foot of the tall masts.

A RACE WITH THE ICE

" Kantusiak is closed. The last boat, the *Commune*, sailed yesterday."

And after my dreams of soon being able to sleep in a warm bunk, after a bath, on the passenger-freighter! What's to be done?

Incredulous, the other passengers decide to continue their journey down the river. If the report is true, they will have to winter there, and wait for the break-up of the ice.

I repeat the reasons given by the telegraphist, which personally quite convinced me.

" But you don't realize that Aralskoie More is nearly four hundred miles further north, and snowed under already."

In the warmth of the crew's quarters on the *Lastotchka* I pay my passage from Kopalik, twenty-one roubles for ninety miles on board an ice-box.

The mate is making up his accounts in a penny exercise book, and gets them signed by the impassive Commander. The grouser is present also. The master of a large cargo boat near-by makes him a present of a carp (sazane). I ask if I may buy one too, and he invites me to go with him. How friendly the short little man seems, with the blue flash in his sparkling eyes, and his high felt boots.

Veritable mountains of cotton are piled in bales on the bank. Pointing to them, he says:

" What a shame; the first mists we get, all this will turn mouldy and be ruined."

His poop is barely visible, so thickly is it covered with strings of drying salted fish.

In the Amu lives a most extraordinary fish, the scaphirhyn-chus. The only other place it is found is in the Mississippi.

" What would be the best way to strike the railway line? " I say to him.

" Well, at Chimbai, on the main channel, you'll find caravans starting for Kazalinsk. That means barely a fort-night in the desert."

" That's just what I should most like. Is it dear? "

" In summer the price generally charged is eighty roubles,

307

but without a 'chuba' and 'valinki' (an enormous pelisse and boots of stiff felt) you'd freeze to death if the 'buran' began to blow. Anyhow, try and get a dozen pounds of bread for yourself at the bakery here. There's the baker just coming out."

Nukuss

To get to Chimbai I have first to cross the river. I am told there is a ferryman within a stone's throw, at the point.

I walk past pyramids of stacked sacks of grain. Some 'beidarkas' are aground against the bank, where the crew have set up their tents. I ask if they are going to Chimbai. No, they are going in the opposite direction, towards Tashauz.

On a projecting spit unharnessed carts are waiting, but I do not see for what. Here the 'beidarkas' moor after their passage, the route they have followed having the shape of a circumflex accent. They help themselves along by a pointed sail bent to a fine lateen yard. When I step on board I break through the ice that covers the planks.

On the other bank there is nothing. . . . Yes, a man muffled in a sheepskin praying and bowing his head down to the sand. I pass by without him noticing me, and now the setting sun is red at his back.

With every step I sink deep into the yielding track, and so, when an arba appears from behind a dune, I give it no chance to escape. After a couple of miles we come to the village of Nukuss.

I get off at the chai-kana and keep my arbakesh to take me next day to Chimbai. Three or four people are sitting in the dark room, silent in the cold.

Anxious to spend a comfortable night, I pay a visit to the postmistress, a Russian.

"I can't put you up," she says: "there are already four of us in this tiny room. We have a housing crisis in Nukuss. There are workers flooding the place from all over the country: they say a new town is going to be built here."

A RACE WITH THE ICE

As I rummage about in the chai-kana I happen to open a door. A gust of warmth comes out to meet me; I see an oil lamp, table, books, newspapers, and two young men, and smell meat simmering on the stove.

" Can I warm myself here a bit? "

" Why, yes, of course. Where do you come from? Where are you going? How do you manage about food? "

They are a couple of surveyors living in the place to make a survey of this part of Karakalpakia.

" You know that Turt Köl is doomed to disappear in two or three years, eaten away by the river? "

" But why does the water scour principally east? "

" We don't really know. Dominant winds or the earth's rotation? But anyhow, there was a competition, and now the plans have been selected for a city of two hundred thousand inhabitants to be constructed here, a hundred and twenty-five miles north of Turt Köl. It is going to cost eighty to a hundred and eighty million roubles, and will be magnificent. For the moment, however, only the hospital is being put up."

" But where is the material coming from? "

" All the wood for the scaffolding is to be brought from the Urals, across the Sea of Aral."

They invite me to sup with them, and I eat to repletion, this time my excuse being that I am soon going to cross the Kizil Kum. The vodka makes everything go down.

" But you have no coat! "

" No! but in the arba I generally sit in my sleeping-bag, and I shall surely find a ' chuba ' in the bazaar at Chimbai."

" Take mine," says the bearded young man with the clear, frank eyes. " I've got one that reaches down to the heels, but it's so heavy I never use it: I prefer the short one, and the cold is not so piercing here as where you're going."

" But I could never pay you for it. I must keep the money I've got, for I don't know how much the camels are going to cost me."

" That's all right: when you've sold it again you can send me the money: it's only worth about sixty roubles."

CHAPTER XVIII

Towards the Unknown North

I climb up on the arba. It is not an easy thing to scale the wheel with my long sheepskin coat, and I curl myself warmly up, enormously cheered by the kindness of my surveyor.

Never has any morning in my life seemed lovelier. If only I could find some cry that would express all my feeling!

To set off! That is like being born again. Everything begins anew: I do not know what lies in front of me. The sun rises red, as it set last night. The air sparkles with frost, and I advance into a reality more lovely than a fairy tale.

Yet yesterday, how difficult it had been to open the door of the *Lastotchka,* and turn my back on that warm cabin, before making the athletic gesture of heaving my sack upon my shoulder.

My arbakesh is a likeable fellow and does not spare his beast. There is an honest look in his eyes when they gaze at me from between the tiny, loose black curls of his ' chugurma.'

An arm of the desert lies between us and Chimbai, twenty-eight miles away. Because of the wind, the big right wheel sprinkles me with sand as it turns. When the track crosses some too-soft ground, my Karakalpak beckons me to go on foot.

We stop at noon, in the street of a hamlet, and I find myself wondering where the plantations lie hidden. Here we eat shashlik. The vendor takes up a lipiotchka and clasps it round the steaming skewer: then he draws, and the metal spike pulls free, shining with fat.

The monotonous route continues. To water our white horse, my man takes him out of the shafts when we get near the main canal, and with his heel breaks a hole in the ice in which the water lies imprisoned. It seems that the natives were opposed to the construction of a straight canal on the grounds that " water to flow well, should not be seen."

It is dark night when we enter the narrow alleyways of Chimbai, where the drab houses seem built of the papier mâché used for stage scenery.

The chai-kanas are shut. At the ' Soyustrans ' they do not want to put me up. The office is shut for the night. Opposite is the ' Soyusarbakesh,' with a yard for vehicles, and an office-chamber where some natives are settling down on a platform for the night. A stove purrs, heating a copper pitcher.

Sour faces greet my kind driver. He does not belong to the Union, and the thirty-five roubles he has charged me is less than the tariff.

In the morning, after a night spent on the table, I go to the ' Raispolkom ' to make inquiries. A very civil native tells me that the camels leave from Takhta Koupir, twenty-five miles farther east.

There's not a moment to be lost if I want to complete my journey that day. But I have to wait till a horse can be brought. Then the cashier is absent who should sign the receipt. Then I am charged forty-five roubles for the journey.

In a very bad humour, because of all the delays, I refuse to settle in advance. I am determined not to put myself at the mercy of these accursed arbakeshes who are making me pay so dearly for having run into them.

It avails nothing, however; I have to submit. Bitterly I complain about the emaciated horse they bring me, saying:

" But I must absolutely get to Takhta Koupir this evening, not to miss a caravan that leaves to-morrow."

" But you will certainly get there in time," replies the cashier.

The road is good, hard; but we are barely out of the city when the horse stops trotting and seems to dawdle along. I am at the mercy of an elegant arbakesh, with a fur cap lined with rose-coloured velvet: extraordinary the things people

think of ! His insolent nonchalance gets on my nerves. I
burst into scornful criticisms every half-hour. If it is a tip
he is waiting for, in order to whip his horse into a trot, he is
very much out in his reckoning.

All round lie dreary fields of sparse cotton bushes where
the picking is all but over.

During the afternoon, as we pass near a hamlet, the arbakesh suggests having tea.

" Agreed, but quickly. Takhta Koupir is still a long way."

In a yard in which are two smoking yurts I am directed to
a large chamber that might be eight yards by four. There are
mats on the ground and a tiny tin stove. That is all.

The tea is a long time coming. And then my arbakesh
appears bringing my equipment after him. I protest furiously,
and in short sentences repeat :

" I will not spend the night here. I shall hire a horse if
necessary. I insist on being taken there to-night. That is
what I paid for."

Then I resign myself. Why appear undignified if nothing
is to be gained by it ?

A fillet of carp fries in my pan, and the little stove turns
red-hot immediately the sticks begin to flare in the grate.

Two elegant couples of Karakalpak riders stop for a
moment, keeping their ' kamtchas '—whips with chased
handles—strapped to their wrists, as they drink their bowl of
tea. The men are in camel-hair chapans, their boots are of
felt, and they wear huge petals of fur that flower on their
heads. The young women wear velvet mantles and silk
scarves.

Emigrants

As night falls, small groups of pilgrims arrive *en route* for
the south. They sit down on the ground, untwist the complicated wrappings that serve them for footwear, and rub their
tired feet. Then the haversack is opened and a wooden bowl
is filled with small round golden grain.

I taste it : it is roasted millet seed, and they moisten it with tea. My neighbour is Russian :

" I've come from Kazalinsk," he says.

" Across the desert then ? "

" Yes, a sixteen-day crossing with my ass : I paid a hundred and twenty roubles for it over there, and here it's not worth more than sixty."

" But don't they sink in the sand ? "

" There's snow not far away and that hardens the track."

" At least that solves the water problem for you, there's no need to bother about the ' kuduks '—wells of brackish water. But where are you bound for ? "

" I'm taking advantage of my holidays to buy grain, which I shall sell again in the north for twice what it costs me."

A single smoky lamp throws a dim light into the now full room. The new arrivals hardly know where to stack themselves. Standing, three tiny children stay hidden in their mother's skirts. Then they are taken off elsewhere.

Tired of listening without understanding what is said, I settle down and fall asleep. Later, waking for a moment, I see the servant bringing full pans of steaming pilav, into which all plunge their fingers.

Then, in the middle of the night as it seems to me, the wanderers put on what serves them for boots, and start out again.

Towards eight, when I wake, it is still almost dark. I am alone, and the arbakesh is putting his horse into the shafts. As usual, I lift my pillow to take up my thick mountain boots which serve me as a bolster, and . . . they are no longer there.

Catastrophe! Hurriedly I move my belongings about, but it does not take long in the empty room to make a thorough inspection. In the neighbouring room groups are still asleep on the floor. I appeal to the servant, who spreads what is news of importance in a region where real boots are something of a rarity.

Perhaps it is the arbakesh. No, his surprise cannot be simulated; but all my rage falls on him.

" It's your fault. You only had to drive your horse. I did not want to sleep here."

More than the irreparable loss, what exasperates me most is that the fat-headed brute had all the time done exactly as it pleased him.

In itself the situation is comical enough: to be in socks and crossing the Kizil Kum in the very depths of winter!

No, it is not the depths of winter yet. I must absolutely get to Kazalinsk before the end of December, and its 35° below zero. " Come on! Faster than that. And don't imagine that I paid the ' mardjia ' of the chai-kana for your pilav last night."

Sand, bushes, dry ariks, caravans loaded with faggots and dead wood. A long street of low huts. Our destination at last.

Takhta Koupir

At the ' Raispolkom ' (The Executive Committee of the Region), the secretary, Bai Muhammedov, a fine Mongol head under a Soviet cap, listens to me with interest.

" In three days there will be a market, and then possibly you may find some camels going north. But it's not very usual in winter. As it happens, a family left this very morning for Kazalinsk, where they live."

" Ah! I knew I should have got here yesterday."

Bai Muhammedov has telephoned to the Co-operative.

" No! " he says. " There is not a single pair of valinkis available to put you in. New, they're worth sixty roubles. You might possibly find a cheap pair in the market."

There is an incessant coming and going of human beings disappearing under pelisses as monumental as my own. The leather is tanned sand colour, and stuff triangles, amulets, are sewn on behind the neck.

A Russian, wrapped in the immense official khaki woollen overcoat of the 100 per cent Bolshevik, observes me.

" If you don't know where to stay," he says, " you can come

back with me. I share a tiny room with my ‘ dziguite,’ but we have just had a small brick stove put in which makes it very agreeable.”

With the exception of the main street, the houses seem to have sprung up at hazard, each at a distance from the other, with the same desolate, flat horizon behind them. I have an astonishing impression of having come to the ends of the earth.

The Russian who takes charge of me, yellow eyes sparkling in a face pitted with smallpox, is in control of the transport of the region. He has been here six months trying to speed up the evacuation of the cotton, the output of which closely concerns him. He is rearing a couple of turkeys in his yard, fattening them up for the 1st of January. The cotton campaign will then be over, and he will be back in Turt Köl, where his wife and children live. She is very lovely, according to her husband, with degrees in all sorts of things.

There are two rooms opposite each other. In that on the left is the family of Mustapha, a young Komsomol; on the right that of the Russian. Thick walls, a little window, a table, two mattresses on low platforms, and a good roaring fire. The ‘ dziguite ’ is a Caucasian who knows the region thoroughly. He acts as Kisseliov’s interpreter. The earth walls are hidden by posters whose crude yellows, reds, and blues, show a native of Turkestan at work in a filature, and another at a tractor steering-wheel, contributing to ‘ The Five-Year Plan in Four.’

Outside, adjoining the shelter put up for the cow, is a cubbyhole in which two women live. One wears a turban and long ear-rings: the other is ill in bed. I never see her, but only hear her coughing. In lieu of a door an old sack hangs in front of it. But though they say baby Kazaks are washed in ice-cold water in the first forty days—does that have to suffice for the whole of their lives?—this invalid must certainly suffer from the cold.

Mustapha’s mother looks very imposing with the turban that also frames her chin. She is very weak and has been fasting for days: it must be the month of Ramadan.

And then there is also Safar, the eldest son, with drooping moustaches, and his wife; and in the traditional cradle their baby Rakhmatulla, spoilt by them all. All day long a little hand mill is being turned, grinding jugara seed into flour.

When I hand them some potatoes to cook for me the old lady asks me what they are : she has never seen them before.

I pass six days in Takhta Koupir in a state of intense exasperation. Camels have completely disappeared from the region. Five hundred have been mobilized outside the village to go and collect cotton and saxual wood. Forty have been sent from Kizil Orda—the ancient capital of Kazakstan on the Tashkent line—to seek bread, but the Soviet of Takhta Koupir will not give them any.

Whenever I perceive three beasts in the village, I rush off to tell the Soyustran's office, which has promised to inform me immediately there is anything setting out for the north. Mustapha also makes inquiries on all sides. I enter into negotiations with a middleman who says he knows where two beasts may be obtained: his man arrives and we arrange a meeting place. He asks for a deposit of twenty roubles . . . and never returns. But Kisseliov forces the middleman to repay the money.

Sometimes in the evening I pay a visit to the woman doctor.

" I came here in 1929 with my boy," she says. " I was then the first European woman ever seen in the region."

On an average she has sixty visits a day.

" Yes, the Kazaks are easy to look after. But there is such a lot to do with 80 to 90 per cent syphilis. It is the life in the yurt that's responsible."

" I happen to have a ' Record ' syringe and some ampoules of neosalvarsan that I should be glad to sell. I'm worried in case I might be short of money when I buy my ticket at Kazalinsk."

" If they're in good condition I'll buy them, though I have those things already."

" Then it's not like it was two years ago when such articles were lacking completely? They're just as I bought them: I thought I might possibly need them during my Mongolian trials and tribulations."

Mustapha has found me a pair of odd valinkis for forty roubles, and now there is nothing to distinguish me from a real Kazak. I go about as they do, broader than long, and when we knock into each other in the deafening, dust-covered crowds of the bazaar it is only a couple of mattresses that bump together.

At the butcher's, standing at the side of his great impaled carcasses, for four roubles I buy a kilo of camels' meat which I cut up at once and begin cooking before it can freeze, for then it turns as hard as a stone. For seven roubles I also buy a kilo of mutton fat to take the place of the non-existent bacon. Of bread, biscuits, tea, dried ouriouks, I have all that I need.

In a Co-operative depot I see more than twenty cases, all identical and all containing an article unprocurable in Moscow: silk stockings! Unprotesting, and obedient to what strange political object have these packing-cases been stranded in this ' bled,' which makes me think of some sort of Arctic Africa?

I begin to wonder whether at night, out in the desert, it is best to sleep close to the verminous camels to get some protection from the cold. Then I see myself bumping through the day in an enormous felt nest, roped to the camel's back, like that caravan I saw at Turt Köl. . . . But mostly I feel afraid they will not want to take me with them: I must behave as though accustomed to crossing deserts in winter.

In the end however, a Kazak turns up, who asks me to hold myself in readiness if I wished to leave with his brother sometime at evening on market day. This time Mustapha wants to take the Kazak's coat as a hostage, but the latter objects and assures us he is honest.

To bid a last farewell to the Asiatic swarms which I am now leaving for the last time, I go to get a good bumping at the bazaar. Almost every head I see might be that of Inkijinof, the Mongol hero of *Storm over Asia.* Which among them carries in his amulet the table of his ancestors beginning with Jenghiz Khan?

In the narrow street that leads to the open space of the market, squatting women are selling yoghourt, pancakes, red peppers. One, sitting by a heap of rice piled on a handkerchief, has a silver ring on her finger like that worn by most of the women. For four roubles I buy it, an amount equal to what I spend a day on lipiotchkas. In order to pay for it I have to get at my trouser pocket, moving aside my heavy pelisse and lifting my jacket and woollen sweater up.

I am barely home again, a hundred yards away, when I feel that my pocket-book is no longer in my pocket. It must have fallen into the dust when I thought I was putting it away again: no one could have stolen it under all the clothes I am wearing.

Luckily I had divided my roubles and put them away in various places: and my pocket-book had only contained fifteen. But horror of horrors! there were thirty-five dollars in the last pocket set aside for Moscow and Berlin.

The woman whose ring I bought is gone. Not a sign of the pocket-book. Who in this place would even understand that my green-backs were real money? And no one, in any case, could change them here: useless, they would be bound to end in the fire. Besides, it had also contained a complete series of aerial postage stamps which I was taking to my brother, and three negatives of the enormous fish hauled up on the shores of the Amu.

At the police station I pay the public crier to announce my loss by beat of drum; forty roubles reward for whoever brings back the leather pocket-book containing the foreign papers. To top it all, there in our yard stands an enormous camel waiting for me. I had so emphatically demanded immediate departure, and night marches. . . that now I must leave without delay.

The camel's saddle consists of an oval mattress, held in place by two stout rods, placed lengthwise on each side of the two humps. One takes one's seat on the loaded sacks with feet resting on the rods that stick out near the neck: then one clings tightly and the great camel suddenly gets up.

Thus I bid farewell to Takhta Koupir, a Kazak leading my camel.

A new departure. Joy inundates me!

But immediately the difficulties that may be in store for me begin to gnaw away at my pleasure and fill me with anxiety.

CHAPTER XIX

THREE HUNDRED MILES THROUGH THE 'DESERT OF RED SANDS'

OUR ROUTE LEADS north. Soon we shall catch up with the rest of our caravan. The country is covered with stunted bushes cut by well-worn tracks. A dyke borders the main frozen arik: women descend the slopes with yokes on their shoulders from each end of which swings a pail. Round patches mark places where holes have been broken in the ice.

Three large yurts stand in a triangle and my camel kneels in the midst of them. It is night. I get off. They unload it. I enter the yurt of Akhmetali.

His daughter Alma is kneading a thick dough of jugara flour, small pieces of which she then casts into a cauldron of boiling water. Toibazar is quite young, and looks very elegant in a necklace of twelve-kopek pieces and ear-rings. Akhmetali, the ancient, is as gnarled as a saxaul, wrinkled, with restless eyes and a few odd hairs to his chin. His son remains silent. His son-in-law Nurman, Alma's husband, is small too, and has a nice round face.

The old man and I have the right to eat from a bowl containing a mixture of meat and the cooked dough. Instead of dessert, we take up a handful of prossa, millet flour mixed with ground 'djida,' small berries with smooth russet skin that are white, sweetish, and flabby inside like the flesh of a mushroom.

Then the men take off their 'chubas,' kneel on them by the fire, and say their prayers.

We stretch out and sleep for three hours.

About midnight we begin to get ready.

Sacks of grain woven of camel-hair are loaded on the three beasts that look like kneeling mountains among the yurts. The yurts themselves seem like giant hedgehogs in the dark.

A hedge of tall bushes protects them against possible sand-storms and the imminent snow.

Buckets are fastened on, and spades. Not an unnecessary word! Departures seem always much the same, whether at the sea or in the desert. It is always the last sleep, the last meal one thinks of, mingled with apprehension of what may be in store.

The wind stings, stars seem like rockets, we depart in silence.

The hoofs of the great beasts pad slowly. With every step the upper part of my body rotates first forward and then back: to diminish the amplitude of the movement I round my back. Then all I think about is how to keep my lovely warmth with the least effort.

Every hour we have to walk a little to get warm: a couple of hundred yards suffices. I linger a moment behind a bush, and when I seek my people again, the night has already swallowed up their silhouettes and the sound of the bells.

I call . . . no reply. There seems no carrying power in my voice, stifled immediately by the immense void. According to the stars my direction is right. I meet tracks: we were not following any. Suddenly my blood runs cold.

" Ohé. . . . O-o-ohé ! "

Feebly comes a reply. But it is impossible to guess from what direction. Damnation! I shall be more careful in future about losing sight of the camels. There they are, motionless, barely visible against the black night.

Akhmetali talks of setting up his yurt here later, there being plenty of brushwood for fires. Day begins to appear, turning from grey to red, then gold, then white. We hear barking and see the fires of distant yurts. There are still traces of ariks.

We leave the brush, and on the left gain a long, sandy slope at the foot of which lie holy tombs. A cavalier outstrips us, visiting his traps for hares.

Now we are in among the sand-dunes, at times in ripples as though left by some receding sea, more often as smooth as suède. We stop for a meal in a sheltered hollow. The old man sits down, takes off his boots. Abouish, the young son, brings up armfuls of brushwood, so dry that it breaks like glass: the wood is impregnated with salts and gives out a bitter, pungent, and medicinal odour. With one hand Nurman milks a camel and with the other holds the wooden bowl.

Now we cross the beds of a series of crackled lakes covered with green patches. Above us swans pass, their wings beating hugely. On the bed of one of the lakes covered with red patches we see the carapaces of dead tortoises and myriads of pink shells.

" Is that the reason why this desert is called Red Sands, ' Kizil Kum ' ? "

We are a long way from the tracks frequented, it is said, by the Bassmatchi. The route will be longer, but we shall find wood for our fire.

So we go on, day after day, at times coming upon the tracks of camels, twin lozenges. Late at night we halt. After a long absence Abouish brings back the bucket filled with water, and the long rope. By what magic did he make his way to the water-hole or kuduk? The water is brackish, tastes of magnesium, and makes me almost vomit my tea. One morning, after having searched for a long time in the hollow of a dune, we find another kuduk bordered with ice in the midst of many converging tracks. There, with untiring energy, our Kazaks drew up pail upon pail, which were as immediately emptied, sucked up by our camels. Each beast must have swallowed a good twenty pails, making twenty gallons: filling their tanks, for thereafter we could count only on snow.

Our Three Camels

At our head leads the large bearded camel, reflective, as woolly as a negro, tears of ice hanging from its long lashes, and bearing two enormous sacks on which are perched Nurman and the old man. It marches well, and rarely is it made to feel the kamcha. This morning Nurman happens to fall asleep on·his perch, and rolling off hits the ground like a ball: some seconds pass before he is able to come to and stand up again.

The pelt of Big Fellow, as we proceed, lengthens and curls down the long, sinewy hocks. Every day the three horizontal lines that stripe his fetlocks are more clearly defined, and every day I see his shadow journey from left to right and pass under his nose. A hair rope makes two half-hitches over the middle of his triangular tail, and joins up with the wooden peg passed through the nose of my own camel, known as the Bastard. Its hump lacks definition somewhat: being the result of crossing a camel with a dromedary.

Such a cross produces a type which is fertile and much appreciated by the Kazaks.

Behind me follows the young female camel: slim, elegant, fair, and with a fine clean-cut muzzle. Her black eye is surrounded by horizontal lashes. At every step she wheezes complainingly, a guttural cry whose expressive intonations are intended for her calf:

"Come! Where are you? It's beyond everything, I protest. Shall I ever see you again?"

I see the sun pass under the delicate curve of her nose and through the almond-slitted nostrils. At the velvety point where the nostrils come closest to each other, rise three frosty hairs like precious blades of grass, or some conventionalized spurt of water.

Day after day, in somnolent stupefaction, my mind emptied by the monotony of the movement, I cease to think of anything but eating and sleeping. The hoofs of Big Fellow: resilient pads, spreading wide with every step, engrave themselves on my retina.

I learn to hoist myself aloft as the Kazaks do, while my Bastard remains standing. Bearing on the nose-rope, I make him bend down his neck, then put a foot on the nape, worn smooth by constant rubbing, and grip hold of the saddle. The head and neck straighten out taking you up with them, then regaining your balance you drag yourself up on the load. I happen, however, to catch my knees in my chuba, swing right over and fall on my head: now I shall have a somewhat unusual excuse when I say something stupid.

This evening, on the shores of the Aral, the landscape, nothing but grey sky and grey ice, is grandiose in its desolation. Nurman collects a block of ice to make our tea, which turns out a filthy salt beverage. I thaw some meat in my frying pan.

To the north the sky is lilac: but of a tinge so tenuous and delicate that I weep, intoxicated with lyric emotion, as I declaim, " Lilac, does lilac really exist somewhere on this earth, honeyed stars stretched aspiring to the bees? Lilac, shall I some day see lilac in flower again? "

This morning we met a camel bearing a crying baby, an ass under a woman wrapped up in a square-patterned table-cloth, her feet tied in rags, and a man. He followed us for a long time, begging our old man to sell him some grain.

Then three men appear. They see our sacks and hang on to the nose of Big Fellow. In spite of our old man's cries, they insist on getting two buckets of grain, for which they pay us twenty-two roubles. They are so muffled up that even their noses cannot be seen. The main trail, it appears, is one continuous procession of wayfarers coming from the north.

We cross a frozen arm of the sea, but the camels do not like it for it makes them skid.

To the north of each little mound the snow has everywhere deposited bright patches. The mouths of the rabbit-runs are ringed with hoar frost. This evening we have to sweep the snow away for ourselves and our camels; otherwise they would refuse to kneel, and would wander about all night.

These nights, that I so much feared, pass wonderfully well. We settle down to sleep in a circle round the large fire. Always the old man takes the best place for himself in the lee of the smoke. Clearly, I am merely a woman to him, a negligible quantity.

The hard saxaul gives a fire of leaping bright flames, with embers that glow for a long time. It is the wood of the desert, and its roots go four feet and over down into the ground. It takes a hundred years for its short trunk to grow as thick as the leg of a man.

In front of the fire, our boots off, we warm our feet: the men take off their boots and dry the steaming bands of stuff they wrap around their legs. The down-at-heel boots of the old man are as stiff as boards and have holes in them: he has quite a system for replacing the soles and unyielding uppers on each occasion. He will certainly have his feet frozen should the ' buran ' blow.

Then, in front of the fire, they take their pelisses off, and pulling their shirts out of the puckered trousers begin investigating the inside. Before each meal they slay a good dozen of the pale crawling beasties. When we wake we shake off the snow that has covered us; but we have to wait for daybreak to depart. One of the camels cannot be found, and the night is so dark that not a thing is to be seen.

At midday, on a dune, I see a cube of faggots. It is a tomb dominated by its buntchuk. Nurman kneels and prays from a distance. We are now half across the desert. The most we can do is thirty miles a day.

The cold intensifies. The bushes no longer ' unfrost,' and look like enormous tufts of white and grey ostrich feathers. It is impossible to face the slight breeze squarely, for it covers your face with a too tight mask that cuts your eyelashes off. My large flannel body belt, converted into a turban, hides my nose, and gets lined with ice around my chin. Now I realize the usefulness of the ' t'maks,' the bonnets with fur flaps that reach half-way down one's back.

During the night I think I am seeing lighthouses flashing all round me.

When we halt, and there is too much snow to sweep away, we make a hole, dig enough sand to cover our camp, and cut down bushes to provide a floor. Abouish sets up a wooden tripod over the fire, from which he hangs the bucket full of snow. Before the embers that roast my face, I make wonderful toast for myself with mutton fat.

The huge beasts kneel near the fire and gaze at us while they ruminate. At night, their necks, like those of birds of prey make me dream of the prow of a ' drakkar.' It seems the Big Fellow bites and spits in the mating season.

I give up trying to understand what determines our irregular halts. Is it to sleep during the daytime and journey at night in order to avoid some possible attack . . . or rather to profit by whatever wood we can find . . . or to make a fire invisible from the main trail.

Every evening my Bastard goes on strike, stops suddenly, so that Big Fellow, going on, tears out the wooden mushroom that passes through his nostrils. He roars softly when the implement is put back into the flesh . . . and a few drops of blood redden the snow.

The pretty female camel luckily has her nose unpierced, but wears a kind of muzzle. Her delicate ×-like legs, and her undulating gait, make her skid on the rime in the track. She falls on her knees, but gets up immediately and looks askance at us with a shocked expression. " But I haven't done anything wrong; you've made a mistake," is what she seems to say. And it is she who has discovered a way of gathering up the snow in her lower lip, without interrupting the steadiness of her gait.

Fugitives

Still the trail continues, unendingly, with numerous dark spots coming gradually to meet us: whole families, crying babies borne on asses, loaded lads with laughing faces, mothers bowed under the weight of their blankets, children in overcoats trailing on the ground, old women sitting down to get their breath again.

All move forward under the same impulse: sustained by the hope of reaching the south, where food is cheaper and the weather warmer, and where a new town is being built, some with no conception of the distance, and having already exhausted their grain. A woman carries a heavy samovar,

THE 'DESERT OF RED SANDS'

another the crown of a yurt: another stalwart laughs, carrying her baby on her back. They travel by short stages. At night they lie down by the side of the trail, and the snow can be seen trodden down near a handful of ashes. There are no more bushes for firewood by the roadside.

Asses that have expired, lie with parallel ribs bordering the trail. Always when we meet them my Bastard takes fright. Here are three men busily engaged cutting up a camel that has broken a leg. The knives have laid bare the spinal column and the base of the two humps: the enormous pouch of the peritoneum spreads round limply.

We now carry our saxaul with us. Round us is unbroken steppe.

Here Nurman's home was, in the days when his father owned eight hundred sheep. In winter he camped in the Kizil Kum, but more to the east, where saxaul abounds. In summer he passed to the west of the Aral into the Kara Kum, where water is nearer the surface, and the summer pasture grounds are to be found.

The moon sinks, an orange melon swallowed suddenly by the earth. Our fire attracts a father and his son, both black with filth. He relates his story:

" I've left Kolkhoz 6 at Aktioubinsk, I want to go to Chimbai. They didn't pay me my seventy roubles a month and how otherwise can I feed my five children? The Kolkhoz said to me: ' We haven't got any money and no produce either, you can go and look for work somewhere else.' "

" Then you must have a paper to show you were free to leave."

" Yes, yes! " he answers.

All the same he is unable to produce any paper. Like the others, he sets out because he is a nomad in his soul.

Like Nurman, who had been so rich, he would rather eat sorghum all his life and never see meat or sugar than have a master over him.

327

Before daybreak, earth and sky are the same livid black. But the black of the earth turns velvety and the sky glimmers greyly like watery ink. Then at its base the grey thickens to an intense mahogany brown. The whole sky turns the colour of 'raspberry drops,' and when orange becomes the dominant colour it is day. I lie out on the sacks of the load to relax my back, and high above me the same succession of colours is reflected on a single cloud.

The cold has never been so piercing. One's eyes water and the insides of one's nostrils stick together. That must mean the temperature is at least 25° below zero, Centigrade.

The mane of Bastard is now as white as the beards one sees hanging from ancient firs: his lashes, brow, and nose are a hoar-frost posy. A constant layer of ice covers his breast-bone. The kneeling camel rests on the box of its thorax which bears down on an enormous oval callous.

Nurman hums incessantly to keep himself awake. This morning he wanted to know how bread was made, seeing me eating some.

The procession of emigrants continues.

We are nearing Kazalinsk and overtake a string of camels disappearing under loads of reeds.

I notice a solitary house. Nurman leaves the main road, and we come to a farm where his cousin lives and where there are many people.

My Kazaks would like to end their journey here. They all chatter together like so many magpies, taking their revenge for all the long days of silence. The house is magnificently situated, but I am saturated with beauty. I long to meditate in warmth, far from this place, and take a standing leap beyond the bitter days that go by the name of return.

It appears that this very day a camel has broken its leg while crossing the Syr Daria which separates us from the city. But I insist on being taken to Kazalinsk, and, the cousin refusing to lend his ass, it is the female camel that bears me off at last.

As a matter of fact, I seem to gather that my Kazaks are

loath to attract attention in the city. It is here they will resell, at seventy roubles the pood, the grain they bought at twenty in Takhta Koupir. I am not sure either that they have an official permit to engage in private commerce.

Here at last are the tall poplars of the city. There is no likelihood of anything unexpected happening now : the real journey is over.

SALEVE, *November* 1933.

BIBLIOGRAPHY

BACH, L.: *Orient Sovietique.* Librairie Valois, 1931.
Revue du Monde Musulman, vol. 50, 51, 59, 63.
Revue des Etudes Islamiques, 1929. II. Emancipation de la femme
musulmane en Orient.
BREHM, A.: *Brehms Tierleben.* Band IV, Leipzig und Wien, 1916.

GAYET, ALBERT: *Art Persan.* Paris, 1895.
GROUSSET, RENE: *Histoire de l'Asie.* Tome III.
Le Réveil de l'Asie. Plon, 1924.
Sur les traces du Bouddha. Plon, 1924
Voyages faits en Asie au XIIIe-XVIe siècles (Plan Carpin, Rubruquis,
etc.). La Haye, 1735.

KISCH, E. E.: *Asien gründlich verändert.* Reiss Verlag, 1932.
KOUZNIETZOFF: *Luttes des Langues et Civilizations en Asie Centrale.*
Paris, 1912.
KUHNEL, E.: *Art Islamique.* Kroner. Leipzig, 1929.

LAVISSE ET RAMBAUD: *Histoire Universelle.* Tome II.

MERZBACHER, G.: *Forschungsreise in dem Zentralen Tian Chan.* Gotha
Justus Perthes, 1904.
MOSER: *A travers l'Asie Centrale.*

PIERRE, A.: *U.R.S.S.* Delagrave, 1932.
PILNIAK, B.: *La septième République.* Rieder.

RICKMERS, W. R.: *The Duab of Turkestan.* Cambridge University Press,
1913.

SKRINE, F. H.: *The Expansion of Russia.* Cambridge University Press,
1903.
SMOLIK, DR. J.: *Die Timurischen Baudenkmäler in Samarkand* (Krystal).
SUAVIA, A.: *Le Khiva ou Khorezm.* Paris, 1873.

VAMBÉRY, A.: *Travels in Central Asia.*
Journal of the Royal Central Asia Society, July 1931.
Asiatic Review, April 1928.

WOLFF, REV. J.: *Narrative of a Mission to Bokhara in 1843-5.*
Illustrated Missionary News, 1873; Captain Burnaby's Ride to Khiva.

INDEX

INDEX